ELEMENTARY HARMONY

Theory and Practice

Second Edition

ROBERT W. OTTMAN

Professor of Music
North Texas State University
Denton, Texas

PRENTICE-HALL, INC., Englewood Cliffs, New Jersey

TO PATRICIA

Printed in the United States of America

13-257451-9

Library of Congress Catalog Card No.: 70-105451

Current printing (last digit):

19   18   17   16   15   14   13

PRENTICE-HALL INTERNATIONAL, INC., London
PRENTICE-HALL OF AUSTRALIA, PTY. LTD., Sydney
PRENTICE-HALL OF CANADA, LTD., Toronto
PRENTICE-HALL OF INDIA PRIVATE LTD., New Delhi
PRENTICE-HALL OF JAPAN, INC., Tokyo

Preface

Elementary Harmony: Theory and Practice and its companion volume, *Advanced Harmony: Theory and Practice,* are designed to meet the needs of college courses in basic music theory, including instruction in the four related areas: written harmony, keyboard harmony, ear training and sight singing. The subject matter of each chapter and its application to each of these four areas are so presented that they can be taught successfully either in the correlated class (all four areas in one class) or in several classes, each devoted to one or more of these areas.

The texts are based on the techniques of composers of the seventeenth to nineteenth centuries. They include a comprehensive survey of the harmonic materials used in these historical periods, from the simple triad through seventh chords, altered chords, ninth, eleventh, and thirteenth chords, and simple and complex methods of modulation. The historical limitation in no way implies that teaching of music theory must be limited to this period. But for the undergraduate student, knowledge of the practices of the seventeenth and nineteenth centuries should serve as a point of departure for his study of both pre-seventeenth-century music and twentieth-century music.

In addition to the theoretical presentation, a comprehensive practical application of these harmonic materials is presented. Concurrent studies in melodic and rhythmic analysis and composition, in harmonic analysis, in instrumentation, and in analysis of form (small forms only) implement this application. With these materials, the student is not only asked to solve traditional figured bass exercises, but is led ultimately to accomplishments in arranging given melodies and in creating original music, in both vocal and instrumental styles. Ample material is given for student work, allowing considerable latitude in choice of assignments.

To aid the student in placing his theoretical studies in both pedagogical and historical contexts, Chapter 2 of this volume presents a survey of the materials to be covered in the two-year theory sequence, while Appendix 3 relates in brief the history of the use of harmony in Western music from the period of organum, c. A.D. 900, to the historical period covered in these texts. The final chapter of *Advanced Harmony*, revised edition, will provide a survey of twentieth-century compositional practices and their relationships to the student's study of harmony.

There are several other features that will be of particular interest:

Rudiments. A comprehensive review of the rudiments of music is furnished, so that members of a beginning class in college music theory will be able to find a common starting point.

Part-Writing. The principles of part-writing are codified, making possible easy reference to any part-writing procedure. (See Appendix 1.)

Musical Examples. Hundreds of examples covering a wide range of composers, nationalities, and periods are presented. Examples early in the course are principally in four-part vocal structure. As the text advances, more of the examples are in instrumental style.

Terminology. Unfortunately, there is no standard terminology in music theory. Students often complete a theory course or even attain a degree in music but are unable to understand many articles in the literature of music theory or musicology. This text lists and describes at appropriate places the more important of these varying terminologies.

The method of identification of chords by Roman numeral symbols is explained in Chapter 2 and at appropriate places in later chapters. Teaching procedures and materials, especially in keyboard harmony and ear training, require chord symbols which, when stated alone and without reference to staff notation, will spell the given chord (diatonic or altered) when the key is known. Chosen for this purpose are the "quality" symbols, where the quality of the sound is reflected in the symbol (I = major, i = minor, etc.), combined with the "functional" symbols for certain altered harmonies (V of V, etc.).

Self-Help in Ear Training. Most chapters contain projects in self-help in ear training, enabling the student to work on this vital aspect of his theoretical training outside of class.

Assignments and Exercises. Material for student participation is divided into "Assignments"—that which can be committed to paper—and "Exercises" —that which can be demonstrated only by speaking or singing or at the keyboard.

Supplementary Materials. Assignments in sight singing and in melodic analysis and melody harmonization are made from the author's *Music for Sight Singing.* Many references besides those illustrated are made to the collection of 371 Chorales by Johann Sebastian Bach; also, a number of assignments in harmonic and melodic analysis are made from this collection.

In appropriate places throughout both volumes, assignments in harmonic analysis are made from these five additional collections of music: Beethoven, Sonatas for Piano (numbers 1-12 only); Chopin, Mazurkas; Mendelssohn, *Songs Without Words;* Mozart, Sonatas for Piano; and Schumann, *Album for the Young,* Op. 68. Many students will already own some or all of these.

All the procedures and materials in these texts have been tested for many years through use in the music theory courses at North Texas State University. The author acknowledges his indebtedness to the many hundreds of undergraduate and graduate students whose participation in the presentation and study of these materials has made the final form of the text possible. Particular thanks are due the members of the NTSU theory faculty, Frank Mainous, Alan Richardson, and William Gardner, for their cooperation in teaching these materials on an experimental basis and for their many able suggestions and constructive criticisms resulting from this classroom experience.

Robert W. Ottman

Contents

19

THE DOMINANT SEVENTH
AND SUPERTONIC SEVENTH CHORDS
RHYTHM: SYNCOPATION, 284

20

ELEMENTARY MODULATION
SECONDARY DOMINANT CHORDS:
THE DOMINANT OF THE DOMINANT, 309

APPENDIX 1

THE ESSENTIALS OF PART-WRITING, 330

APPENDIX 2

INSTRUMENTATION:
RANGES, CLEFS, TRANSPOSITION, 333

APPENDIX 3

HARMONY, SCALES, AND KEYS
IN WESTERN MUSIC, 337

INDEX, 353

1

The Fundamentals of Music

A Review

Before embarking upon a study of harmony, it is essential that the student be well-acquainted with the basic aspects of pitch, rhythm, and music notation. This information is acquired by many students through instrumental or vocal lessons and through readings in music history and music literature. For others, a formal course in this material is desirable, either in secondary school or as a one-semester college-level course, identified by titles such as Fundamentals of Music or Rudiments of Music.

The fundamentals of music are represented in this chapter only in the form of an abbreviated review. Students to whom this material is unfamiliar should avail themselves of a formal course or a textbook[1] covering these elementary aspects of music theory.

For the student of harmony, it is particularly important that he be knowledgeable in keys, key signatures, and scale spellings to the extent that he can do the following with absolute accuracy and without hesitation:

1. Name both the major and minor key for any given key signature.

2. State the number of sharps or flats in the signature of a given key, and spell these accidentals in their correct order on the staff.

3. Spell any major scale and the three forms of any minor scale, ascending and descending.

4. Sing a major scale and each of the three forms of the minor scale on "la," or sing any of these scales in any key with letter names when the name of the key is given.

---

[1] *Rudiments of Music* by Robert W. Ottman and Frank Mainous (Englewood Cliffs, N.J.: Prentice-Hall, Inc., 1970) is especially designed to precede the study of harmony beginning in Chapter 3 of the present volume.

Pitch

1. PITCH NAMES. Pitches are named with the first seven letters of the alphabet, A B C D E F G.

2. STAFF. The staff (plural, *staves*) consists of five lines and four spaces.

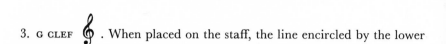

3. G CLEF 𝄞 . When placed on the staff, the line encircled by the lower

loop of the clef sign is designated G. This clef sign is commonly used to designate the second line as G, and in this position it is known as a *treble clef*.

4. F CLEF 𝄢 . When placed on the staff, the line between the dots is

designated F. This clef commonly designates the fourth line as F, and in this position it is known as a *bass clef*.

5. STAFF SPELLINGS. Adjacent lines and spaces use adjacent pitch names from the alphabet.

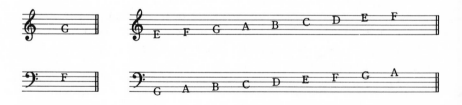

6. LEDGER (LEGER) LINES AND SPACES. Ledger lines are short lines written above or below the staff for the purpose of extending the staff. Spaces between ledger lines are ledger spaces.

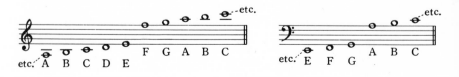

7. GREAT STAFF (GRAND STAFF). The treble and bass clefs joined together constitute the great staff.

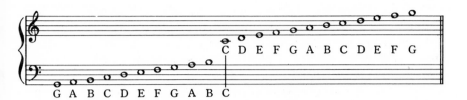

C D E F G A B C D E F G

G A B C D E F G A B C

8. HALF STEPS AND WHOLE STEPS. Two pitches from the musical alphabet or from the piano keyboard as close together as possible constitute a half step. In the musical alphabet, E-F and B-C are half steps, since no pitch sound is found between them. Other adjacent pairs of letter names are whole steps (two half steps). On the keyboard, any two adjacent keys sound a half step.

9. ACCIDENTALS (CHROMATICS)

A *sharp* (♯) raises the pitch of a note one half step. (C♯ is one half step higher than C.)

A *flat* (♭) lowers the pitch of a note one half step.

A *double sharp* (✗) raises the pitch of a note a whole step.

A *double flat* (♭♭) lowers the pitch of a note a whole step.

A *natural* (♮) cancels out a previously used accidental.

The relative pitch relationships of the accidentals are

(low) ♭♭   ♭   ♮   ♯   ✗ (high)

10. THE KEYBOARD. Names of the keys on the piano can be seen in the figure below.

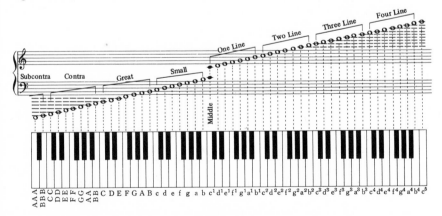

11. OCTAVE REGISTERS. This is a system in which identical pitch names in various octave positions may be differentiated from each other. Middle C is designated c^1 (read "one-line C"). Each pitch is designated in the figure above. (For other systems of pitch differentiation, see "Pitch names" in *Harvard Dictionary of Music*.)

12. SCALES. A scale is a series of pitches using, in order, the seven letter names of the musical alphabet, beginning on any one letter.

Major scale. A series of eight tones (8 being the pitch-name repetition of 1) in which the relationship between successive tones is as follows (1 = whole step, 1/2 = half step):

Scale tones	1	2	3	4	5	6	7	8
Step size		1	1	1/2	1	1	1	1/2

Using C on the keyboard as 1, the major scale makes use of the white keys exclusively.

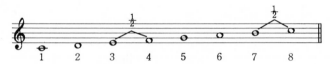

When beginning the major scale on any other letter name, it is necessary to add accidentals to maintain the relationship of half steps and whole steps.

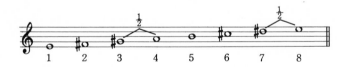

Minor scales. A series of eight tones in which the relationship between successive tones differs from that of the major scale. There are three forms of minor scales.

a) Pure (natural) minor scale. The relationship between successive tones is as follows:

Scale tones	1	2	3	4	5	6	7	8
Step size		1	1/2	1	1	1/2	1	1

Examples of the pure minor scale starting on A (no accidentals) and G:

b) Harmonic minor scale. The harmonic form of the minor scale is similar to the pure form, with the seventh scale degree raised one half step. This results in a distance of 1 1/2 steps between 6 and 7 and a half step between 7 and 8.

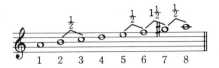 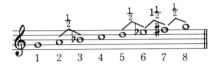

c) Melodic minor scale. Ascending only, the melodic form of the minor scale is similar to the pure form with the sixth and seventh degrees each raised one half step.

The descending form of the melodic minor scale is identical to that of the pure minor scale.

8	7	6	5	4	3	2	1
A	G	F	E	D	C	B	A

Chromatic scale. A scale consisting exclusively of half steps.

C C♯ D D♯ E F F♯ G G♯ A A♯ B C   ascending
C B B♭ A A♭ G G♭ F E E♭ D D♭ C   descending

13. SCALE DEGREE NAMES

Scale degree	Name: major key	Scale degree	Name: minor key
1	Tonic	1	Tonic
2	Supertonic	2	Supertonic
3	Mediant	3	Mediant
4	Subdominant	4	Subdominant
5	Dominant	5	Dominant
6	Submediant	6	Submediant
7	Leading tone	♯6	Raised submediant
		7	Subtonic
		♯7	Leading tone

(♯6 and ♯7 mean raised sixth scale step and raised seventh scale step.)

14. INTERVALS. An interval is the distance between two pitches. It can be measured by the number of half steps and/or whole steps it contains and then identified by an interval name.

Intervals are named according to the number of letter names encompassed in the interval. For example, C up to F is a *fourth* since four letter names (C, D, E, and F) are encompassed. Interval names are qualified by the terms *major, minor, perfect, diminished,* and *augmented.* Major, minor, and perfect intervals above C are

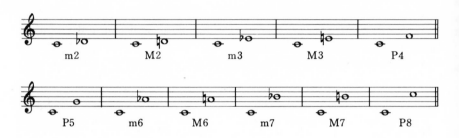

m2—minor second, a half step.
M2—major second, a whole step.
m3—minor third, a whole step plus a half step (three half steps).[2]
M3—major third, two whole steps (four half steps).
P4 —perfect fourth, two whole steps plus one half step (five half steps).
P5 —perfect fifth, a major third plus a minor third (seven half steps).
m6—minor sixth, a perfect fifth plus a half step (eight half steps).
M6—major sixth, a perfect fifth plus a whole step (nine half steps).
m7—minor seventh, an octave less one whole step (ten half steps).
M7—major seventh, an octave less one half step (eleven half steps).
P8 —perfect octave, two pitches with the same name separated by twelve half steps.

Minor intervals are one half step smaller than major intervals. Diminished intervals are one half step smaller than minor or perfect intervals (e.g., C up to F♭, diminished fourth). Augmented intervals are one half step larger than major or perfect intervals (for example, C up to A♯, augmented sixth).

In addition, there are two other intervals, the *perfect prime* (PP), no distance between pitches, and the *augmented prime* (AP), a half step in which both pitches use the same letter name.

---

[2]Not to be confused with the interval between the sixth and seventh scale steps of the harmonic minor scale. This latter interval also consists of a whole step plus a half step, but encompasses only two letter names, and is therefore called an *augmented second.* Intervals that sound the same but are spelled and named differently are known as *enharmonic* intervals. The term *enharmonic* also applies to pairs of single pitches (C♯-D♭) or pairs of chords (F♯ A♯ C♯-G♭ B♭ D♭) that sound the same but are spelled differently.

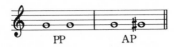

15. INVERSION OF INTERVALS. Intervals may be inverted by placing the lower note one octave higher, or the higher note one octave lower. In this process, major intervals invert to minor intervals, and minor intervals invert to major intervals. Perfect intervals remain perfect when inverted, hence their name.

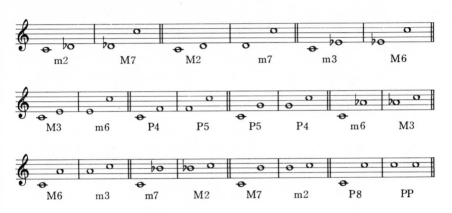

16. KEY AND KEY SIGNATURE. A key signature is a grouping of those accidentals found in the scale and placed on the staff immediately after the clef sign. For example, from the E major scale shown in the discussion of the major scale, the four sharps may be extracted and placed on the staff.

These accidentals ordinarily need not appear thereafter in the musical composition. For minor key signatures, accidentals from the pure minor scale are used. The pure minor scale on C♯ also has four sharps.

In music of the seventeenth to nineteenth centuries, the key signature is commonly used to identify the tonic note of the scale used at the beginning and end of the composition. Thus a signature of four sharps will indicate to the performer that the tonic note is either E of the E major scale, or C♯ of the C♯ minor scale.

A given piece is said to be in a certain *key*, the name of which is identical with the letter name of the tonic note of the scale. These are the key signatures, together with their tonic notes and names.

Major keys

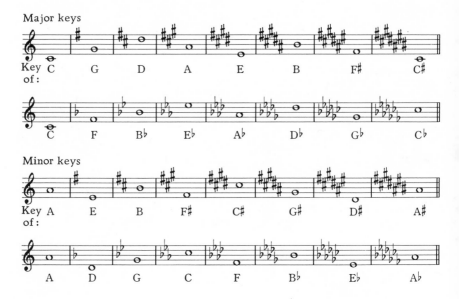

Key of: C G D A E B F♯ C♯

C F B♭ E♭ A♭ D♭ G♭ C♭

Minor keys

Key of: A E B F♯ C♯ G♯ D♯ A♯

A D G C F B♭ E♭ A♭

In the bass clef, the accidentals of the key signature are arranged as follows:

Relative keys. Two keys, each using the same key signature, are known as relative keys, for example, G major (1 sharp) and E minor (1 sharp).

Parallel keys. Two keys, each using the same letter name for tonic note, are known as parallel keys, e.g., G major and G minor.

17. CIRCLE OF FIFTHS. Keys whose tonic notes are located at the interval of a perfect fifth (or its inversion, the perfect fourth) from each other will show one accidental difference in their key signatures. Upon this principle, all keys may be shown in a circle of fifths.

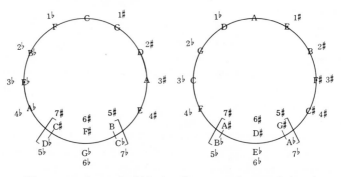

(Key names located within brackets are enharmonic keys.)

18. CHORD. A chord is a group of different notes, usually three or more, sounded simultaneously or in rapid succession (*broken chord*). Chords in the music of the seventeenth to nineteenth centuries are ordinarily found spelled in thirds, for example, C E G, D F♯ A C, and so on.

19. TRIAD. A three-note chord spelled in thirds is called a triad. Triads may be constructed from any combination of major and minor thirds. Four such combinations are possible.

a) two minor thirds: diminished triad
b) two major thirds: augmented triad
c) one major third and one minor third, in that order from the lowest note up: major triad.
d) one minor third and one major third, in that order from the lowest note up: minor triad.

Duration

20. NOTES AND RESTS. Durations of pitch or silence are indicated, in part, by characteristic note-shapes or rest signs.

Double Whole Note	‖o‖	Double Whole Rest	▬
Whole Note	o	Whole Rest	▬
Half Note	♩ ρ	Half Rest	▬
Quarter Note	♩ ♩	Quarter Rest	𝄽 or ɼ
Eighth Note	♪ ♪	Eighth Rest	𝄾
Sixteenth Note	♬ ♬	Sixteenth Rest	𝄿
Thirty-Second Note	♬ ♬	Thirty-Second Rest	𝅀
Sixty-Fourth Note	♬ ♬	Sixty-Fourth Rest	𝅁

The whole rest is also used to indicate a complete measure rest regardless of the number of beats in the measure.

These note-shapes do not indicate actual duration of time until combined with a tempo indication and a time signature (see below). They do indicate relative relationships of duration as expressed by their names. For example, a whole note (or rest) is equal in duration to two half notes (or rests) or to four quarter notes. Any note value is equal in duration to two notes of the next smaller value.

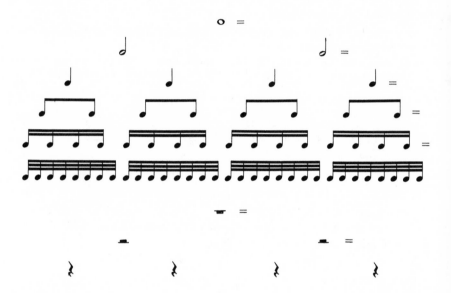

21. BEAT. A beat is a unit of musical time. It can be represented visibly by the movement of a conductor's hand, or audibly by the ticking sound of a metronome. A beat may be represented on the staff by any note value indicated above. (See also "dot" and "time signature" below.)

22. BAR. This is a vertical line appearing on the staff (sometimes called "bar-line").

23. DOUBLE BAR. Two vertical lines on the staff at the close of a composition or a major division of a composition are called a double bar.

24. MEASURE. A measure is a group of notes or rests found between two bars (bar-lines). Usually each measure represents a fixed number of beats as indicated by the time signature (see below). The word "bar" is often used to mean "measure."

25. DOT. A dot appearing after a note or rest, for example, ♩., increases the value of the note by one half: ♩. = ♩ + ♪ . A dotted note or rest is equal in value to three notes of the next smaller value: ♩. = ♪ ♪ ♪ , ♪. = ♬♪ , ♪. = ≀ ≀ ≀ . Any dotted note can be used to represent the beat.

26. TIE. A curved line joining two successive notes of identical pitch is a tie. The two tied notes sound as one note. ♩‿♩ = ♩

27. TEMPO. Tempo is the rate of speed of a composition. It may be expressed at the beginning of a composition or during a composition by musical terms such as *allegro* or *adagio* or by a metronome marking such as ♩ = 60 M. M. (M.M. is Maelzel's Metronome). "60" on the metronome indicates one tick per second. The marking ♩ = 60 means that the duration of each quarter note will be one second.

28. TIME SIGNATURE. The time signature consists of two Arabic numerals, arranged vertically, found at the beginning of a musical composition following the clef and the key signature.

In its simplest definition, the upper number of the time signature states the number of beats to be found in each measure, while the lower number indicates which of the possible note values will receive one beat.

²⁄₄ , two beats in a measure, a quarter note receives one beat.

³⁄₄ , three beats in a measure, a quarter note receives one beat.

Very often, certain time signatures in certain situations will convey other meanings. In a slow tempo, ⁶⁄₈ may be interpreted as above, but in a fast tempo it invariably indicates two beats in a measure with a ♩. note receiving one beat (two ♩. = six ♪ notes). In any case, the upper number always indicates how many of the note values expressed by the lower number will be found in one measure. Clarification of this situation will be found in Chapter 4.

Although the time signature can be made up of many combinations of two numbers, the following are the combinations most often used.

Upper number: 2, 3, 4, 6, 9, 12
Lower number: 2, 4, 8, 16

The sign **C** (often called *common time*) is a substitute for $\frac{4}{4}$.

The sign **₵** (often called *cut time* or *alla breve*) is a substitute for $\frac{2}{2}$

Elementary Notation

29. THE SINGLE NOTE. A note is drawn with one, two or three parts:

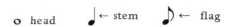

    o head   ← stem   ← flag

An ascending stem is found on the right side of the head ♩ .
A descending stem is found on the left side of the head ♩ .

30. NOTES ON THE STAFF. *a*) When writing notes for a single part (one voice or one instrument) on the staff, place descending stems on notes found on the middle line or above, and ascending stems on notes below the middle line.

When the note on the middle line is the highest note of the measure, it is often found with an ascending stem.

b) When writing for two parts on a single staff, notes for the upper part use ascending stems and notes for the lower part use descending stems, regardless of their location on the staff.

c) To indicate two parts performing the same pitch on a single staff (unisons), use a single note head with both ascending and descending stems. For two whole notes in unison, use two overlapping whole notes.

31. NOTES USING LEDGER LINES OR SPACES. Above the staff, do not write ledger lines above the highest note. Below the staff, do not write ledger lines below the lowest note

right   wrong

32. DOTTED NOTES. When the note head is on a space, the dot is found in the same space. When the note is on a line, the dot is usually found in the space above, though it is sometimes in the space below.

33. VERTICAL ARRANGEMENT OF NOTES. All notes sounding simultaneously must be written so that a line drawn through the note heads will be perpendicular to the lines of the staff.

right   wrong   right   wrong

right   wrong

34. HORIZONTAL ARRANGEMENT OF NOTES. Space between notes should be in proportion to their time values.

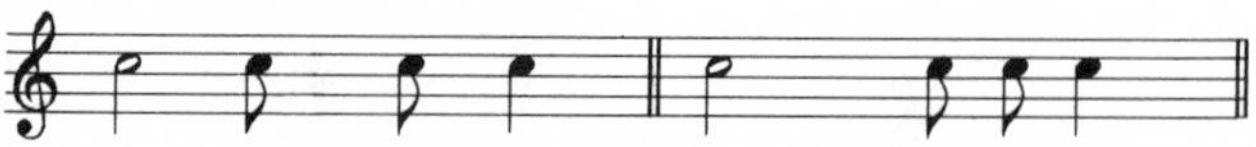

wrong right

35. PLACEMENT OF ACCIDENTALS. An accidental before a note is placed on the same line or space as the note head.

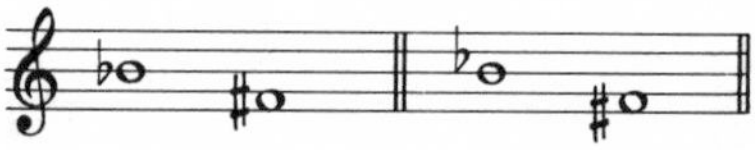

right wrong

The effect of an accidental lasts until the following bar-line unless it is cancelled by a natural sign, or unless the note is tied into the following measure or measures.

36. BEAMS. Notes employing flags may be grouped together with beams.

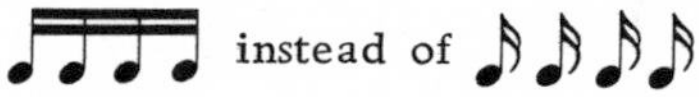

Notes ordinarily should be beamed in terms of beat units. 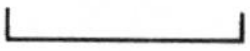 indicates a beat unit.

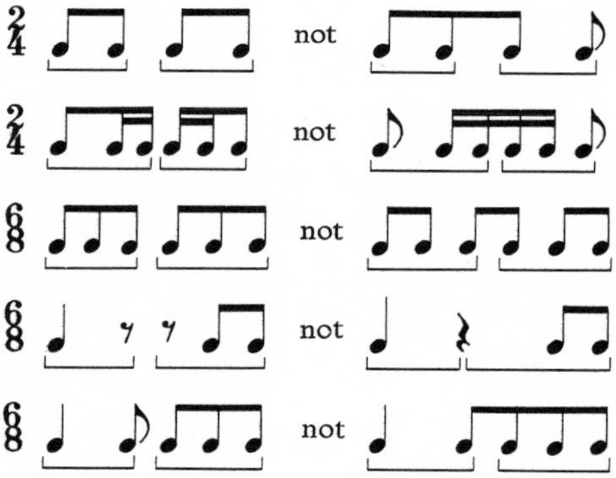

When a group of beamed notes is placed on the staff, use a stem direction that is correct for a majority of the notes in the group.

In most vocal music, beams are used only when two or more notes are found on a single syllable.

Santa Lucia

Now 'neath   the   sil - ver moon   o - cean   is   glow - ing,

The curved line connecting two or more notes of different pitch is known as a *slur*.

2

A Survey of Harmonic Materials

In the preceding chapter, the section entitled "Pitch" ended with definitions of intervals, triads, and chords. It is here that the study of harmony begins, for harmony is basically a study of chords: (1) their construction, (2) their relationship to a key center, (3) their relationships to one another, and (4) their use in melodic, rhythmic, and formal[1] contexts. Our study will be made in relation to the music of the seventeenth, eighteenth, and nineteenth centuries (c. 1600—c. 1900), a period when a system of harmony was the basis of most music composition.

In this chapter we will survey the basic types of harmonic materials used by composers during this particular chronological era. A survey such as this will of necessity include some of the technical language and symbols required to describe the materials under discussion. But it is not necessary at this time to attempt to learn or to comprehend fully these technicalities. Detailed and comprehensive study of harmonic materials begins in Chapter 3, which presents the major triad, with subsequent chapters of this and the following text, *Advanced Harmony: Theory and Practice*, covering additional harmonic materials in progressive order.

As a further aid in orienting yourself to the subject of harmony, you will find in Appendix 3 a brief survey of the use of harmony in the music of Western civilization. You are urged to read this essay before continuing with the present chapter, and to read it several times during the year, at which times it will become more meaningful as a result of your increasing experience in music theory, music history, and music performance.

---

[1]"Formal" refers to *form* in music, discussed further in Chapter 5.

The Triad

The simplest type of chord is the triad, a three-note chord built in thirds. It may be constructed above any letter name of the music alphabet simply by selecting the third and fifth letter names above the given letter name. For example, choosing A, we construct the triad A C E; choosing G, we construct the triad G B D. When arranged in thirds, as these are, the lowest note is known as the *root*, above which are the *third* and *fifth*.

Fig. 2.1.

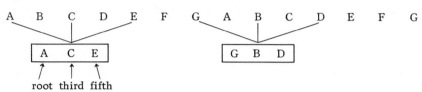

Constructing triads above each of the seven letter names of the musical alphabet will produce three different types of triads, major, minor, or diminished, according to the arrangement of thirds within the triad (review Chapter 1, section 19).

A	C	E	minor triad
B	D	F	diminished triad
C	E	G	major triad
D	F	A	minor triad
E	G	B	minor triad
F	A	C	major triad
G	B	D	major triad

The Triad in a Key

In the same way, triads can be built above each note of any major or minor scale, as in Figure 2.2. When used in a key, the number of the scale step serving as the root of the triad may also be an identifying number for the triad, but expressed in Roman numerals.

Fig. 2.2.

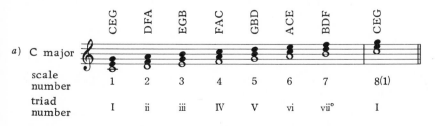

b) A minor, natural form

scale number	1	2	3	4	5	6	7	8 (1)
triad number	i	ii°	III	iv	v	VI	VII	i

The Roman numeral not only designates the scale step location of the root of the triad, but also indicates triad construction:

Large numeral = major triad (I in C major = C E G)
Small numeral = minor triad (ii in C major = D F A)
Small numeral with small° = diminished triad (vii° in C major = B D F)
Large numeral with + = augmented triad (not found in diatonic[2] scales or triads; I+ in C major = C E G♯).

Thus, for example, IV indicates a major triad built on the fourth scale degree, while iv indicates a minor triad built on the fourth scale degree.

A triad in a key may also be designated by the name of the scale step on which it is built; for example: I = tonic triad, V = dominant triad.

Fig. 2.3. Triads in the Major Scale

			Spelling in	
Scale Degree	Scale Degree Name	Triad Number	C Major	G Major
1	Tonic	I	C E G	G B D
2	Supertonic	ii	D F A	A C E
3	Mediant	iii	E G B	B D F♯
4	Subdominant	IV	F A C	C E G
5	Dominant	V	G B D	D F♯A
6	Submediant	vi	A C E	E G B
7	Leading Tone	vii°	B D F	F♯A C

In minor keys, the harmonic and melodic forms of the scale make use of both lowered and raised sixth and seventh scale degrees. When raised, these notes are actually *altered* (review footnote 2) in relation to the key signature, but as members of frequently used scale patterns they are ordinarily classified and studied as diatonic tones. Inclusion of these tones in the scale produces more "diatonic" triads in minor than in major.

---

[2] Triads, chords, scale passages, and other note groupings using only notes of the scale are known as *diatonic*. The triads so far listed are diatonic. When pitches not in the scale are used, the note grouping is known as *altered;* for example, in C major, C E G♯ and D F♯ A are examples of altered triads. See Figure 2.4 for exceptions in minor.

Fig. 2.4. Triads in the Minor Scale

			Spelling in	
Scale Degree[3]	*Scale Degree Name*	*Triad Number*	*A Minor*	*D Minor*
1	Tonic	i	A C E	D F A
2	Supertonic	ii°	B D F	E G B♭
		ii	B D F♯	E G B
3	Mediant	III	C E G	F A C
		III+	C E G♯	F A C♯
4	Subdominant	iv	D F A	G B♭ D
		IV	D F♯A	G B D
5	Dominant	v	E G B	A C E
		V	E G♯B	A C♯E
6	Submediant	VI	F A C	B♭ D F
♯6	Raised submediant	vi°	F♯A C	B D F
7	Subtonic	VII	G B D	C E G
♯7	Leading tone	vii°	G♯B D	C♯E G

To demonstrate the use of triads in actual music, we will first look at the beginning of a well-known hymn often known as the "Doxology" (Figure 2.5). Here we see a series of triads, each with its root in the bass, or, as we may say, a series of triads in *root position*. The series of chord numbers below the music is known as the *harmonic analysis*. You will also notice that although triads are used, four tones are always sounding simultaneously because this is written for the usual combination of four human voices: soprano, alto, tenor, and bass.

Fig. 2. 5.

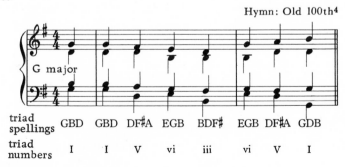

Hymn: Old 100th[4]

G major

triad spellings	GBD	GBD	DF♯A	EGB	BDF♯	EGB	DF♯A	GDB
triad numbers	I	I	V	vi	iii	vi	V	I

---

[3]♯6 and ♯7 means raised 6 and raised 7.

[4]"Old 100th" is the name of the hymn tune. Various hymns (poems) may be set to the same tune. Old 100th may be found with the hymns "Praise God From Whom All Blessings Flow" ("Doxology") and "All People That on Earth Do Dwell," among others. Most hymnals include an "Index of Tunes," which will locate all settings of a given tune. In this text, each hymn will be identified by the name of the hymn tune.

The first triad, G B D, contains two G's, and we say that the G is *doubled*. Triads may contain one doubling, as here, or more as required by the musical situation, such as in Figure 2.6.

Fig. 2.6.[5]

At the other extreme, a composition consisting of only two voices[6] (or only a single voice, as will be shown later on) can imply the presence and use of triads (Figure 2.7).

Fig. 2.7.

Triads in Inversion

The complete triads shown and identified so far have been in root position. Triads are also commonly used when the third or fifth of the triad is the lowest note. The triad is then said to be in *inversion: first inversion* when the third is the lowest note and *second inversion* when the fifth is the lowest note.

In harmonic analysis first inversion is indicated by a "6" and second inversion by a "$\frac{6}{4}$", as will be explained in Chapter 11. (See Fig. 2.9)

---

[5]The latter part of the harmonic analysis is not included because it contains chords other than triads.

[6]In music analysis, *voice* refers to a melodic line, whether sung or played on an instrument.

Fig. 2.8.

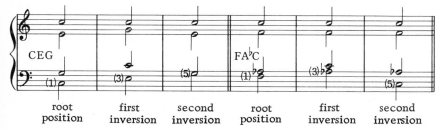

| root position | first inversion | second inversion | root position | first inversion | second inversion |

Fig. 2.9.

Hymn: Tappan

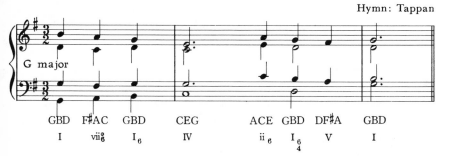

Non-harmonic Tones

Music compositions are not limited to pitches that can be identified as parts of triads or other chords. Pitches other than members of the chord may sound simultaneously with the chord; these are called *non-harmonic tones*. The notes circled in Figure 2.10 are non-harmonic tones because they

Fig. 2.10.

Bach, *Liebster Jesu, wir sind hier* (♯131)[7]

---

[7]The number in parentheses refers to the number of the chorale in the collected editions of J.S. Bach's chorales, such as *The 371 Chorales of Johann Sebastian Bach*, edited, with English texts, by Frank D. Mainous and Robert W. Ottman (New York: Holt, Rinehart & Winston, Inc., 1966). These chorales will be used extensively for illustration and analysis in this text.

are not members of the triads with which they sound. To comprehend more fully the significance of non-harmonic tones, play or listen to the chorale as written (Figure 2.10); then play or listen to Figure 2.11, in which the non-harmonic tones have been replaced by notes in the triad (harmonic tones).

Fig. 2.11.

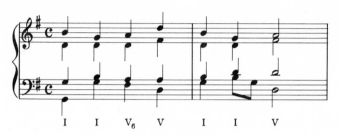

I   I   V₆   V   I   I   V

Seventh Chords

Chords larger than triads can be constructed by the same method used to construct the triad, that is, by the addition of thirds. Adding two thirds together produced a triad; adding another third to the triad will produce a *seventh chord*, so named because the new note is the interval of a seventh above the root of the chord:

A   B   **C   D   E   F   G   A   B**   C   D   E   F   G

            C   E   G   B

    root   3rd   5th   7th

Like triads, seventh chords may be built above any note of the scale: in C major, for example, $C E G B = I^7$, $D F A C = ii^7$, $E G B D = iii^7$, $F A C E = IV^7$, etc. Notice that the chord number still indicates the root location and type of triad, while the superscript 7 is added to indicate that there is an interval of a seventh above the root.

Fig. 2.12.

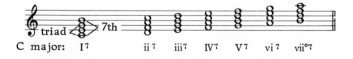

C major: I^7 ii^7 iii^7 IV^7 V^7 vi^7 $vii°^7$

Fig. 2.13.

Hymn: Millennium

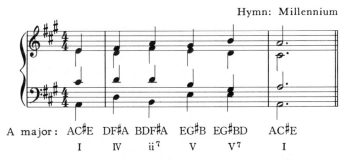

A major: AC#E   DF#A   BDF#A   EG#B   EG#BD   AC#E
            I   IV   ii⁷   V   V⁷   I

Also like triads, seventh chords may be inverted, that is, some note other than the root may be the lowest note. When the *third* is the lowest note, the chord is in *first inversion,* indicated in harmonic analysis by $^6_5$; when the *fifth* is the lowest note, the chord is in *second inversion,* $^4_3$; when the *seventh* is the lowest note, the chord is in *third inversion,* $^4_2$, explained further in Chapter 19.

Fig. 2.14.

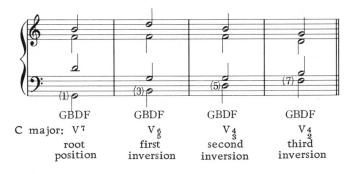

GBDF   GBDF   GBDF   GBDF
C major: V⁷   V$_6^6$ V$_3^4$ V$_2^4$
          root   first   second   third
        position   inversion   inversion   inversion

Fig. 2.15.

Beethoven, Sonata for Piano
Op. 2, No. 3

E major: EG#B   BD#F#A   EG#B   BD#F#A
            I   V$_2^4$ I₆   V$_3^4$ I₆ V₆ I   ii₆ V

Chords Larger Than the Seventh

Chords more complex than seventh chords can be created by superimposing additional thirds above the seventh. These chords, called *ninth* chords, *eleventh* chords, and *thirteenth* chords, are infrequently used, particularly in music relatively easy to analyze. They are included in your study of advanced harmony.

Fig. 2.16.

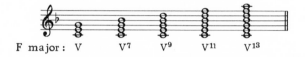

F major : V   V⁷   V⁹   V¹¹   V¹³

Broken Chord Style

Up to this point, all music illustrations have shown chords in "block" style, that is, all the notes are found vertically on the staff, indicating that all notes are to be sounded simultaneously. Any chord, however, may be written with single tones in succession or with pairs of tones and single tones in various combinations in succession. This method of presenting chords is known as "broken chord" style; in piano music, the broken chord can appear in either hand or in both hands simultaneously.[3]

Fig. 2.17.

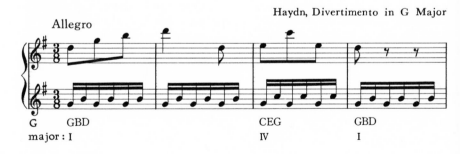

Haydn, Divertimento in G Major

Allegro

G   GBD   CEG   GBD
major : I   IV   I

---

[3]When it occurs in the left hand, the broken chord pattern is often referred to as an *Alberti bass*, after Domenico Alberti (1710–40?) who used this device extensively in his compositions.

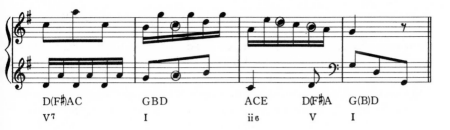

D(F♯)AC   GBD   ACE   D(F♯)A   G(B)D
V⁷   I   ii 6   V   I

Fig. 2.18.

Mozart, Sonata for Piano, K. 282

E♭ major: E♭GB♭   FA♭C   E♭GB♭ B♭DFA♭ E♭GB♭)
        I 6   ii 6   I 6/4   V⁷   I

Fig. 2.19.

Schubert, *Ständchen (Serenade)*

D   DFA   EGB♭D   AC♯EG   DFA
minor: i   ii°4/3   V⁷   i

Altered Chords

Chords at times include notes not belonging to the scale of the key in which the composition is written. Known as *altered chords*, each will display one or more notes preceded by an accidental to indicate the alteration. For ex-

ample, in C major, D F A is diatonic, but is commonly altered to become
D F♯ A, D♯ F♯ A, D F A♭, or D♭ F A♭. Three excerpts, Figures 2.20—2.22,
show first the use of a single altered triad, followed by two examples of
several altered chords within the limits of a few measures. Since much of the
analysis in these figures is part of advanced study in harmony, chord symbols[9] and spellings will appear quite complex to the beginner. At this time
we need only acquaint ourselves briefly with the appearance and sound of
a few representative altered harmonies.

Fig. 2.20.

Bach, *Es ist das Heil uns kommen her* (♯248)

AC♯E

G major : I   V6   IV6   I   ii6   II6   V   I
(VofV)

The single altered triad in Figure 2.20 is spelled A C♯ E (II) instead of its
diatonic spelling A C E (ii).

Fig. 2.21.

Hymn: Everyland

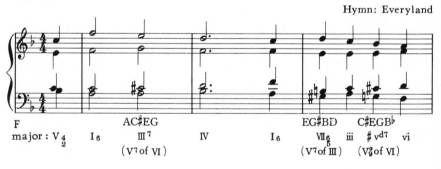

F
major : V4/2   I6   III7   IV   I6   VII6/5   iii   ♯v d7   vi
            AC♯EG   EG♯BD   C♯EGB♭
         (V7of VI)   (V7of III)   (V3/5of VI)

---

[9]A complete presentation of these will be found at appropriate times. In parentheses in the
figures are alternate symbolizations frequently used in analysis of altered harmonies. Differences in terminologies in music theory are common and will be included throughout the
text where appropriate.

For those interested, here is a brief explanation of the symbols in Figures 2.20–2.22. V of:
a major triad, or major triad with seventh added (V7 of), whose root is a perfect fifth above
the assumed root of the following chord; V0/9: a ninth chord built on the fifth scale degree
but with its root missing; ♯ preceding a number: the chord is built on a raised scale degree
(♯iv° in F major is built on B natural); d7: the chord is a diminished seventh chord, composed of three minor thirds; –7: the seventh of the chord is lowered in relation to the key
signature (in C major, C E G B♭ = I⁻7).

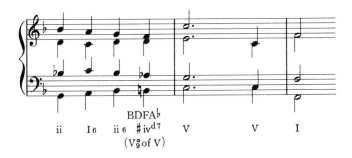

The altered chords in Figure 2.21 are:

F major:

$$A\ C\sharp\ E\ G\ (III^7)\ \text{instead of}\ A\ C\ E\ G\ (iii^7)$$
$$E\ G\sharp\ B\ D\ (VII^7)\ \text{instead of}\ E\ G\ B\flat\ D\ (vii^{\circ 7})$$
$$C\sharp\ E\ G\ B\flat\ (\sharp v^{d7})\ \text{instead of}\ C\ E\ G\ B\flat\ (V^7)$$
$$B\ D\ F\ A\flat\ (\sharp iv^{d7})\ \text{instead of}\ B\flat\ D\ F\ A\ (IV^7)$$

The next excerpt, in broken chord style for keyboard, includes one rather complex chord spelling because of the number of accidentals (five sharps) in the key signature.

Fig. 2.22.

Chopin, Nocturne, Op. 32, No. 1

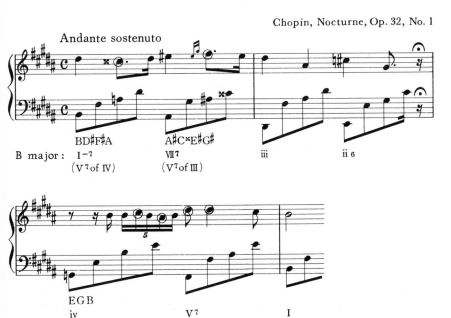

The altered chords are:

B major:

B D♯ F♯ A (I⁻⁷) instead of B D♯ F♯ A♯ (I⁷)
A♯ C × E♯ G♯ (VII⁷) instead of A♯ C♯ E G♯ (vii°⁷)
E G B (iv) instead of E G♯ B (IV)

Detailed study of altered chords, or as sometimes known, *chromatic harmony*, will be a part of your advanced study in harmonic materials.

Modulation

For most composers of the seventeenth-nineteenth centuries, the basic source materials for musical composition were the two forms of a scale, major and minor. Although there are fifteen major scales, each sounds like the others. A C major scale sounds the same as an E major scale, for example, except that each starts on a different pitch level. The same is true of the fifteen minor scales. When we say that a piece is in C major, we mean that it uses the resources of the major scale, and that the starting point of the scale is C. We could play the same piece in D major and it would sound the same, except a step higher. So we have just two systems in which to write music: major and minor. In all the music excerpts presented so far, each has been in one particular major or minor key.

It is not necessary, however, that a piece remain in its starting key. During the course of a composition, the music may progress from one key to another by a process known as *modulation*. Any major or minor key may progress by modulation to any other major or minor key, though, as we will see, certain modulations are much more frequently used than others.

In Figure 2.23, an excerpt from the familiar "Moonlight" Sonata, we see an example of a frequently used modulation from a minor key to a major key whose tonic is located a minor third higher (to the relative major), in this case from C♯ minor to E major. Both use the same key signature (four sharps); both use the same pitches in their scales except that in C♯ minor, the sixth and seventh scale steps, A and B, may be raised to A♯ and B♯.

C♯ minor:	C♯	D♯	E	F♯	G♯	A(♯)	B(♯)	C♯		
E major:			E	F♯	G♯	A	B	C♯	D♯	E

The most frequently used method of making such a modulation as this is through the device known as a "common chord" or a "pivot chord." This is a single chord that can be analyzed as one chord number in the original key and as a different chord number in the new key. In our example, the common or pivot chord is F♯ A C♯, which is iv in C♯ minor and ii in E major.

Why this is so, and how to find or create for yourself the pivot between two keys, will be studied later in a chapter on modulation.

Fig. 2.23.

Beethoven, Sonata for Piano, Op. 27, No. 2

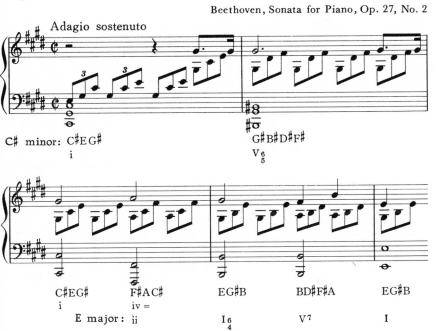

In our other illustration, Figure 2.24, we see a much more complex modulation. This song of Brahms started in D major; as we pick it up in measure 30, it has already modulated to F major and, at the end of Figure 2.24, will modulate again to D♭ major through the key of F minor.

Fig. 2.24.

Brahms, *So willst du des Armen*, Op. 33, No. 5

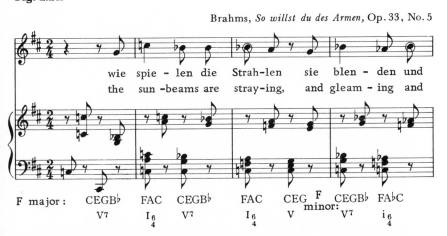

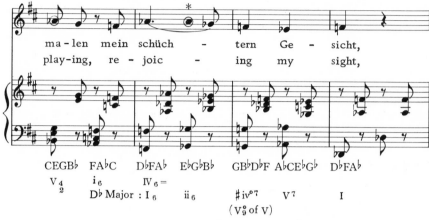

ma - len   mein   schüch   -   tern   Ge   -   sicht,
play-ing,   re - joic   -   ing   my   sight,

CEGBb   FAbC   DbFAb   EbGbBb   GBbDbF   AbCEbGb   DbFAb

V 4/2   i 6   IV 6 =
    Db Major : I 6   ii 6   ♯iv°7   V7   I
            (V 0/9 of V)

* at this point the Ab is a non-harmonic tone
(against Eb Gb Bb)

The use of modulation in a music composition may be limited to a single instance, or it may occur at frequent intervals. Modulation may range from *closely related keys* (keys whose signatures show not more than one accidental difference) to *remote (foreign)* keys (keys whose signatures show more than one accidental difference). It is a most important device for producing variety in a system of music composition that utilizes only two basic scale structures, major and minor.

Chord Choice and Functions of Harmony

If you should attempt to calculate how many different chord structures (the diatonic chords plus all possible alterations of each chord) are available to a composer, and then should attempt to calculate the number of different progressions of one chord to another, the totals could easily run into many thousands.[10] Fortunately, for ease of listening as well as for harmonic study, only a relatively small proportion of these harmonic resources was used regularly by composers during the three centuries under study. As an example, in a major key, the progression ii-V can be found frequently, while the progression ii-vi is quite rare; in C major, the altered chord D F♯ A is very common, while the altered chord D F♯ A♯ is hardly to be found at all. Your study of harmony will show you what chords are most often used by com-

---

[10]For example, the C major triad alone can be found in 25 altered forms, using only single sharps or flats to alter triad members (not using double sharps or double flats).

posers and, when once selected for use, how a chord functions in relation to the key center and to its preceding and following chords.

Melody and Harmony

Melody has always been one of the principal characteristics of the music of Western civilization, from the earliest known music, which was entirely melodic, to that of the present time. In the period of our study (c. 1600— c. 1900), melody is as important as harmony, a fact that is obvious when hearing or performing almost any composition from this period. During this era, one important aspect of music composition is the fact that a melodic line implies both specific harmonies and successions of harmonies. We will not attempt here to enter into an argument of long standing: does melody dictate the choice of chord progression, or does chord progression dictate the characteristics of melodic writing? Whether either or both possibilities are correct, there can be no denying that there is a very close correlation between melody and the harmonic system of this period. By understanding these relationships, you will easily be able to write good melodies and to supply vocal or instrumental harmonizations to these or other unharmonized melodic lines.

Part-Writing

For purposes of displaying triads or other chords, you have been shown figures taken from hymns (Figures 2.5, 2.9, 2.13, and 2.21) and from J.S. Bach's chorales (Figures 2.10 and 2.20). In studying these excerpts, we have looked at the pitches on the staff from the bottom up (or the top down); that is, we have analyzed the music vertically.

Just as important is the horizontal aspect. The highest note of each chord (stem up) is part of the tune, or principal melody, which is read by the soprano singer horizontally across the score. Below this soprano line and on the same staff is another melodic line (stems down), which is sung by the alto voice. In the bass clef are two additional melodic lines, sung by the tenor and bass voices. These hymns and chorales, then, are not simply a succession of chords; they are just as importantly a simultaneous sounding of four melodic lines. The art of writing a succession of chords (vertical) and at the same time connecting these with good melodic lines (horizontal) is known as *part-writing*. The principles of good part-writing apply to the combination of any number of voices, from two to as many as twelve or more, or in an extreme case, forty (see Appendix 3, footnote 2). In addition, the principles of vocal part-writing apply, in general, to all forms of instrumental writing, such as piano, string quartet, symphony, and many others. An important part of our study, therefore, will be the art of part-writing.

Counterpoint

Counterpoint is the art of combining two or more independent melodic lines for simultaneous performance. We have just seen that our four-voice hymns are made up of four horizontal lines, though in hymn style the lower voices are sometimes not really tuneful, and in almost all cases, each voice part moves with the same rhythmic values as the three others. In the chorale excerpts, you can observe that the voice lines are slightly different from each other rhythmically and so show a little more independence from each other than do the voice lines in the hymns. In true counterpoint, the voices are much more independent of each other, melodically and rhythmically. Figure 2.25 shows a contrapuntal composition made up of three voice lines. Each voice is independent from the others both melodically and rhythmically, and each is an interesting line in itself, while the three combine to make a single unified composition. In this excerpt, the two voices in the treble clef are in *canon*,[11] rhythmically one beat (half note) apart, and melodically an interval of a sixth apart.

The practice of counterpoint is actually the oldest art in the history of music composition for more than one voice line, as shown in the historical survey, Appendix 3. In the period we are studying, it is still a very important factor in music composition. It differs from pre-seventeenth-century counterpoint in that the combined voice lines produce chords and chord progressions that conform to the principles discussed earlier in this chapter. This is illustrated in the harmonic analysis given below the contrapuntal music of Figure 2.25. Part-writing, as discussed in the previous section, can be considered a most elementary type of contrapuntal writing, since several voice lines sound simultaneously, though in part-writing, these melodic lines do not need to show the same degree of rhythmic and melodic interest and independence as in true counterpoint. As you develop your skills in setting melodic lines simultaneously through the study of part-writing, you will be preparing yourself for the more advanced skills required in counterpoint.

---

[11]Well-known *rounds*, such as "Row, Row, Row Your Boat," represent the simplest type of canon. In a round, the second and subsequent voices sing the same tune and start on the same pitch as the first voice. In a canon, the second and subsequent voices may begin at a pitch or pitches other than that of the first voice; these voices may also be altered in pitch or rhythm or both by special devices, descriptions of which can be found in articles entitled "Canon" in music dictionaries.

Fig. 2.25.

Bach, *Goldberg Variations,* Var. 18

Rhythm

Rhythm, the ever-changing pattern of longer and shorter note values in a music composition, is a characteristic feature of virtually all music. It is possible, and even probable, that rhythm antedates melody as the earliest expression of music in the history of civilized man. It is obvious that knowledge of rhythm is necessary in the understanding, reading, or composing of melodic lines. Perhaps not so obvious is the fact that the use of chords in succession is also based upon principles of rhythm and meter. Thus, your study of harmony will include rhythm and meter and their effect upon melodic and harmonic aspects of music composition.

Form

After the opening notes of a composition, the music must obviously continue for a length of time until the composition ends. Having established the outside limits of a composition, its beginning and ending, we must now consider whether the melodic, rhythmic, and harmonic elements of the composition will proceed at random within these limits or whether these elements should be organized into some recognizable patterns. Randomness in music composition is extremely rare; from earliest times, written music is usually found in some orderly arrangement, or patterns of musical construction. The pattern used in the construction of the piece is known as its *form*. In addition, most music displays a succession of shorter patterns within the piece as a whole; each of these patterns is also known as a form.

The principle of form can most easily be shown by first looking at a stanza of a well-known poem:

Flow gently sweet Afton, among thy green braes,
Flow gently, I'll sing thee a song in thy praise,
My Mary's asleep by thy murmuring stream,
Flow gently sweet Afton, disturb not her dream.

(*Robert Burns*)

Each verse (line) of the stanza contains eleven syllables. The end of each verse is marked by a "breathing" point or stopping point, the first three without coming to a definite stop, while the fourth comes to a full stop. In terms of rhyme scheme, the stanza consists of two couplets, the first ending in "braes" and "praise," and the second ending in "stream" and "dream." The form of the stanza can then be said to be a quatrain (four lines) made up of two couplets each consisting of eleven-syllable lines with regular recurring accents.

In combining this poem with the melody that is traditionally associated with it (Figure 2.26), we can observe the following:

1. The music comes to a resting place or pause at the same places as in the poem. In music, these points are known as *cadences*, and, as in poetry, the cadence may give the feeling of a temporary stop or a full stop. The cadences on "braes," "praise," and "stream" are temporary cadences (in music, called *imperfect* or *half* cadences, studied in Chapter 8), while the last cadence is a full stop (*perfect* cadence.)

Harmonically, the cadence consists of two successive chords. At the words "green braes," for example, we find the triads IV—I, which constitute an *imperfect plagal* cadence, while at the words "her dream," the chord progression V^7—I constitutes a *perfect authentic* cadence. When analyzing a

Fig. 2.26.

James E. Spilman, *Flow Gently Sweet Afton*

a = phrase
b = phrase
ab = period
abab' = double period

melody without its harmony, the last two melody notes at the stopping point constitute the melodic cadence, for example, the notes G—Ab at the final cadence.

2. The cadences enable us to recognize and identify the form or forms of a piece of music. The music up to and including the first cadence is known as a *phrase*, and since there are three more cadences, there are three more phrases. Like a period (.) in sentence structure, the perfect cadence marks the end of a form in music, while the other types of cadence mark off phrases more or less comparable to clauses in sentence structure.

So we see we have a piece containing four phrases, the last marked by perfect cadence. In looking further, we can see that melodically the first phrase and the third phrase are practically identical, and that the second and fourth are similar to each other, in that each begins in the same way. By calling the first phrase *a* and the second phrase (different melody) *b*, the four phrases can be called *a b a b'* (*b'* indicates similar but not identical melody).

This particular arrangement of phrases is called, in the language of music form, a *double period*. The double period is one of a number of music forms, some larger, some smaller, that describe the construction of a piece of music. These terms can describe any musical construction from a two-note melodic element to a complete movement of a symphony.

Our study of form, correlated with that of harmony, melody, and rhythm, will begin with cadences and phrases and continue with larger forms. The results of these correlated studies will enable you to understand and describe the music you are performing or hearing, to compose your own original music in various melodic and harmonic styles, and to make effective vocal and instrumental arrangements of original or folk melodies.

Having read this chapter and Appendix 3 you should have a good general understanding of the history and principal features of harmony. Beginning in the next chapter, with the tonic triad in major keys, we will systematically study one element of harmony at a time, and in each chapter apply the knowledge gained in several ways: in writing music, in listening in order to be able to identify harmony and melody by ear, in making useful application of harmony at the piano keyboard, and learning to comprehend the sound of music visually and demonstrating this skill through sight singing.

3

The Major Triad
The Tonic (I) Triad in a Major Key

THEORY AND ANALYSIS

Now that we have had a preview of the materials of harmony, our procedure from here on will be to investigate and study one element of harmony at a time, describing the function of each in music as a whole, and, as we progress through each chapter, to add the known elements together, thereby enabling us to analyze, to arrange, and to write music, ranging from utmost simplicity at first to considerable complexity at the end of the course.

We will begin with one of the simplest harmonic elements, the major triad and its use as the tonic (I) triad in a major key.[1]

The importance of the tonic triad lies in the fact that it is the triad that identifies the key in a piece of music. A key is usually established by a tonic triad appearing early in a composition, very often as the opening chord, as shown in Figures 2.5, 2.6, 2.10, 2.15, and 2.17, and as the final chord, as examination of almost any piece of music will show. To emphasize the tonic of the key, composers commonly repeat the final tonic triad in a composition, as you have undoubtedly noticed in playing or listening to music, and as shown in Figure 3.1.[2]

Although the use of a single triad would seem insufficient for a complete composition, this has been done on at least one occasion. The prelude to the opera *Orfeo* (1607) by Claudio Monteverdi (1567–1643), though only sixteen

---

[1]Review construction of triads, Chapter 1, paragraph 19, and Chapter 2, Figure 2.1. Review relation of the tonic triad to the major scale, Figures 2.2 and 2.3.

[2]See also Smetana, *The Moldau*, which, except for the penultimate dominant chord, ends with 31 measures of repeated tonic triads.

Fig. 3.1.

Beethoven, *Leonore Overture* No. 3, Op. 72a[3]

measures long, makes use of the tonic triad exclusively, together with non-harmonic tones. The only notes in the prelude not part of the tonic triad are non-harmonic tones (review Chapter 2, page 21). In a later time, Richard Wagner (1813–83) opened his music drama, *Das Rheingold* (1869), with 48 measures of tonic triad only (no non-harmonic tones), followed by an additional 88 measures based principally on the tonic triad, a device used to illustrate in music the quiet majesty of the Rhine river.

---

[3]Op., abbreviation for *Opus* (Latin), *work*; the number of a composition in a complete list of a composer's output.

The tonic triad is one of the most commonly used triads in music, but it is more often found dispersed among other chords rather than concentrated in passages of great length as in the exceptional examples just quoted. In a progression of chords, the goal of the chord movement is usually the tonic triad, and it is this feeling of reaching the tonic that imparts a sense of "key" to a musical composition. When listening, we can always feel the key of a piece of music as the sound of the root of the final tonic triad. Upon inspecting this final triad in the printed music, we can identify that sound as a triad spelling, and we say that the piece has a *key name* identical to the spelling of the root of the final tonic triad. Play again or listen to the last phrase of Figure 2.26: the final tonic triad is spelled A♭ C E♭, a major triad; therefore, we say that the composition is in the key of A♭ major.[4]

Spelling the Major Triad

Method 1. If you can already spell intervals with facility, as shown in Chapter 1, paragraph 14, you can spell any major triad simply by spelling a major third and a perfect fifth above any given pitch name designated as the root of a triad, or by spelling a major third above the root of the triad and a minor third above the third of the triad. Examples:

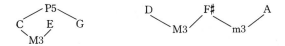

Method 2. Students lacking facility at this time in spelling intervals will find the following method convenient until such facility is developed.

There are seven basic triad spellings, using each of the seven letter names of the musical alphabet as a root. These are ACE, BDF, DFA, CEG, EGB, FAC, and GBD. Three are already major, three are minor, and one is diminished.

Group I (major)	Group II (minor)	Group III (diminished)
C E G	D F A	B D F
F A C	E G B	
G B D	A C E	
- - -	- ↑ -	- ↑ ↑

Group I. These triad spellings will be major when each letter carries the same accidental, as indicated by the symbol - - -.

C E G,   C♯ E♯ G♯,   C𝄪 E𝄪 G𝄪,   C♭ E♭ G♭,   C♭♭ E♭♭ G♭♭
- - -   - - -   - - -   - - -   - - -

Group II. These triad spellings will be major when the third carries an accidental one half step higher than the root and the fifth (- ↑ -).

A C♯ E,   A♯ C𝄪 E♯,   A♭ C E♭,   A♭♭ C♭ E♭♭
- ↑ -   - ↑ -   - ↑ -   - ↑ -

Group III. This single triad is major when the third and fifth carry an accidental one half step higher than the root (-↑ ↑).

B D♯ F♯,   B♯ D𝄪 F𝄪,   B♭ D F,   B♭♭ D♭ F♭
- ↑ ↑   - ↑ ↑   - ↑ ↑   - ↑ ↑

Assignment 3.1. Major triad spelling. Use either method. This assignment may be followed or combined with Assignment 3.5.

a) Spell with letter names the major triad when each of the following is the root: C, F, E, G♭, E♭, A♯, B♭, F♯, D♭, B♯.

b) Spell the major triad when each of the following is the third: B, E♯, F♯, C, D, G♯, A♭, D♭, A♭♭, F   (Example: A—F A C).

c) Spell the major triad when each of the following is the fifth: D, C♯, E♭, B♯, A, F, F♯, D♭, E♭♭, F♭ (Example, A♭—D♭ F A♭).

Intervals in the Major Triad

The major triad contains a number of intervals, which can be found by extracting and combining any two notes from the three-note triad.

1 up to 3	Major Third (M3)	3 down to 1
3 up to 5	Minor Third (m3)	5 down to 3
5 up to 1	Perfect Fourth (P4)	1 down to 5
1 up to 5	Perfect Fifth (P5)	5 down to 1
3 up to 1	Minor Sixth (m6)	1 down to 3
5 up to 3	Major Sixth (M6)	3 down to 5
1 up to 1 ⎫		⎧ 1 down to 1
3 up to 3 ⎬ Perfect Octave (P8)		⎨ 3 down to 3
5 up to 5 ⎭		⎩ 5 down to 5

Assignment 3.2. Based on a given triad, spell each of the intervals in the table of intervals. Example: D major triad (D F♯ A):

M3	D up to F♯	M6	A up to F♯
m3	F♯ up to A	m6	F♯ up to D
P4	A up to D	P8	D up to D
P5	D up to A		F♯ up to F♯
			A up to A

Do the same with the following triads, or others, as assigned: G, F, B♭, E♭, A, B, F♯, C♭, D♯, D♭. This assignment may be followed or combined with Assignment 3.6.

Assignment 3.3.   Spell all the intervals in the table of intervals from a given note. Example, given the note G:

M3 up	G—B	P4 down	G—D	m6 up	G—E♭
M3 down	G—E♭	P5 up	G—D	m6 down	G—B
m3 up	G—B♭	P5 down	G—C	P8 up	G—G
m3 down	G—E	M6 up	G—E	P8 down	G—G
P4 up	G—C	M6 down	G—B♭		

Do the same from any given note.

Intervals in Melodic Writing

Those intervals that are found in triads, together with scale steps, are the intervals most often used in melodic writing. For the present, we will study only the intervals used in the tonic triad in major keys. Figure 3.2 shows how intervals in a melodic line may imply a major tonic triad.

Fig. 3.2.

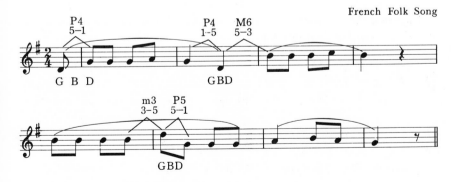

Assignment 3.4.   Identify intervals from major tonic triads in melodies 1—44 and 58—73, as assigned, from *Music for Sight Singing*. In these melodies

all intervals are in the tonic triad. Copy out melody and indicate intervals by number and by name as shown in Figure 3.2.

APPLICATION

Written Materials

Assignment 3.5. Write major triads on the staff. Referring to triads listed in Assignment 3.1, write each in the treble and bass clefs as shown in Figure 3.3.

Fig. 3.3.

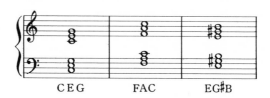

      C E G   F A C   E G♯ B

Assignment 3.6. Write intervals on the staff. Refer to Assignment 3.2. Place each interval, ascending and descending, on the treble or bass staff as assigned, and as shown in Figure 3.4.

Fig. 3.4.

      Major third   Minor third   Perfect fourth

Assignment 3.7. Fill in the second note of the interval according to the direction given for each interval.

   P5 up   M3 up   P4 up   P4 down   m3 down

   M6 up   M6 down   P5 down   m6 up   m6 down

   P5 down   P4 up   m6 up   m3 down   m3 up

Ear Training and Music Reading

Singing the Major Triad

Exercise 3.1.   Singing the C major triad.

a) Sing the first five notes of the C major scale. Then, starting with 1, sing only the notes 1, 3, and 5.

Fig. 3.5.

b) Starting on 5, sing the descending scale, followed by 5, 3, and 1 only.

Fig. 3.6.

c) Sing the C major triad ascending and descending.

Fig. 3.7.

Exercise 3.2. a) Singing any major triad. Listen to major triads played at the piano. After each triad is sounded, sing the pattern 1–3–5–3–1.

b) Listen to the triad. Sing the root only.

Fig. 3.8.

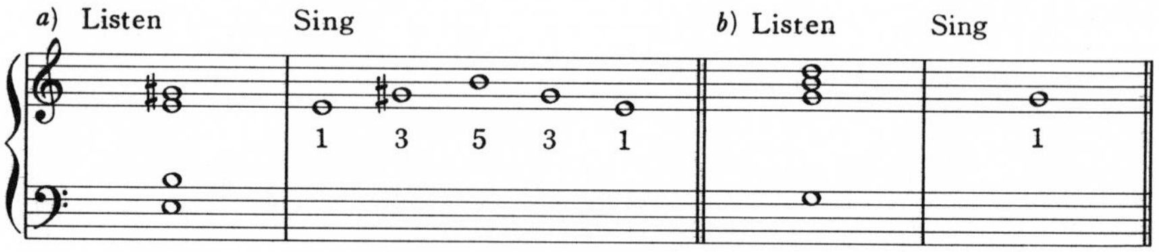

Exercise 3.3. Singing any major triad from its root. Play or listen to any given pitch. Call this pitch 1. Sing a major triad from this pitch.

Fig. 3.9.

Exercise 3.4. Singing any major triad from its fifth. Play or listen to any given pitch. Call this pitch 5. Sing the triad pattern 5–3–1–3–5.

Fig. 3.10.

Exercise 3.5. Singing any major triad from its third. Play or listen to any given pitch. Call this pitch 3. Sing the triad pattern 3–1–3–5–3.

Fig. 3.11.

Exercise 3.6. Repeat exercises 3.3, 3.4, and 3.5. Instead of singing numbers, sing with letter names when the name of the first pitch is given. (When latter name includes an accidental, sing repeated note, as in "D flat.")

Fig. 3.12.

Identifying the Soprano Note in a Major Triad

The goal of this series of exercises (3.7—3.11) is to identify the soprano (highest) note of a triad, either by number or by letter name. Students able to achieve immediate satisfactory results in Exercise 3.11 may dispense with the preliminary exercises.

Exercises 3.7—3.10 are designed to aid those not immediately able to cope with Exercise 3.11. The exercises are based on the ability to hear the melody line in a chord progression, as in Figure 3.13, and to identify the soprano notes in the cadence of a phrase (review Chapter 2, pages 34–36).

Exercise 3.7. Identify the final soprano (melody) note in the cadence.

a) Listen to a phrase of music, with harmony. (Instructor: phrases from hymn tunes or improvised phrases as in Figure 3.13 may be used. The final two triads of each phrase should be major triads.)

b) Sing the melody line while the exercise is played at the piano.

c) Listen to the final triad of the phrase; sing the melody note.

d) Sing the triad pattern, 1–3–5, and identify the soprano note as 1, 3, or 5 by singing the soprano note with a number or by reciting the number of the soprano note.

Fig. 3.13.   Example for Exercise 3.7.

Exercise 3.8.   Follow directions for Exercise 3.7, but at *b*), sing the melody line without the piano. This will help develop your musical memory, a skill necessary in taking melodic dictation, which begins in Chapter 4.

Exercise 3.9.   Identify soprano notes in the harmonic cadence.

a) Listen to a phrase of music. Sing back the last two soprano notes.

b) Listen to each triad of the cadence separately. Sing the triad pattern from each soprano note.

Fig. 3.14.   Example for Exercise 3.9.

Exercise 3.10.   Identify soprano notes from two-chord cadential progressions. Example:

Fig. 3.15.

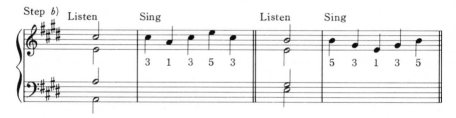

Exercise 3.11.   Identify the soprano note of a single triad. Listen to a single triad and identify soprano note as 1, 3, or 5

a) by singing the soprano note with its correct number, *or*

b) by reciting the correct number of the soprano note, *or*

c) by writing the correct number of the soprano note.

Exercise 3.12.   Spell the major triad when the letter name of the soprano note is known. The letter name of the soprano note will be given. Identify the soprano note by number and then spell the triad. Example: F♯ is given as the soprano note. Listen to the triad. If the soprano note is identified as the third of the triad, the triad is spelled D F♯ A.

Self-Help in Ear Training

Upon completion of Exercise 3.20 (playing the major triad at the keyboard), students working in pairs can practice Exercises 3.11 and 3.12 outside the classroom. One student will play a triad while the other proceeds with either of the two exercises. After approximately ten triads have been played and identified or spelled, the students should change places. Both students will derive much valuable practice in both keyboard harmony and ear training.

Intervals

Exercise 3.13.   Singing intervals from the major triad by number.

a) Sing a major triad from a given pitch, using the numbers 1–3–5–3–1. Then sing two-note combinations (intervals) from this triad, as directed. Example:

Fig. 3.16.

b) Sing the triad with additional upper or lower tones, as many above and below the given triad as lie in a comfortable singing range. Example:

Fig. 3.17.

Exercise 3.14.   Sing a given interval from a given pitch, using triad numbers. Sing aloud, or mentally, the basic triad before singing the interval. For example: G is given; sing 3 up to 5 from G.

Fig. 3.18.

Exercise 3.15. Identify melodic or harmonic intervals aurally. (An interval in which the two notes are sounded simultaneously is known as a *harmonic interval*; when the two notes sound in succession it is known as a *melodic interval*.)

  a) You will hear a triad at the piano.

  b) You will hear an interval (melodic or harmonic) from that triad.

  c) Sing the interval on *la*.

  d) Sing the complete triad, using 1–3–5–3–1.

  e) Sing the interval again, using correct numbers. Example:

Fig. 3.19.

With continued practice, eliminate steps *a)*, *c)*, and *d)*.

Exercise 3.16. Identify intervals aurally by writing number relationships. Follow procedure for Exercise 3.15. For the problem given in Figure 3.19, write the answer 1 up to 5, or 1 ∧ 5, or 1 ↑ 5.

Exercise 3.17. Identify intervals aurally by naming the interval. Follow procedure for Exercise 3.15. For the problem in Figure 3.19, state or write the answer: perfect fifth (P5).

Exercise 3.18. Sing interval when name of interval is given and one note of interval is played at the piano. Sing the triad on 1–3–5–3–1 first, if necessary. Example: sing a minor sixth down from G.

Fig. 3.20.

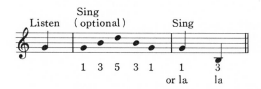

Exercise 3.19. Write intervals on the staff from dictation. The first note of the interval will be given; place this on the staff. Listen to the interval, then

write:

   a) the numbers of the interval

   b) the name of the interval

   c) the triad spelling

   d) the second note of the interval. Example:

Fig. 3.21.

After sufficient practice, continue drill by omitting steps *a*) and *c*).

Self-Help Procedure for Intervals

Upon completion of Exercise 3.20 (playing intervals at the keyboard), students working in pairs can aid each other in mastering Exercises 3.16— 3.19. One student will play the interval while the other student identifies the interval.

Keyboard Harmony

Exercise 3.20. Playing the major triad with the root in the bass at the keyboard.

   a) Spell the triad.

   b) Find the root of the triad in the left hand. Do not play.

   c) Place the little finger of the right hand on the given soprano note. Do not play.

   d) Find the other two notes of the triad immediately below the soprano note, using the right hand. Do not play.

   e) Play all four notes of the triad simultaneously. Sample problem: Play the D major triad with the third in the soprano.

Fig. 3.22.

	(silent)			Play:
a) Spell D F♯ A	*b*)	*c*)	*d*)	*e*)

The triad is commonly played and written in four parts, as above. In adding the extra note, one of the members of the triad is *doubled*, that is, there will be two of that member. The root of the triad is usually doubled.

Exercise 3.21.   At the keyboard, play any interval based on a given triad.

Procedure	*Example*
a) Listen to directions.	*a*) Play 5 up to 1 in the A♭ major triad, or play an ascending perfect fourth in the A♭ major triad.
b) Spell the triad.	*b*) A♭ C E♭
c) Spell the interval.	*c*) 5 up to 1 is E♭ up to A♭, or, a perfect fourth up is E♭ up to A♭.
d) Play the interval.	*d*) 

4

Rhythm (I)[1]

Since music exists in time, a given pitch must sound for a certain length of time until it is replaced by another pitch, which may sound for the same or a different length of time. These durations need to be measured before they can be set down on paper to become part of the music score.

The Beat

The standard of measurement in musical time is the *beat*. The beat is not a fixed length of time; it can be long or short according to the character of the particular musical composition. The nature of the beat is commonly experienced by most persons when listening to music. For example, when walking to the accompaniment of a military march, your footsteps mark off equal measurements of time, which can be considered as beats. The slower the music, the longer the beat, and conversely, the faster the music, the shorter the beat. The metronome set at 80 establishes a beat of moderate speed; beat durations range from a beat of long duration (approximately M.M. 50) to a beat of short duration (approximately M.M. 140). The tempo of a composition is directly related to the length of the beat—music in a slow tempo is comprised of beats of long duration, music in a fast tempo of beats of short duration.

---

[1] The material of this chapter properly belongs in the study of the rudiments of music; it is covered in a similar manner in *Rudiments of Music* by Robert W. Ottman and Frank Mainous. Students who have completed this text or comparable material from other sources may wish to use this chapter as a review or to continue with Chapter 5.

Exercise 4.1.   Listening for beats. Listen to music played by the instructor. With the right hand, make taps of equal time durations. Be sure not to tap the unequal durations you may hear in the melody or other prominent part; your taps should be of equal duration and conform comfortably to the tempo of the music.

Grouping of Beats

It will be noted that beats tend to group themselves, one beat assuming more importance than following beats. The more important, or stronger, beat recurs regularly, usually marking off groups of 2, 3, or 4 beats.

Fig. 4.1.

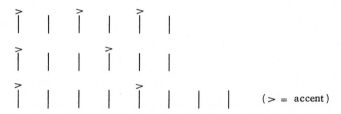

(> = accent)

Exercise 4.2.   Listening for beat groupings. Listen to music, as in Exercise 4.1. When the strong beat is located, count aloud 1–2 or 1–2–3, as the case may be. (In listening, it is difficult to distinguish between the two-beat and four-beat groupings.)

Varieties of the Beat

Two varieties of the beat exist. These can best be illustrated by listening to two different folksongs, Figures 4.2 and 4.4 In each folksong, the beats are in groups of two, but the nature of the beat differs in each of the two songs.

Fig. 4.2.

Spanish Folk Song (MSS 4)[2]

Allegro

---

[2]MSS refers to *Music for Sight Singing*, 2nd ed. (Englewood Cliffs, N.J.: Prentice-Hall, Inc., 1967). The number refers to the melody number.

Listen to the melody in Figure 4.2. Note that each beat in this melody can be divided into two parts. This can be demonstrated by tapping the beats in the right hand and, with the left hand, making two taps for each beat in the right hand.

Fig. 4.3.

Fig. 4.4.

German Folk Song (MSS 194)

Listen to the melody in Figure 4.4. Note that each beat in this melody can be divided into three parts. This can be demonstrated by tapping the beats in the right hand and, with the left hand, making three taps for each beat in the right hand.

Fig. 4.5.

The above procedure is known as dividing the beat. A beat that can be divided into two parts is known as a *simple* beat, a division often called "background of two." A beat that can be divided into three parts is known as a *compound* beat, often called "background of three."

Exercise 4.3. Listen to music examples: *a*) determine whether the background of the beat is simple or compound and, *b*) as in Exercise 4.2, determine whether the beats are in groupings of 2 or 3.

Meter

The meter of a piece of music is the basic scheme of beat groupings used; most music has a meter of two, three, or four beats per measure. Meter is not to be confused with rhythm. The term "rhythm" indicates the pattern of longer and shorter note values used; the sum total of the note or rest values in each measure will be equal to the number of beats per measure.

Fig. 4.6.

Hungarian Folk Song (MSS 32)

The Time Signature

It is the function of the time signature (meter signature) to indicate the meter of the piece (how many beats per measure) and the kind of notation to be used (what kind of a note gets one beat).

Simple Time. Music in which the beat is a simple beat is said to be in simple time. Since a simple beat is divisible into two parts, any note value divisible into two parts may be used to represent a beat. Therefore, any undotted note may be used to represent a beat.

Each time signature in Table 4.1 is derived by multiplying the number of beats per measure by the value of the note (indicated here as a fraction) assigned to receive one beat. Theoretically, this table could be extended indefinitely. Signatures with denominators of 4, 2, 8, and 16 are those most used, and in that order of frequency.

TABLE 4.1.

SIMPLE TIME SIGNATURES

Beat note	2 beats per measure (Duple)	3 beats per measure (Triple)	4 beats per measure (Quadruple)
$\circ\left(\frac{1}{1}\right)$	$\frac{2}{1}$	$\frac{3}{1}$	$\frac{4}{1}$
$\natural\left(\frac{1}{2}\right)$	$\frac{2}{2}$ or $\math혼{C}$	$\frac{3}{2}$	$\frac{4}{2}$
$\natural\left(\frac{1}{4}\right)$	$\frac{2}{4}$	$\frac{3}{4}$	$\frac{4}{4}$ or C
$\natural\left(\frac{1}{8}\right)$	$\frac{2}{8}$	$\frac{3}{8}$	$\frac{4}{8}$
$\natural\left(\frac{1}{16}\right)$	$\frac{2}{16}$	$\frac{3}{16}$	$\frac{4}{16}$
$\natural\left(\frac{1}{32}\right)$	$\frac{2}{32}$	$\frac{3}{32}$	$\frac{4}{32}$

Observe from Table 4.1 that in simple time, the numerators of time signatures are 2, 3, and 4.

2 = duple simple time (meter)
3 = triple simple time
4 = quadruple simple time

Therefore, the time signature $\frac{2}{4}$ is to be interpreted as follows: 2 indicates that the music is in duple simple time, meaning that there are two beats in the measure, each beat divisible into two parts; 4 indicates that the quarter note is used to represent the beat, and it is divisible into two eighth notes.

Fig. 4.7.

Exercise 4.4. Explain verbally, or by diagram as in Figure 4.7, the meaning of the following time signatures.

$$\frac{3}{4}, \quad \frac{4}{4}, \quad \frac{3}{8}, \quad \frac{3}{2}, \quad \frac{3}{8}, \quad \frac{4}{16}, \quad \frac{4}{2}$$

Compound Time. Music in which the beat is a compound beat is said to be in compound time. Since a compound beat is divisible into three parts, any note value divisible into three parts may be used to represent a beat. Therefore, any dotted note may be used to represent a beat.

Each time signature in Table 4.2 is derived by multiplying the number of beats in a measure by the value of the note (indicated as a fraction) assigned to receive one beat. Signatures with denominators of 8, 4, and 16 are most commonly used, and in that order of frequency.

Compound time signatures do not indicate the number of beats per measure and the note value receiving one beat as conveniently as do the simple time signatures. Actually, the upper number of the compound time signature indicates the number of *divided beats* per measure, while the lower number states the kind of note used to represent a *divided beat*. The beat note is therefore equal in value to three of the notes indicated by the lower number, for example, $\frac{6}{8}$: the beat equals three eighth notes, or a dotted quarter note.

TABLE 4.2.

COMPOUND TIME SIGNATURES

Beat note	2 beats per measure (Duple)	3 beats per measure (Triple)	4 beats per measure (Quadruple)
○· $\left(\frac{3}{2}\right)$	$\frac{6}{2}$	$\frac{9}{2}$	$\frac{12}{2}$
♩· $\left(\frac{3}{4}\right)$	$\frac{6}{4}$	$\frac{9}{4}$	$\frac{12}{4}$
♪· $\left(\frac{3}{8}\right)$	$\frac{6}{8}$	$\frac{9}{8}$	$\frac{12}{8}$
♬· $\left(\frac{3}{16}\right)$	$\frac{6}{16}$	$\frac{9}{16}$	$\frac{12}{16}$
♬· $\left(\frac{3}{32}\right)$	$\frac{6}{32}$	$\frac{9}{32}$	$\frac{12}{32}$

Observe from Table 4.2 that in compound time the numerators of the time signatures are 6, 9, and 12.

6 = duple compound time
9 = triple compound time
12 = quadruple compound time

Therefore, the time signature $\frac{6}{8}$ is interpreted as follows: 6 indicates that the music is in duple compound time, meaning that there are two beats in the measure, each beat being divisible into three parts; 8 indicates that the eighth note is a divided beat, three of which equal the beat note, a dotted quarter note.

Fig. 4.8.

Occasionally, twentieth-century composers will write a compound signature with the actual number of beats in the numerator and a note value in the denominator: $\frac{2}{}$. instead of $\frac{6}{8}$; $\frac{3}{}$. instead of $\frac{9}{16}$ and so on.

Fig. 4.9.

Paul Hindemith, String Trio, Op. 34

Sehr lebhaft

pp

(instead of $\frac{6}{4}$)

Copyright 1924 by B. Schott's Soehne, Mainz; by permission of Associated Music Publishers, Inc., Sole U.S. agents.

If this were standard practice, most of the confusion about compound signatures would cease to exist.

Exercise 4.5. Explain verbally, or by diagram as in Figure 4.8, the meaning of the following time signatures.

$\frac{6}{4}, \quad \frac{9}{8}, \quad \frac{12}{8}, \quad \frac{6}{16}, \quad \frac{12}{4}, \quad \frac{9}{2},$

Exceptions. In any time signature, the upper number always indicates how many of the note values expressed by the lower number will be found in any one measure. Usually, the time signature expresses rhythmic concepts just as presented, but exceptions do exist.

  a) Numerator of 4. In a fast tempo, there may be actually two beats per measure. In a fast $\frac{4}{4}$, the beat may be a half note, two half notes per measure. Sometimes this is indicated in the music by the term "alla breve" or by the signature ¢ . (See *Music for Sight Singing, 321.*)

  b) Numerator of 3. In a fast tempo, there may be actually one beat per measure. In a fast $\frac{3}{4}$, the beat may be a ♩., divisible into three quarter notes. Thus the effect is that of compound time, one beat per measure. The *scherzo* movements from the various Beethoven symphonies illustrate this effect. (See *Music for Sight Singing, 142–145.*)

  c) Numerator of 2, 3, or 4. In a slow tempo, the division of the note value indicated in the denominator may become the beat note. In a slow $\frac{2}{4}$, the eighth note may become the beat, with four beats per measure. (See Beethoven, Sonata for Piano No. 3, Op. 2, No. 3, second movement; also *Music for Sight Singing,* Chapter 20.)

  d) Numerator of 6, 9, 12. In a slow tempo, the numerator may indicate the number of beats per measure. These beats are rarely equal in stress. Usually the first note and every third note thereafter receives a stress; this preserves the impression of compound time.

Fig. 4.10.

(See Beethoven, Sonata for Piano No. 7, Op. 10, No. 3, second movement; also *Music for Sight Singing,* Chapter 20.)

Terminology Variant[3]

Simple time refers to metric groups of 2 or 3 $(\frac{2}{2}, \frac{2}{4}, \frac{2}{8}; \frac{3}{2}, \frac{3}{4}, \frac{3}{8})$. Compound time refers to combinations of the following metric groups:

---

[3]See Preface, *Terminology*

$$\frac{4}{4} = \frac{2}{4} + \frac{2}{4} \qquad\qquad \frac{6}{8} = \frac{3}{8} + \frac{3}{8}$$

$$\frac{4}{2} = \frac{2}{2} + \frac{2}{2} \qquad\qquad \frac{9}{8} = \frac{3}{8} + \frac{3}{8} + \frac{3}{8}$$

$$\frac{3}{2} = \frac{2}{4} + \frac{2}{4} + \frac{2}{4} \qquad \frac{12}{8} = \frac{3}{8} + \frac{3}{8} + \frac{3}{8} + \frac{3}{8}$$

$$\frac{3}{4} = \frac{2}{8} + \frac{2}{8} + \frac{2}{8} \qquad \frac{6}{4} = \frac{3}{4} + \frac{3}{4} \quad \text{etc.}$$

$\frac{3}{4}$, among others, appears both as a simple group and as a compound group; these are differentiated for reasons of tempo.[4]

APPLICATION

Written Materials

Assignment 4.1.   Place a correct time signature before each musical example. The first measure of an example may be incomplete, in which case the last measure is also incomplete; the two partial measures equal one complete measure in time value. In a few cases, more than one correct signature is possible.

---

[4]See Paul Hindemith, *Elementary Training for Musicians* (New York: Associated Music Publishers, 1946), pp. 98–101.

Assignment 4.2. Find examples of time signatures in music scores, particularly those other than the commonly used $\frac{2}{4}$, $\frac{3}{4}$, $\frac{4}{4}$, and $\frac{6}{8}$. Copy out one or two measures of the music, including the time signature; indicate source of music including composer, title, publisher, and page number.

Rhythmic Transcription

Music written with a given time signature may be rewritten following any other time signature with the same numerator.

Fig. 4.11.

Performance of examples in each pair would be identical, assuming both have the same tempo indication.

Assignment 4.3. From Part I of *Music for Sight Singing*, transcribe each melody listed below using the time signature indicated.

a) No. 1 in $\frac{4}{2}, \frac{4}{8}$

b) No. 29 in $\frac{3}{8}, \frac{3}{16}$

c) No. 41 in $\frac{4}{4}$

d) No. 44 in $\frac{4}{4}, \frac{4}{2}$

e) No. 59 in $\frac{6}{4}, \frac{6}{16}$

f) No. 72 in $\frac{6}{8}, \frac{6}{4}$

g) No. 135 in $\frac{12}{4}, \frac{12}{16}$

h) No. 199 in $\frac{9}{4}, \frac{9}{16}$

Ear Training and Music Reading

The Conductor's Beat

The ability to read rhythm demonstrates comprehension of the meaning of the printed rhythmic symbols. This ability is one of the two required for successful sight singing, the other being comprehension of the printed pitch symbols.

Use of the conductor's beats of 2, 3, and 4 will facilitate the development of rhythmic reading ability. Each of these conductor's beats is characterized by a preparatory upbeat, followed by a downbeat on the first beat of the measure. The upbeat is the preparation for the following downbeat; the downbeat drops in a straight line and describes a small bounce at the instant the first beat occurs. After the downbeat, each of the conductor's beats follows a different course.

Fig. 4.12.

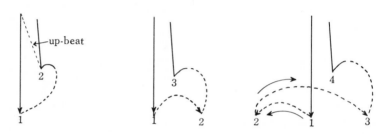

At the completion of one measure, the last beat of the measure is the upbeat of the next measure.

Exercise 4.6. Practice each of the conductor's beats before a mirror and with a metronome. Set the metronome at a slow rate at first (about M.M. 50). These movements must become completely automatic, so that when you read rhythm or sing at sight, your attention can be devoted to the musical notation.

Exercise 4.7. Add simple background to each of these conductor's beats by tapping twice with the left hand to each beat of the right hand. In doing so, you are conducting duple simple, triple simple, and quadruple simple times. Follow all directions given in Exercise 4.6.

Exercise 4.8. Practice the conductor's beats (2, 3, and 4) adding a compound background by tapping three times with the left hand to each beat in the right hand. In doing so, you are conducting duple compound, triple compound, and quadruple compound times. Follow other directions given in Exercise 4.6.

Rhythmic Reading

Reading should be done with rhythmic syllables. For notes that fall on the beat use the number of the beat in the measure. When the note is held for more than one beat, hold the number of the beat on which the note started.

Fig. 4.13.

German Folk Song (MSS 1)

Simple Time.   When the beat is divided into two equal parts, the second half of the beat may receive the syllable *ta* (*tah*).[5]

Fig. 4.14.

a)

Spanish Folk Song (MSS 29)

b)

German Folk Song (MSS 43)

Compound Time.   When the beat is divided into three parts, the second and third division of each beat may receive the syllable *ta.*

Fig. 4.15.

a)

German Folk Song (MSS 66)

b)

American Folk Song (Indiana) (MSS 73)

---

[5]Syllables other than *ta* may be used to read durations shorter than the beat, if desired. Rhythmic reading is more precise, and therefore more likely to be accurate, if the rhythmic syllable begins with an explosive consonant.

Before reading, make the following preparations:

a) Review the meaning of the time signature.

b) Choose the appropriate conductor's beat.

c) Start the conductor's beat and background at least one measure before beginning to read.

Try to read each piece of music through without stopping. If you make an error, do not stop to correct it, but keep going. The conductor's downbeat always coincides with a bar-line in the music, and it will help you keep your place. At the end of the piece, go back to review the reasons for any errors you made and reread those places to correct the errors.

Exercise 4.9.[6] Rhythmic reading in simple time. Ample material may be found in *Music for Sight Singing*, using all melodies in Chapters 1, 3, and 6, and all other melodies in Part I that are in simple time. These melodies in simple time use the beat and its division into two parts only.

Exercise 4.10. Rhythmic reading in compound time. Material may be found in *Music for Sight Singing*, using all melodies in Chapters 2, 4, and 7, and all other melodies in Part I that are in compound time. These melodies in compound time use the beat and its division into three parts only.

Rhythmic Dictation

This is the converse of rhythmic reading. In rhythmic reading the rhythmic symbols are converted into sound. In rhythmic dictation, the rhythmic sounds are converted into notation. At this point, rhythmic dictation will contain the same problems as studied in rhythmic reading.

Exercise 4.11. Rhythmic dictation, simple time.

Follow this procedure in taking rhythmic dictation.

a) The time signature will be announced. Write this on your paper.

b) At the given signal, make the proper conductor's beat and tap the background.

c) Listen to the melody played, while conducting.

d) Sing back the melody, aloud or silently as directed, still using the conductor's beat.

e) Write rhythmic notation on your paper.

Had melody number 1 from *Music for Sight Singing* been dictated, your solution would be as follows:

 etc.

Exercise 4.12. Rhythmic dictation, compound time. Follow directions listed in Exercise 4.11.

---

[6]Upon completion of Exercise 4.9., you may begin work in Chapter 5.

Self-Help Procedures

In listening to a melody being dictated, it is of utmost importance that the student *memorize* the melody as soon as possible, since it is impossible to write on paper that which cannot be recalled to mind. The ability to remember the sounds heard will be equally important in later studies, such as melodic and harmonic dictation.

Students working in pairs can be of great assistance to each other in training melodic memory or rhythmic dictation outside regular classroom time. These procedures may be followed.

Memory. Using *Music for Sight Singing*, Student A chooses a melody. From this melody he plays one to four measures. Student B immediately sings the phrase back. If there is an error or if it is incomplete, the procedure is repeated until a correct response is achieved. Continued practice will reduce the number of hearings necessary to achieve a correct response. When the number of playings is reduced to one, extend the length of the melody.

Dictation. Using *Music for Sight Singing*, Student A chooses a melody and announces the time signature. Student B makes the appropriate conductor's beat, with background. Student A plays one phrase, which Student B sings back using rhythmic syllables. Repeat playing and singing until phrase is sung back correctly. Then write the rhythmic notation only on paper. Aim to reduce the number of hearings necessary and to extend the amount of material heard at one time.

5

The Melodic Line (I)

THEORY AND ANALYSIS[1]

A melody consists of a succession of tones. The pitches of this succession may consist of repeated notes, notes adjacent to each other, as in a scale, and intervals larger than scale steps. Rhythmically, these notes display varying degrees of duration. Melodies may be simple or difficult depending upon the simplicity or complexity of their pitch and rhythmic elements. In most melodies, these elements are contained within a formal structure.

Pitch

A melody in its simplest form may consist of adjacent scale steps only. These are comparatively uncommon except for ecclesiastical chants. More usual is a melody incorporating both scale line passages and intervals larger than the scale step. Having studied intervals in the major triad, we will begin study of melodic lines that consist of adjacent scale steps and skips in the tonic triad, and melodic lines such as are found in Chapters 1 and 2 in *Music for Sight Singing*.

Rhythm

The simplest kind of rhythmic pattern in a melody would be the use of single note value. Such melodies are uncommon. Melodic interest is heightened by contrast in the durations of pitches. This contrast can be very simple, as

---

[1]Study of this chapter may begin upon completion of rhythmic reading and rhythmic dictation in simple time from Chapter 4. It is suggested that the study of sight singing and melodic dictation precede that of melodic composition.

demonstrated by the melody of Figure 5.4, which consists of eighth notes only except for a single quarter note at the beginning of measures 4 and 8. The melody in Figure 5.6 is only slightly more complex. In rhythmic reading, observe how few rhythmic patterns are used in any one melody and how often rhythmic patterns are repeated.

Form

Most music is written in some orderly arrangement. In the music of Western civilization, certain patterns or plans of musical construction have come to be commonly (though not exclusively) used. These patterns are known as musical *forms*.

The term *form* refers to the shape or structure of the object or concept being described. In music, a form usually ends at a cadence point; a form begins either at the beginning of the piece or immediately after a cadence. Since a musical composition usually has more than one cadence, it usually contains a series of forms. These smaller forms, in turn, will often combine to make up a larger kind of form, the nature and description of which are determined by the number and nature of the material between cadences.

From this general description, we can turn our attention to the smallest of the forms, the *phrase*. In melodic writing, the phrase is a group of notes leading to a cadence (review Chapter 2, page 34). The distance from the first note of a phrase to the cadence may be any number of measures, though usually not more than eight. A frequently used phrase length in music is the four-measure phrase, as shown in Figure 5.1. Because it is so commonly used, it is useful to consider the four-measure phrase as a standard length to which other varying phrase lengths may be compared.

Fig. 5.1.

Gaily

German Folk Song (MSS 18)

In this melody, the first phrase ends with a cadence on the tonic note, and the whole phrase is marked off with a phrase-mark extending from the first note to the last note of the phrase. A phrase may also consist of two or more distinct units, called *motives*. The phrase in Figure 5.2 is composed of two

Fig. 5.2.

Moderato

German Folk Song (MSS 1)

two-measure motives; the motives combine to make a phrase. The motive can be identified by the fact that it is a unit of melody smaller than a phrase, usually identifiable by a pause in the melodic line or in the rhythm. Note that the phrase-mark is used to indicate the length of the motive.

Two phrases may combine to form a *period*. In a period, the first phrase, called the *antecedent phrase*, usually ends on a temporary cadence (lacking a feeling of complete finality), and called a *half cadence*. This is accomplished by ending the phrase on a note of the V triad[2] (Figure 5.3, measure 4) or, less often, on the third or fifth of the tonic triad, called an *imperfect cadence* (Figure 5.4, measure 4). The second phrase, called the *consequent phrase*, then ends usually on the tonic note, called a *perfect cadence*, or less often, on an imperfect cadence.

Periods may be *parallel* or *contrasting*. A period is parallel when the two phrases are similar in some respect. Usually the beginnings of each phrase are identical, as in Figure 5.3, but any marked melodic similarity in the two phrases, such as the similar melodic contour in Figure 5.4, will justify analysis as a parallel period. When the two phrases of a period lack any specific or general similarity, the period is contrasting, as in Figure 5.5.

Fig. 5.3.   Parallel Period

Fig. 5.4.   Parallel Period

---

[2]The V triad is a major triad (in both major and minor keys) built on the fifth scale step (C major: V = G B D). The fifth, seventh, or second scale step can be used at the end of the antecedent phrase to imply a V triad, thereby creating a temporary or half cadence.

Fig. 5.5. Contrasting Period

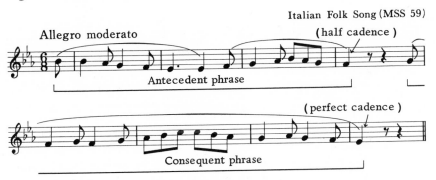

At times, successive phrases will each end with the tonic note. Since the perfect cadence marks the *end* of a formal pattern, these phrases cannot be combined into a larger form. The folksong in Figure 5.6 contains two four-measure phrases, each ending on the tonic note. Therefore, the song is not a period, but simply two phrases.

Fig. 5.6.

Phrases are also classified according to the rhythmic placement of their first and last notes. Phrases beginning on a strong beat are said to have a *masculine beginning*, phrases beginning on a weak beat a *feminine beginning*. Similarly, phrases ending on a strong beat have a *masculine ending* and phrases ending on a weak beat a *feminine ending*. The four possible combinations of masculine and feminine beginnings and endings can be found in Chapter 1 of *Music for Sight Singing*.

Fig. 5.7.

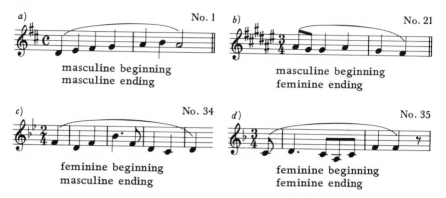

Parts *a*), *b*), and *d*) of Figure 5.7 are motives. The principle is the same for entire phrases. Usually each phrase of a period is found with the same type of beginning and ending, though exceptions may be noted, as in melody number 15 from *Music for Sight Singing*, where the first phrase has a feminine beginning and the second phrase a masculine beginning, or in melody number 16, which shows the reverse: the first phrase with a masculine beginning and the second with a feminine beginning.

There are many exceptions to these statements concerning musical form. A careful study of the melodies used for sight singing will reveal many variations of musical forms, including phrases of lengths other than four measures, cadences on tones other than those previously indicated, and combinations of repetitions of either phrases or parts of phrases. But for the first attempts in melodic analysis and melody writing, the student should be satisfied to confine his efforts to the four-measure phrase and to the parallel or contrasting eight-measure period.

Assignment 5.1. Analyzing form in melodies. From Chapters 1 and 2 of *Music for Sight Singing*, analyze any of the following melodies, as assigned: 1, 2, 6, 14, 15, 16, 20, 28, 35, 40, 42, 44, 61, 64, 66, 70, 72, 73. Each is an eight-measure melody and may be *a*) a parallel period, *b*) a contrasting period, or *c*) two phrases.

Copy out the melody and indicate *a*) location and name of each cadence, *b*) phrase lengths, *c*) name of the entire form, and *d*) the nature of the beginning and the ending of each phrase. Use this example as a guide:

Fig. 5.8.

Fr. Silcher (MSS 26)

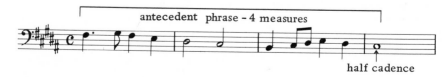

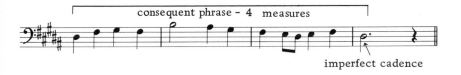

consequent phrase – 4 measures

imperfect cadence

Each phrase has a masculine beginning and a masculine ending. The two phrases make a contrasting period.

APPLICATION

Written Materials

Melodic Composition

The simplicity of *writing* a good melody can be observed through careful study of the melodies in Chapters 1–2 of *Music for Sight Singing*. These demonstrate how effectively a limited amount of technical material can produce a pleasing musical composition. These materials already studied are

    a) The scale.

    b) Intervals in the tonic triad.

    c) Rhythm—no note value smaller than the beat note and its division into two parts (in simple time) and into three parts (compound time).

Before writing a melody, special characteristics of the melodic line must be investigated.

    a) Scale-wise progressions are always good, but avoid more than five or six scale tones in the same direction. Figure 5.2, starting with six scale tones ascending, demonstrates the usual limit of successive scale tones in one direction.

    b) Skips (intervals of a third or larger) are usually limited to not more than two in the same direction, after which the melodic line progresses in the opposite direction.

Fig. 5.9.

English Folk Song (MSS 10)

Infrequent exceptions are illustrated in melodies 30 and 34 in which, after two leaps in the same direction, the melodies continue scale-wise in the same direction for one or two pitches.

    A large skip (fifth or larger) is usually approached from a direction opposite to the skip and left in a direction opposite to the skip.

Fig. 5.10.

Mexican Folk Song (MSS 33)

See also Figure 5.12, measures 1–2.

   c) Repetition from one phrase to another has already been shown under "Form," Figure 5.3. Repetition of smaller units of the melody are also effective.

Fig. 5.11.

Spanish Folk Song (MSS 4)

A *sequence* is similar to repetition except that the repeated material appears at a new pitch level. In the following example, measures 3 and 4 each are a sequence of measure 2. (See also melodies 17, 31 and 48.)

Fig. 5.12.

German Folk Song (MSS 36)

Sequence need not be exact, but may be modified to some extent. The last two measures below are a sequence of the previous two measures, though differing by one note.

Fig. 5.13.

Spanish Folk Song (MSS 29)

   d) The highest note of a melody (the *climax* note) is usually not repeated during the course of the phrase, and often not repeated during the course of a period. Because it is the highest note, it tends to stand out from the rest of the piece and repetition diminishes its effectiveness. The same rule applies to the lowest note of a melody (*anti-climax* note), though not as strictly.

e) The leading tone (seventh scale step) must be treated with care. As its name implies, it *leads* to the tonic. When approached by step from below, the leading tone must progress to the tonic. When preceded by the tonic note, the leading tone may progress down by step, as in a descending scale, or it may return to the tonic.

Fig. 5.14.[3]

a) leading tone approached by step from below and progresses up
b) leading tone approached from tonic and progresses down by step
c) leading tone approached from tonic and returns to tonic

Assignment 5.2. Write original four-measure melodies demonstrating each of the four possible phrase classifications (masculine and feminine beginnings and endings).

Review the following before writing, and check the melody you have written against these points.

a) Use only scale-wise passages and skips in the tonic triad.

b) Use a simple meter; use no note value smaller than the beat note and its division into two parts. Avoid complex rhythm patterns.

c) Use scale-wise patterns, skips, repetitions, and sequences as discussed in this chapter.

d) Be sure each phrase ends with an appropriate cadence, either half, imperfect, or perfect.

Assignment 5.3. Write original eight-measure periods, following directions given in Assignment 5.2. Phrases already written for the previous assignment may be used as one phrase of the period where feasible.

Assignment 5.4. Write original phrases and periods in compound time, following directions given in Assignment 5.2.

---

[3]Key names will be indicated by letter name under some music examples. A large letter indicates a major key; a small letter indicates a minor key (C = C major; c = c minor).

The test of a good melody is its singability. Playing the melody on the piano will not necessarily reveal a defect, since almost any melody can easily be played. If, in singing, there is an awkward interval or section, try to determine the cause of the defect and rewrite as much as necessary to make the melody easily singable.

Ear Training and Music Reading

Sight Singing

One of the skills demanded of the professional musician is the ability to "hear" a musical score merely by looking at it. This is essential, for instance, to any musician who expects to direct a musical ensemble, whether it be band, orchestra, or choir. The director of such an ensemble must look at his score and know what sounds to expect from his organization. He has to recognize whether the sounds played or sung are the same as those written in his score, and what specific errors are being made by the performers. If the director cannot do this, he is merely a "stick-waver" and unable to offer his musicians any competent assistance in the reproduction of the musical score.

This all-important ability can be developed in several ways: a) through ear-training exercises, already begun in Chapter 3, b) through exercises in dictation, begun in Chapter 4, and c) through sight singing. In sight singing, the student is asked to look at a piece of music he has never seen before and then sing that music without recourse to any instrument. When this can be done correctly, it demonstrates the student's ability to comprehend mentally the symbols on the printed page. Reading music on an instrument does not prove this skill conclusively; a pianist, for example, may interpret a note on the staff as a fingering and play the note correctly without knowing beforehand what it will sound like.

Sight singing involves the simultaneous use of two reading skills—the reading of rhythm and the reading of pitch. The former skill has been studied in Chapter 4; at this point the study of the skill of reading pitches will be added to that of reading rhythm. Initial sight singing experience may be gained from *Music for Sight Singing*, Chapter 1, sections a—e, and Chapter 2, section a. These melodies contain only scale steps and intervals in the tonic triad.

Melodic Dictation

In melodic dictation, the student is asked to write on the staff a melody he hears performed. This is a skill closely related to sight singing; while in sight singing, the student interprets notation as pitch, in melodic dictation the student interprets pitch as notation. Melodic dictation is also a continuation of the skills learned in rhythmic dictation, with the added ability to write the correct pitch. As in sight singing, at this point all dictated melodies will be diatonic and scale-wise, with occasional intervals in the tonic triad, and with rhythm no more difficult than that of previous rhythm dictation exercises.

Exercise 5.1.   Melodic dictation, simple time. Follow this procedure. After sufficient practice, eliminate steps *d*) and *e*).

a) The name of the key will be given. Write the key signature on the staff, treble or bass, as assigned.

b) The time signature will be given. Write it on the staff.

c) While making the conductor's beat and tapping the background, listen to the melody played by the instructor.

d) On the second playing, sing the melody with the piano.

e) Sing the melody without the piano, still conducting and tapping.

f) Sing aloud or mentally, as directed, the tonic triad (1–3–5–3–1) and determine the letter name of the first note of the melody.

g) Write the melody on the staff. If it seems particularly difficult, first write the rhythm above the staff.

h) Listen to a final playing and check your work.

As an alternate procedure, the instructor may give only the letter name of the first note instead of giving the name of the key. After hearing the melody (step *c*), sing the tonic triad and then sing the first note of the melody. From this, determine the key and write the signature on the staff. For example, G is given as the first note. Singing the tonic triad after hearing the melody reveals that G is the third of the triad. The key will be E♭ with a signature of three flats.

Exercise 5.2.   Melodic dictation, compound time. Follow directions given in Exercise 5.1.

Success in melodic dictation, as in rhythmic dictation, depends upon the ability to memorize the melody heard. Review the comments and directions for the development of musical memory found on page 65.

Keyboard Harmony

Exercise 5.3.   Play melodies from Chapters 1–2 of *Music for Sight Singing,* melodies written for Assignments 5.2–5.4 or other melodies as assigned, at the keyboard. Before playing the melody, play the tonic triad of the key. While playing, observe the melodic skips and mentally relate each to the tonic triad.

6

The Connection of Chords

Elementary Principles of Part-Writing

Part-writing is the name of the procedure used to connect a series of chords in a musical composition, such as the series of chords shown in the hymn, Figure 6.1.

Fig. 6.1.

Hymn: Hamburg

FAC   FAC CEG FAC   GB♭D F♯AC GB♭D   FAC CEG   FAC

The triad spellings under each of the bass notes constitute an analysis of the vertical structures of the composition, usually referred to as the harmony. But there is present another and equally important element, the horizontal structure, represented in the figure above by four melodic lines: the soprano, alto, tenor, and bass lines. In writing or analyzing music, it is important that both the vertical (harmonic) and horizontal (melodic) aspects of the composition receive equal attention.

The principal aim of part-writing is to produce good individual voice lines when a series of chords is written in succession. Each line should be easily singable, as you have already learned in your work in sight singing, melodic dictation, and melodic composition. Placing individual notes of a given triad in one voice part or another at random will not produce good melodic lines, except perhaps accidentally. If we were to rewrite Figure 6.1, using the same melody, the same bass line and the same chords, but filling in the remaining chord tones in the alto and tenor voices at random, an arrangement such as this might result:

Fig. 6.2.

FAC   FAC CEG   FAC   GB♭D   F♯AC GB♭D   FAC CEG   FAC

As this "arrangement" is played at the piano, try to sing the alto line. It is difficult because the alto part is a poor melodic line. Now compare the alto line of Figure 6.2 with that of the original, as shown in Figure 6.3, noting how much easier it is to sing the original alto line. The same comparison can be made between the two tenor lines.

Fig. 6.3.

arrangement

original

This and succeeding chapters will present rules for part-writing, which will aid you in connecting chords so that each voice is smooth and singable, and which will help prevent such poor voice lines as found in Figure 6.2.

Students often question the origin and application of part-writing rules. "Do composers follow the rules?" they ask, or "Why do I find places in the music I perform that do not follow the rules?" A composer of serious music (meaning music such as symphony, opera, art song, string quartet, etc., as opposed to popular or commercial music) is primarily concerned with the exploration of *new* ways of musical expression. He is certainly cognizant of past practices and will avail himself of any earlier techniques that he finds useful, but he will not feel that need to limit himself to procedures already established by earlier composers. In creating new methods of expressing musical ideas, he risks his reputation as a composer of merit through public approval or disapproval of his efforts, as judged by his contemporaries or by posterity. Much music is forgotten soon after it is written, while other music maintains its interest or becomes even better known and accepted as time goes on. In looking back over a period of music composition, the music theoretician attempts to discover, to classify, and to codify the principles and procedures of those composers whose music has stood the test of time.

In surveying the music of c. 1650–c. 1900, music theoreticians have discovered that most of the basic principles and procedures of music composition are similar, so similar, in fact, that the period is often known as the "common practice" period. In harmony, this common practice refers to both the principles of chord progression[1] and the techniques of part-writing. Part-writing rules are simply the result of investigation of part-writing practices of successful composers of the period. This theoretical investigation shows how these composers usually (but not always) handled various problems in moving from one chord to another, and the procedures thus deduced are organized and codified as a set of rules.

It should be understood that these rules exist only for pedagogical convenience in the teaching of part-writing techniques of the common practice period. Although they suggest effective procedures to be used in given situations, there are often times when exceptional procedures must be used or may be used optionally to produce more effective lines. Your work in part-writing will begin with chord connections in which correct application of part-writing rules will produce satisfactory and effective voice lines. As your skill increases, exceptional practices will be presented, including reasons why these exceptions will prevent poor lines or even enhance lines already satisfactory.

Appendix 1 presents eleven rules that cover all the basic part-writing procedures in this volume and its sequel, *Advanced Harmony: Theory and Practice*. Some students find that Rule 11 (General Rule), plus a natural musical instinct or intuition, suffices in producing satisfactory results. Most students, however, will benefit by studying Rules 1—10 individually and carefully applying each new rule as it is presented in this chapter and in those that follow.

Elementary part-writing will be studied through the medium of the four-part vocal style, as shown in Figure 6.1. Examples of four-part vocal writing

---

[1]See Chapter 14.

on an elementary level can easily be found in hymnbooks, in collections containing simple secular pieces as "America!" and "Auld Lang Syne," and, on a more advanced level, in the four-part chorales of J.S. Bach. The principles of music composition inherent in the four-part vocal style are basic to vocal music in other numbers of voices and to all media of instrumental music, such as piano solo, solo voice or instrument with piano, instrumental ensembles, band, orchestra, and so on. The knowledge gained in vocal writing from this volume will be applied in the next volume to music composition in instrumental style. Successful completion of your study of part-writing techniques will serve not only as a basis for arranging and composing music, but will also give you a standard by which to judge the quality and performability of music when selecting it for yourself or for the group under your direction.

Writing a Single Triad

For the first part-writing project, the single triad will be placed on the staff. The triad will be written in four voices—soprano, alto, tenor, and bass, conforming to the four ranges of the human voice. When the treble and bass staves are used, the soprano and alto voices appear on the treble staff, and the tenor and bass voices appear on the bass staff.

In part-writing the single triad, four factors must be taken into consideration, *a*) voice range, *b*) doubling, *c*) triad position, and *d*) distance between voices.

a) *Range.* Each of the four voices should, as a rule, be written in the normal singing range of that voice.

Fig. 6.4.

soprano   alto   tenor   bass

Voices ordinarily should be kept within the ranges outlined by the whole notes. Pitches outside of these ranges are possible, but should be used only sparingly and within the limits of the black notes.

b) *Doubling.* Since four notes will be used, one note of the triad must be doubled, that is, two voices will have to use the same letter name, either in unison or in an octave relationship. The root of the triad is usually doubled.

Fig. 6.5.

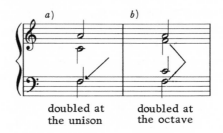

doubled at   doubled at
the unison   the octave

c) Position. Triads may appear in either of two positions, open or close. In *open position*[2] the distance between the soprano and tenor is an octave or more; in *close position,* the distance between the soprano and tenor is less than an octave. In either position, any interval may appear between tenor and bass.

Fig. 6.6.

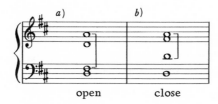

open   close

Note also that in open position another note of the triad could be inserted between the tenor and the soprano, while in close position, the three upper voices are as close together as possible.

d) Distance between voices. The distance between any two adjacent voices (for example, soprano and alto) usually does not exceed an octave, except that an interval larger than an octave may appear between the bass and tenor voices.

Voices should not be crossed, that is, the alto should not be lower than the tenor, the tenor should not be lower than the bass, and so on.

Written Materials

Assignment 6.1. Fill in the inner voices of each triad in both close position and open position, in that order. At present use two roots, one third and one fifth; keep voices in correct pitch range. Here is an example.

---

[2]The terms *open structure* and *close structure* are commonly used synonymously with *open position* and *close position.*

Fig. 6.7.

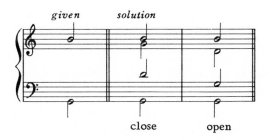

The given note on the bass staff is always the root of a major triad.

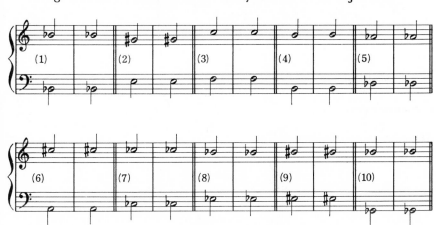

Assignment 6.2. Write each of the following triads on the staff in both close and open position. The bass will carry the root of the triad in all cases. Observe doubling and voice range instructions. The number after the triad indicates the soprano note to be used. **Example: G♭(3).**

Fig. 6.8.

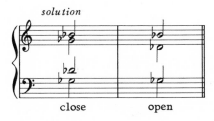

G (3), D (5), E (3), C♯ (5), D♭ (1), B (1), C♭ (1), D♯ (5), A♭ (3), F♯ (3).

The Connection of Repeated Triads

Part-Writing Rule No. 1. When two triads, each with the same spelling and each with its root in the bass, are used in succession with differing soprano notes:

  a) each may be written in the same position by moving the three upper voices in similar motion;

Fig. 6.9.

  b) each may be in a different position; when changing position, two voices, the bass and one other, remain stationary while the other two voices exchange tones.

Fig. 6.10.

Several factors determine which method will be used.

  a) The necessity of keeping voices in a good register. In the example, continuing close position *a*) places both tenor and alto in excessively high ranges. Changing the position *b*) corrects this situation.

Fig. 6.11.

b) Avoidance of large leaps (fifths or larger) in the inner voices. In the example, maintaining the same position *a*) causes large leaps in the tenor and alto. Changing the position *b*) corrects this situation.

Fig. 6.12.

c) The necessity to maintain correct voice distribution (two roots, one third and one fifth). Maintaining the same position *a*) makes it impossible to keep the correct chord distribution. Changing the position *b*) corrects this situation.

Fig. 6.13.

(no 5th)

Often either solution is correct. In the following example, changing position *a*) is correct; maintaining the same position *b*) is also correct.

Fig. 6.14.

Assignment 6.3.   Choose the better of the two solutions in each of the pairs of examples. Explain why you made your choice. State if both solutions are correct.

Assignment 6.4.   Write each pair of repeated triads using whichever method is more appropriate.

7

The Minor Triad
The Melodic Line in Minor

THEORY AND ANALYSIS

Upon examining the minor scale and the triads that can be built upon each of its steps,[1] we find that the triad built upon the first scale step, the tonic, is a minor triad. This minor tonic triad (i) serves the same functions in a minor key as were ascribed in Chapter 3 to the major tonic triad in a major key. One of the most important of these is its function as the final goal of the harmonic progression in a minor key.

Fig. 7.1.

Beethoven, Sonata for Piano, Op. 2, No. 1

Unlike the almost inevitable final major tonic triad in a major key, two alternate final triads can be found in minor keys, especially in music of the sixteenth, seventeenth, and early eighteenth centuries. During this time,

---

[1]Review Figure 2.4 and accompanying discussion.

the minor triad was often felt to be too dissonant for a concluding triad. In its place, composers used either a major triad, called a "picardy third" or "tierce de Picardie"[2]

Fig. 7.2.

Bach, Cantata No. 4
"Christ Lag in Todesbanden"

e: i   i6   V   V   I

or a triad without a third (root and fifth only).

Fig. 7.3.

Handel, Concerto Grosso in B Minor,
Op. 6, No. 12

Adagio

b: iv   i   iv   V   i

The Minor Triad

The minor triad displays both similarities and differences when compared with the major triad. In both, the perfect intervals are identical,

Fig. 7.4.

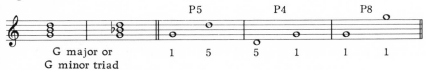

G major or   P5   P4   P8
G minor triad   1   5   5   1   1   1

---

[2]The origin and meaning of this term are unknown.

while the locations of the major and minor intervals are reversed.

Fig. 7.5.

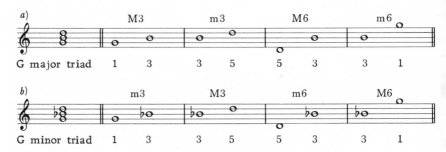

Minor Triad Spelling

With a knowledge of interval names and spellings, the minor triad may be spelled by interval. These are the intervals in the minor triad.

1 up to 3	Minor Third (m3)	3 down to 1
3 up to 5	Major Third (M3)	5 down to 3
5 up to 1	Perfect Fourth (P4)	1 down to 5
1 up to 5	Perfect Fifth (P5)	5 down to 1
3 up to 1	Major Sixth (M6)	1 down to 3
5 up to 3	Minor Sixth (m6)	3 down to 5
1 up to 1⎫		⎡1 down to 1
3 up to 3⎬ Perfect Octave (P8)		⎨3 down to 3
5 up to 5⎭		⎣5 down to 5

Assignment 7.1.   Minor triad spelling.

a) Spell with letter names the minor triad when each of the following is the root. D, A, C, F, E♭, A♭, G♯, B, G♭, B♭.

b) Spell the minor triad when each of the following is the third. F, C, B♭, E, E♭, D, F♯, G♯, A, B, D♭.

c) Spell the minor triad when each of the following is the fifth. A, B, D, G, F♯, B♭, C♯, A♭, F, D♯.

Assignment 7.2.   Based on a given triad, spell each of the intervals in the table of intervals. Example: C♯ minor triad.

m3	C♯ up to E	m6	G♯ up to E
M3	E up to G♯	M6	E up to C♯
P4	G♯ up to C♯	P8	C♯ up to C♯
P5	C♯ up to G♯		E up to E
			G♯ up to G♯

Do the same with triads from Assignment 7.1 *a*, or others as assigned.

Assignment 7.3. Identify intervals from melodies in minor keys from *Music for Sight Singing*, Chapter 1, section *f*. Follow example of Assignment 3.4.

The Melodic Line in Minor

As its name implies, the melodic form of the minor scale is generally used in melodic writing. When a melody ascends through a scale line from the dominant tone to the tonic tone, the sixth and seventh scale steps are usually raised.

Fig. 7.6.

When the melody descends through a scale line from the tonic tone to the dominant tone, the seventh and sixth scale steps are usually lowered, as in the descending form of the melodic minor scale.

Fig. 7.7.

a minor

When either the sixth or seventh scale step is used without the other in a step-wise passage, the seventh scale step is raised and proceeds up (Figure 7.8. *a*), and the sixth scale step is lowered and proceeds down (Figure 7.8. *b*).

Fig. 7.8.

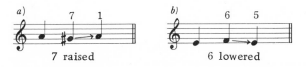

Occasionally, both the sixth and seventh scale steps are found in a step-wise passage but are not found between the tonic and dominant tones. In this case each note in the group of sixth and seventh scale steps is treated alike. If the last note of the group is the seventh scale step, all the notes of the group are raised (Figure 7.9. *a*). If the last note of the group is the sixth scale step, all the notes of the group are lowered (Figure 7.9. *b*).

Fig. 7.9.

Last note of group (7) proceeds up.   Last note of group (6) proceeds down.
Use ascending melodic minor.   Use natural minor (descending
                                          melodic minor).

Fig. 7.10.

Assignment 7.4. Analyze melodies in a minor key as found in *Music for Sight Singing*, Chapter 1 *f* and Chapter 2 *b*. Locate examples of the sixth and seventh scale steps and describe their use as in the following example.

Fig. 7.11.

(MSS 50, meas. 4-7)

1. Scale step 7 is used alone; it is raised and proceeds up.
2. Scale steps 7 and 6 descend between the tonic and dominant tones; they are lowered.

APPLICATION

Written Materials

Part-Writing

Assignment 7.5. Write minor triads on the staff. Using each of the following letters as a root of a minor triad, write the complete triad in four voices, using the number after the letter name as the soprano note. Example: B♭ (3)

Fig. 7.12.

A (1), E (5), G (3), F♯ (5), C♯ (1), B (1), E♭ (5), G♯ (3), A♭ (1), D♯ (5).

Assignment 7.6.   Write intervals from the minor triad on the staff. Using the table of intervals in Assignment 7.2, write all the intervals ascending and descending in each of the triads listed in Assignment 7.5. Example: B♭.

Fig. 7.13.

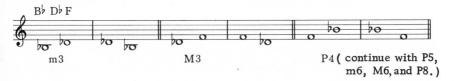

Assignment 7.7   Write each pair of repeated minor triads. Follow all directions for part-writing given in Chapter 6. No new procedures are required.

Melody-Writing

Assignment 7.8.   Writing melodies in minor keys. The discussion of melodic writing in Chapter 5 applies equally to melodies in major and in minor keys. In a minor key, an additional consideration is the treatment of the sixth and seventh scale steps as outlined earlier in this chapter. Melodies in a minor key may now be written as phrases or as periods and in simple or compound time, as assigned. Follow specific directions as given in Assignments 5.2 and 5.3.

Ear Training and Music Reading

The Minor Triad

Ear-training drills for the minor triad listed below are similar in intent and procedure to the drills for the major triad found in Chapter 3.

Exercise 7.1. Singing the minor triad: *a*) listen to minor triads played at the piano. After each triad is sounded, sing the pattern 1–3–5–3–1.

b) Listen to the triad. Sing the root of the triad only.

Exercise 7.2. *a*) Play or listen to any given pitch. Call this pitch "1." Sing a minor triad from this pitch.

b) Call the given pitch "5." Sing the triad pattern.

c) Call the given pitch "3." Sing the triad pattern.

Exercise 7.3. Repeat Exercise 7.2. Instead of singing with numbers, sing with triad spellings.

Exercise 7.4. *a*) Repeat Exercise 7.2, but be prepared to sing either a major or minor triad as directed by instructor.

b) Repeat Exercise 7.3, but be prepared to sing either a major or minor triad with triad spellings.

Exercise 7.5. *a*) Identify the soprano note of a minor triad as 1, 3, or 5 of the triad when the triad is played at the piano.

b) Listen to a series of major and minor triads, mixed. Identify the soprano note and indicate whether the triad is major or minor. For example, the answers to the examples below would be 5M, 3m, 1m, 3M (M = major, m = minor).

Fig. 7.14.

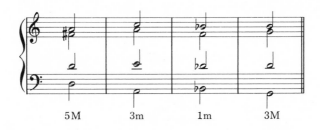

Exercise 7.6. *a*) Spell a minor triad when the triad is played at the piano. Follow directions given for Exercise 3.12.

b) Same as *a*), but triads played will be both major and minor, mixed.

Intervals in the Minor Triad

Ear-training drills for intervals in the minor triad are similar to the drills for intervals in the major triad found in Chapter 3. The intervals studied here are the same as in the major triad, but in different contexts; for example, a major third is found as 3 up to 5 in a minor triad rather than as 1 up to 3 in a major triad.

Each exercise below is based on a similar exercise from Chapter 3, using the minor triad instead of the major triad as its basis.

Exercise 7.7. Singing intervals from the minor triad by number. See Exercise 3.13.

Exercise 7.8. Singing minor triad intervals from a given pitch. See Exercise 3.14.

Exercise 7.9. Identifying intervals from the minor triad aurally. See Exercise 3.15.

Exercise 7.10. Writing intervals from the minor triad on the staff from dictation. See Exercise 3.19.

Sight Singing

Melodies in minor keys may be found in *Music for Sight Singing*, Chapter 1 *f* and Chapter 2 *b*. These melodies consist of scale line passages and leaps in the minor tonic triad only.

Melodic Dictation

Exercise 7.11. Taking melodic dictation in minor keys. Follow directions given for melodic dictation in Chapter 5. When listening to melodies in a minor key, pay particular attention to the use of the sixth and seventh scale degrees. These will conform to the rules given in the discussion on melody writing. The melodies you hear will contain scale line passages and leaps in the tonic triad only and may be in simple or compound time.

Keyboard Harmony

Exercise 7.12. Playing the minor triad. Play any minor triad, as assigned, with the root in the bass and in each of its three soprano positions. Follow directions for playing the major triad in Exercise 3.20.

Exercise 7.13. Play Assignment 7.7 at the keyboard.

8

Authentic and Plagal Cadences

THEORY AND ANALYSIS

The Three Principal Triads in a Key

The tonic, subdominant, and dominant triads are often known as the three principal triads of a key. Cadences, as presented in the following paragraphs, are composed of the tonic triad plus one of the other principal triads. Of all possible cadence formulae, these are by far the most frequently used in music.

The three principal triads are here illustrated in the key center of E. In minor, the three forms of the scale influence the spelling of the subdominant and dominant triads.

E Major	E G♯ B		I	
	A C♯ E	B D♯ F♯	IV	V
E Minor natural form	E G B		i	
	A C E	B D F♯	iv	v
E Minor harmonic form	E G B		i	
	A C E	B D♯ F♯	iv	V
E Minor melodic form	E G B		i	
	A C♯ E	B D♯ F♯	IV	V

Assignment 8.1. *a*) Spell the three principal triads in each major key.

b) Spell the three principal triads in each minor key. These should be spelled in each of the three scale forms.

Harmonic Cadences[1]

The harmonic cadence consists ordinarily of two chords, usually two triads, or a seventh chord and a triad, and marks the end of a phrase or larger formal structure in music. A harmonic cadence can be identified in two ways:

1. By the chords selected for the progression. When tonic and dominant chords are used (V–I, I–V; V–i, i–V), the cadence is known as an *authentic cadence*. When the tonic and subdominant chords are used (IV–I, I–IV; iv–i, i–iv), the cadence is known as a *plagal cadence*.

2. By the degree of finality implied in the sound of the chord progression. The terms *perfect* and *imperfect* identify cadences that end with the tonic triad (V–I, IV–I, etc.). Of the two, the perfect cadence provides the strongest implication of finality. The *half* cadence, ending on a triad other than tonic (I–V, I–IV, etc.) implies that the music must continue until a perfect or imperfect cadence is reached.

A cadence is fully described by combining one of the terms *authentic* or *plagal* with one of the terms *perfect, imperfect,* or *half.*

Authentic Cadences

The authentic cadences are:

1. *Perfect authentic:* The progression V–I[2] or V–i in which the V triad has its root in the bass and the final tonic triad has its root in both bass and soprano. The soprano line connecting the two triads usually proceeds from the leading tone to tonic (7–8) or supertonic to tonic (2–1), illustrated in Figure 8.1 *a* and *b*. Perfect authentic cadences can also be seen in these music excerpts: Figures 2.9, 2.17, 7.2, and 7.3.

2. *Imperfect authentic:* the progression V–I[2] or V–i in which the final tonic triad is found with its third or fifth in the soprano and/or the bass, or in which the bass note of the dominant triad is the third or fifth. The commonly used soprano lines are 2–3, 5–5, and 5 down to 3, as illustrated in Figure 8.1 *c, d,* and *e*. In music excerpts, see Figures 2.5, 2.7 and 6.1.

3. *Authentic half:* the progression I–V or i–V, illustrated in Figure 8.1 *f, g, h,* and *i*. In a music excerpt, see Figure 2.10.

---

[1]Review preliminary survey of cadences in Chapter 2, "Form," and melodic cadences in Chapter 5, "Form." Cadences not discussed in this chapter (including deceptive, Phrygian, and various forms of the half cadence) will be presented in later chapters.

[2]V-I in a major key, or V-I (picardy third) in a minor key. Review Figure 7.2 and accompanying discussion.

Fig. 8.1.[3]

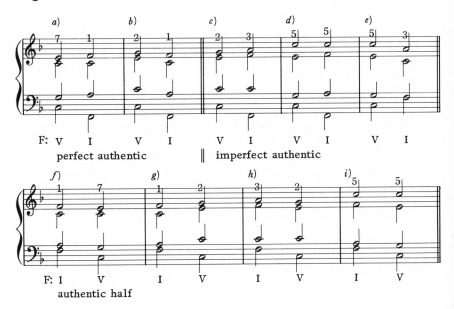

perfect authentic   ‖ imperfect authentic

authentic half

Plagal Cadences

Although not used as frequently as the authentic cadence, the plagal cadence is familiar through its use as the "Amen" following most hymns.

Fig. 8.2.

Hymn: St. Anne

---

[3]Cadences are illustrated in a major key, but are identical in a minor key when appropriate key signature is used. In Figure 8.1, for F minor, place four flats in the signature, add the natural sign before each leading tone (E♮), and use chord numbers V and i. In Figure 8.4, (plagal cadences), place four flats in the signautre and use chord numbers iv and i.

Fig. 8.3.

Handel, *Messiah*, "Lift Up Your Heads"

He is the King of Glo-ry,   of   Glo - ry.

F: IV$_6^4$ I   IV   I$_6$ I   I   IV   I

The plagal cadence is found in the same three forms as the authentic cadence.

1. *Perfect plagal:* the progression IV–I or iv–i in which the subdominant triad has its root in the bass, and the final tonic triad has its root in both bass and soprano. The commonly used soprano line 1–1 is illustrated in Figures 8.2 and 8.4 *a*.

2. *Imperfect plagal:* the progression IV–I or iv–i in which the final tonic triad is found with its third or fifth in the soprano and/or the bass, or in which the bass note of the subdominant triad is the third or fifth. The commonly used soprano lines are 6–5, 4–3, and 1 up to 3, illustrated in Figure 8.4 *b*, *c*, and *d*. See also Figure 8.3 and the cadence at the end of the first phrase of Figure 2.26.

3. *Plagal half:* a little-used cadence, the progression I–IV or i–iv, illustrated in Figure 8.4 *e*, *f*, and *g* and in Figure 8.5.

Fig. 8.4.

Assignment 8.2. Analysis of cadences in Bach chorales. From the *371 Chorales* of J.S. Bach, copy out the cadence triads from the chorale phrases listed below. Place chord numbers (I, IV, V; i, iv) under each triad and name the cadence (e.g., perfect authentic, imperfect plagal) as shown in Figure 8.5.

The term "phrase" when used in relation to a hymn or chorale refers to the music set to a verse (line) of the poem. When using an edition of the chorales that includes texts (see Chapter 2, footnote 7), a cadence will be found at the end of each verse of the poem. In editions of the chorales that do not include texts, the end of the phrase is indicated by a *fermata* (⌢); in this context, the fermata does not mean "to hold." Repeats in the chorales are not considered in the numbering of the phrases.

Chorale No.   1, first phrase
          8, final phrase
          11, second phrase
          12, third phrase
          42, second phrase
          53, first phrase
          98, final phrase
          106, fifth phrase
          107, first phrase (D is non-harmonic)
          166, final phrase (C is non-harmonic)
          236, final phrase (E is non-harmonic)
          255, first phrase

Fig. 8.5.

Bach, *Was frag ich nach der Welt* (♯291)

D: I   IV
                    plagal half cadence

Melodic Use of the Dominant (V) Triad

Intervals from the V triad are commonly used in melodic writing, as illustrated in melodies from Chapter 3 *a–c* in *Music for Sight Singing*.

Fig. 8.6.

German Folk Song (MSS 82)

G:　　　　　　　　　　　　V

Assignment 8.3. Locate melodic intervals from the dominant triad as shown in Figure 8.6. Copy out melodies from Chapter 3 *a–c* in *Music for Sight Singing,* as assigned.

The Dominant Seventh (V⁷) Chord

A seventh chord is a four-note chord consisting of a triad plus an additional note at the interval of a seventh above the root. When built upon the dominant note of the key, it is known as a dominant seventh chord (V⁷), as shown in Figure 8.7. The seventh of the chord is the fourth scale step and is a minor seventh above the root.

Melodies from music literature that contain intervals implying functions other than skips in the tonic and dominant triads, as will be studied in Chapter 10 and subsequent chapters, also frequently include intervals in the dominant seventh chord. This makes it necessary to investigate at least the melodic characteristics of this chord before it will be possible to proceed with the study of melodic intervals implying other functions. But to study in a most efficient manner the harmonic uses of this chord, it is necessary to wait until after a full presentation of non-harmonic tones. So at this time, we will learn to spell the dominant seventh chord in various keys, to recognize its use in melodic lines, and to write melodic lines incorporating skips from this chord.

Fig. 8.7.

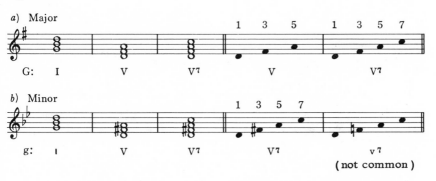

a) Major

b) Minor

Assignment 8.4.   Spell the V⁷ chord in each major or minor key.

Intervals in the V⁷ Chord

The intervals in the list below are from the dominant seventh chord and are those in which the seventh of the chord is involved. The underlined intervals are those most commonly used in melodic writing.

1 up to 7	minor seventh	7 down to 1
3 up to 7	diminished fifth⁴	7 down to 3
5 up to 7	minor third	7 down to 5
7 up to 1	major second	1 down to 7
7 up to 3	augmented fourth⁴	3 down to 7
7 up to 5	major sixth	5 down to 7

Fig. 8.8.

Assignment 8.5.   Spell each of the intervals in Figure 8.8, based on the dominant seventh chord of any major or minor key.

Melodic Use of the V⁷ Chord

Intervals from any note of the V triad to the fourth scale step (the seventh of the V⁷) or reverse are frequent in melodic writing, with the minor third 5 up to 7 or 7 down to 5 being particularly common.

Fig. 8.9.

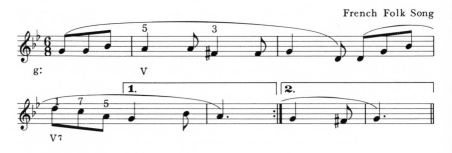

French Folk Song

---

⁴Also known as a *tritone*. See Chapter 14.

Assignment 8.6.   Melodic Analysis. From *Music for Sight Singing*, Chapter 3 *d*, copy out melodies as assigned and identify those intervals found in the V⁷ chord. From Chapter 4 of *Music for Sight Singing*, locate melodies that contain intervals from the V⁷ chord and identify these intervals.

APPLICATION

Written Materials

Figured Bass

Part-writing assignments, beginning in this chapter, will include figured bass lines. Figured bass, as described in Appendix 3, is no longer used as a compositional device by composers or in performance by solo musicians. But it still has a real pedagogical value in aiding students to learn part-writing techniques.

Two primary aims in the study of harmony are (1) the ability to choose effective chord progressions and (2) the ability to connect a series of chords in such a way that the horizontal melodic lines produced are musical and performable. Both of these skills are required simultaneously when writing original music or setting harmonizations to existing melodies. But first it is desirable to learn each skill separately, putting them together when each technique is satisfactorily established. Figured bass is a compact, shorthand device for indicating a given harmonic progression, leaving the student free to concentrate on part-writing techniques until it is time to combine part-writing with harmonic choice.

An Arabic numeral, or figure, under a bass note *always* indicates the size of an interval *above the bass note*. Two or more numbers, together with the given bass note, will spell the entire chord. Certain combinations of numbers will quickly indicate whether the bass note is the root, third, or fifth of the triad. The figuration $^5_3$ indicates that the bass note is the root of a triad.

In Figure 8.10, $^5_3$ indicates that the interval of a third and the interval of a fifth should be placed above the bass note G (the G in the soprano results from normal doubling and is usually not noted in the figuration). Thus, $^5_3$ usually indicates that the bass note is the root of a triad.

Fig. 8.10.

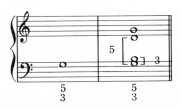

In actual practice, when the bass note is the root of a triad, the $\frac{5}{3}$ is usually not written, but is understood to be below the bass note. If one or more of the notes above the bass require an accidental, then those numbers only, with accidentals, appear. An accidental used without a number always refers to the third above the bass note. A slash through a number means the same as a sharp before a number.

Fig. 8.11.

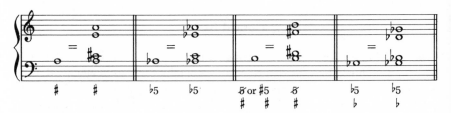

Figured bass does not indicate open or close structure, nor does it indicate soprano position. All possible arrangements of a triad with the root in the bass will be served by the same figured bass symbol.

Fig. 8.12.

With a key signature, the figured bass calls for that letter name above the bass indicated by the signature. A ♮ (natural sign) is used to cancel out an unwanted accidental in the key signature.

Fig. 8.13.

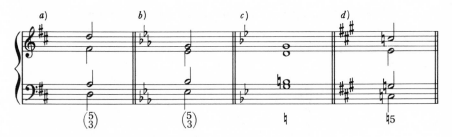

Minor triads (or any other type of chord) can be indicated by figured bass.

Fig. 8.14.

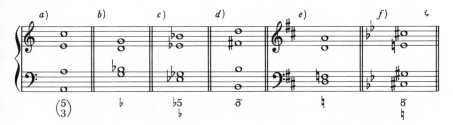

For purposes of part-writing assignments in this chapter (cadences with roots in the bass), the only figured bass required will be an accidental to indicate a major dominant triad in a minor key, or a picardy third in a minor key. Where no figured bass is shown, $\frac{5}{3}$ is implied.

Writing Cadences

Any cadence shown earlier in the chapter displays a pair of roots in the bass, always at the interval of a perfect fifth apart, or the inversion of the perfect fifth, the perfect fourth.

Fig. 8.15.

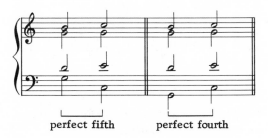

perfect fifth   perfect fourth

Part-writing rules numbered "2" refer to pairs of triads with roots in the bass a perfect fifth or a perfect fourth apart, and are therefore applicable to all authentic and plagal cadences.

Part-Writing Rule 2A. Triads with roots in the bass a fifth apart. In a progression of two triads whose roots in the bass line are a fifth apart, retain the common tone in the same voice and move the other voices step-wise.

Fig. 8.16.

C: V   I

common tone "g" in alto ;
soprano and tenor move stepwise

e♭:   V   i

common tone "B♭" in soprano;
alto and tenor move stepwise.

Assignment 8.7. Writing authentic cadences. Identify each as perfect, imperfect, or half cadence.

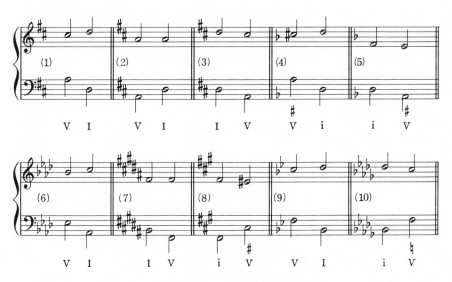

Assignment 8.8. Writing plagal cadences. Fill in alto and tenor voices. Identify each cadence as perfect, imperfect, or half.

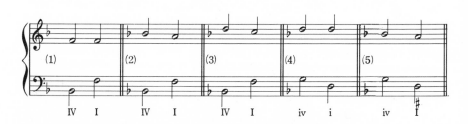

Assignment 8.9. Writing authentic and plagal cadences. Fill in inner voices. Write chord number below each bass note. Identify each cadence by name.

Since it is occasionally impossible to follow Rule 2A when writing two triads with their roots a fifth apart, there must be an alternate method.

Part-Writing Rule 2B. Triads with roots in the bass a fifth apart. In a progression of two triads whose roots in the bass line are a fifth apart, move the three upper voices in similar motion to the nearest tones of the next triad.

Rule 2B is particularly valuable in the authentic cádence when the melody line is supertonic to tonic (2–1) or reverse, or, in either cadence, when there is a leap in the melody.

Fig. 8.17.

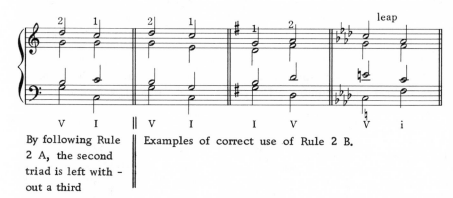

By following Rule 2 A, the second triad is left with - out a third

Examples of correct use of Rule 2 B.

Assignment 8.10.   a) Write cadences using Rule 2B. Choose open or close structure according to needs of voice range.

b) Write cadences using either Rule 2A or Rule 2B as required by part-writing situation. Write chord number below each bass note.

Assignment 8.11.   a) Part-write cadences when bass line only is given. Supply any correct soprano line.

b) Part-write cadences when soprano line only is given. Be sure the bass note is always the root of the triad.

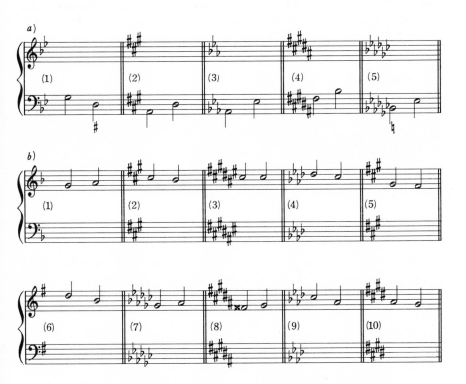

Assignment 8.12. Write any or all of the following cadences in major or minor keys as assigned.

a) The two perfect authentic cadences (soprano line 7–8 and 2–1).

b) The imperfect authentic cadence in two positions (2–3, 5–5).

c) The authentic half cadence in four positions (1–7, 1–2, 3–2, 5–5).

Assignment 8.13. Write the following cadences in major or minor keys, as assigned.

a) The perfect plagal cadence (1–1).

b) The imperfect plagal cadence in two positions (6–5, 4–3).

c) The plagal half cadence in three positions (1–1, 3–4, 5–6).

Melody-Writing Using the V Triad

Skips in the dominant triad are used freely in melodic writing, as your investigation from Assignment 8.6 has shown. You probably noticed that the leading tone (third of the V triad) does not always go directly to the tonic note. The leading tone may skip up or down to another note of the dominant triad. In addition, the two tones of the descending interval 3 to 1 in the dominant triad (leading tone down to dominant) are often filled in with a passing tone to become a scalar passage. In a minor key, this will result in a descending melodic line ♯7–♯6–5, as in Figure 8.18. See also *Music for Sight Singing*, melody 356.

Fig. 8.18.

Johann Crüger (1640) *Herzliebster Jesu*

Assignment 8.14.   Write melodies in phrases or periods as assigned, using intervals in the tonic and dominant triads.

Melody-Writing Using The V⁷ Chord

While observing, singing, or listening to intervals in the V^7 chord, note the special property of the seventh of the chord. It almost always proceeds downwards, either to the scale step below or to another member of the V^7 chord.

Fig. 8.19.

a)   German Folk Song (MSS 109)

7 down by step

b)   American Folk Song (Ohio)(MSS 118)

7 down by skip in
same chord

In rare cases where the seventh is allowed to ascend, the melodic line usually descends immediately after to effect a normal resolution of the seventh.

Fig. 8.20.

French Folk Song (MSS 115)

resolution of 7 delayed

Assignment 8.15.   Write melodic lines using intervals in the V⁷ chord in keys and forms as assigned. Be particularly careful of the resolution of the seventh of the V⁷ chord.

Ear Training and Music Reading[5]

The Dominant Triad

Exercise 8.1.   Singing the V triad in a major key.

a) You will hear a single note played at the piano; this will be the tonic note of a major key. From this note, sing the tonic triad, using letter names. The fifth of the tonic triad is the same pitch as the root of the dominant triad. From this note sing the dominant triad using letter names.

Fig. 8.21.

b) Sing the dominant triad immediately after hearing the tonic note.

Exercise 8.2.   Singing the V triad in a minor key. Follow the same procedure as in Exercise 8.1. The tonic triad will be minor, and the V triad will be major.

Fig. 8.22.

The Authentic Cadence

Exercise 8.3.   Identifying the authentic cadence. You will hear a phrase of music at the piano. The last two triads will comprise an authentic cadence.

a) At the conclusion of the first playing, sing the tonic of the key.

b) During the second playing, sing the roots of the cadence chords.

c) During the third playing, sing the soprano line. Identify the cadence as perfect, imperfect, or half.

---

[5]Dominant harmonies only. The subdominant triad is included in Chapter 10, where you will also find melodic writing with the subdominant triad.

Here is an example:

Fig. 8.23.

With continued practice, identify cadence completely in two hearings, then in one hearing.

Exercise 8.4. Writing the cadence from dictation on staff paper. Follow directions in Exercise 8.3, and in addition place soprano and bass notes on the staff after the key signature has been given. Fill in inner parts according to part writing rules.

Sight Singing, Dominant Triad

In *Music for Sight Singing*, study page 25, followed by practice in sight singing from Chapter 3 *a–c*. These melodies include scale line passages and skips in the tonic and dominant triads only.

Exercise 8.5. Melodic dictation. Listen to melodies containing skips in the V triad and the I triad. Follow directions for melodic dictation as outlined in Exercise 5.1. In addition to these directions, when the name of the key becomes known, spell the I and V triads, and sing them if so directed.

The Dominant Seventh Chord

Exercise 8.6. Singing the V^7 chord. Sing a V triad as in Exercises 8.1.–8.2, but add a minor third above the fifth of the triad to create the V^7 chord. Sing the chord with letter names in all major and minor keys.

Exercise 8.7. Sing intervals from the V^7 chord, as directed.

Sight Singing, Dominant Seventh Chord

Practice singing melodies from Chapter 3, section *d*, of *Music for Sight Singing*. Follow this with Chapter 4, which contains examples of intervals in both the V triad and the V^7 chord in melodies written in compound time.

Melodic Dictation, Dominant Seventh Chord

Exercise 8.8. Melodic Dictation. Dictation exercises will now contain intervals from the V triad and the V⁷ chord.

Keyboard Harmony

Authentic Cadences[6]

You have already played single triads, both major and minor at the keyboard. To play a cadence, simply play two triads in succession, the choice of triads and position determined by the type of cadence and soprano line. For example, play a perfect authentic cadence in G major, soprano line 2–1, $\left(\begin{smallmatrix} 2 & 1 \\ V—I \end{smallmatrix}\right)$.

    a) Spell the dominant and tonic triads.

    b) Locate the second scale step of G major on the piano; locate lower notes of the dominant triad, as in Exercise 3.20.

    c) Play dominant triad.

    d) Locate tonic note on the piano; locate other notes of the tonic triad.

    e) Play tonic triad.

Fig. 8.24.

---

[6]See Chapter 10 for plagal cadences.

By using close position in the right hand, part-writing procedures will always be correct, and at the same time the cadence can easily be played. Open position (two notes in each hand) may be used, but this is slightly more difficult. Students should never resort to playing three notes in the left hand; although this may seem easier, it is impossible to follow normal voice leading procedures, resulting in harsh and unpleasant sounds.

Exercise 8.9.   Playing authentic cadences at the keyboard. In practicing each cadence below, use the circle of fifths. Start at any key and play the cadence in that key. Go to the next key of the circle and continue around the circle until you arrive at the key from which you started.

    a) Play the perfect authentic cadences:

        Major: 2 1   7 1   Minor: 2 1   7 1
                V—I   V—I   V—i   V—i

    b) Play the imperfect authentic cadences:

        Major: 2 3   5 5   Minor: 2 3 5 5
                V—I   V—I   V—i V—i

    c) Play the authentic half cadences:

        Major: 1 7   1 2   3 2   5 5
                1—V   I—V   I—V   I—V

        Minor: 1 7   1 2   3 2   5 5
                i—V   i—V   i—V   i—V

Harmonizing Melodic Cadences

Many melodic phrases end with cadences consisting of the scale steps practiced in Exercise 8.9. As a first step in learning to harmonize an entire melody, we will learn to harmonize these melodic cadences with harmonic authentic cadences. In Figure 8.25, we see two motives from a folk song with melodic cadences using scale steps 2–3 and 2–1, which can be harmonized with an imperfect authentic cadence and a perfect authentic cadence, respectively.

Fig. 8.25.

Vermont Folk Song

Exercise 8.10. Harmonizing melodic cadences. In the melody numbers from *Music for Sight Singing* listed below, play the entire melody, and harmonize each melodic cadence, found at the end of each phrase-mark. When a melody appears in the bass clef, play it one or two octaves higher, as necessary. Use Figure 8.25 as a guide. 10, 11, 16, 26, 29, 33, 42, 45, 47, 49, 56, 58, 59, 63, 135.

For additional practice, play melody and harmonize cadence only in those phrases indicated in parentheses. For example, "3, 4" means the third and fourth phrase-marks. 6(3, 4), 15(2, 4), 20(1, 2, 4), 25(1, 2), 34(1, 2), 38(1, 2), 51(1, 2, 4), 66(2, 4), 94(1, 2), 125(1, 3, 4), 127(1, 2, 4).

9

The Alto and Tenor Clefs

THEORY AND ANALYSIS

The C clef is universally used in music, though not as commonly as the treble and bass clefs. The C clef sign ║ꓭ or ║ꓘ indicates the location of Middle C on the staff. It is particularly useful for those instruments whose range extends from the middle part of the bass clef to the middle of the treble clef.

Fig. 9.1.   **Fig. 9.2.**

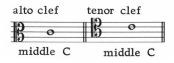

alto clef   tenor clef

middle C   middle C

When the C clef is found on the third line of the staff, it is known as the *alto clef*, used by the viola and by the trombone. When the C clef is found on the fourth line of the staff, it is known as the *tenor clef*, and is often used by the violoncello, the bassoon, the trombone, and occasionally by the double bass. Illustrations of actual usages of these clefs follow.[1]

---

[1]A score in which each part or voice line is on a separate staff, as in Figure 9.3, is known as an *open score*.

Fig. 9.3.

Beethoven, Quartet, Op. 18, No. 1,
first movement

Fig. 9.4.

Dvořák, Concerto for Violoncello and Orchestra
in B minor, Op. 104, second mvt.

Fig. 9.5.

Tschaikowski, Symphony No. 6, third mvt.

These two clefs, together with the treble and bass clefs, are the only ones remaining in common use today from a system of ten different clef signs used in music before 1750. The other six clefs are seen in Figure 9.6.

Fig. 9.6.

These clefs can be found in very old editions of music and in many modern publications of pre-nineteenth-century music.

Exercise 9.1. *a*) Learn the names of the lines and spaces of the alto clef. Be able to name any line or space correctly, for example, name the fourth line—answer, E. In addition, be able to locate any pitch name in the alto clef.

b) Learn the names of the lines and spaces of the tenor clef, as above.

Sharps and flats for the key signatures are placed as follows on the alto and tenor clefs.

Fig. 9.7.

Assignment 9.1. Write the signature for each major and minor key in both the alto and tenor clefs.

APPLICATION

Written Materials

Assignment 9.2. Writing cadences in open score. Choose several cadences from Assignments 8.7–8.13 and rewrite in open score, placing the alto part in the alto clef and the tenor part in the tenor clef. Here are solutions for example (1) from Assignment 8.7; *a* in open position and *b* in close position.

Fig. 9.8.

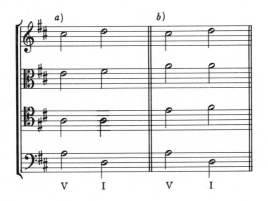

Ear Training and Music Reading

Sight Singing

Sing melodies from Chapter 5 in *Music for Sight Singing*. To facilitate the learning of these clefs, the student should sing the letter name of each note (do not sing the word sharp or flat). Study methods of clef transposition discussed at the beginning of Chapter 5 of *Music for Sight Singing* and apply to melodies from Chapters 1-4.

Melodic Dictation

Exercise 9.2. Melodic dictation. Dictation exercises will now be given in the alto and tenor clef. Remember that "C" in these clefs is middle C; be careful not to write your solution an octave too high or too low.

10

Further Use
of the Three Principal Triads

THEORY AND ANALYSIS

The three principal triads are not, of course, limited solely to use in cadences as described in Chapter 8. These three triads are used freely and frequently in the course of most music compositions. But they are usually interspersed with other chords, or, should the three be found without other harmonies, they will be found in inversions or with added sevenths (particularly V⁷) or with added nonharmonic tones, as in Figures 2.7 and 2.10. It is not common to find even a phrase using only the three principal triads with roots in the bass. It occurs in a short excerpt from Wagner, Figure 10.1, and, except for two chords in measure 4, in a phrase from Chopin, Figure 10.2. But for our opening studies in the technique of part-writing in phrase lengths, it will be advantageous to minimize the number of technical problems by writing the three principal triads only in root position.

Fig. 10.1.

Wagner, *Das Rheingold*, Prelude to Scene 2.

Ruhiges Zeitmass

pp

D♭:   I   IV   I   V   I

Fig. 10.2.[1]

Chopin, Nocturne, Op. 37, No. 1

Eb: I IV IV I   IV I V I   V I IV I   V (vi) (V7) I

In our study of cadences, the subdominant and dominant triads have progressed directly to or from the tonic triad. In addition, the progression subdominant to dominant is also commonly used (IV-V, iv-V). The reverse of this progression (V-IV, V-iv) is not commonly used and will not be considered at this time.

Fig. 10.3.

Hymn: Toulon (Old 124th)

IV V I

Fig. 10.4.

Coventry Carol

iv V I

Melodic Use of the Subdominant Triad

Intervals from the subdominant triad can be used effectively in melodic writing, though they are used less frequently than intervals from the tonic and dominant triads.

---

[1]Chord numbers in parentheses in this and subsequent figures represent harmonies not yet studied.

Fig. 10.5.

Memel Folk Song (MSS 175)

A: (IV=DF♯A)   IV

Assignment 10.1. Analyzing melodic intervals from the subdominant triad. Copy out melodies from *Music for Sight Singing* from the following list, as assigned. Indicate location of intervals from the subdominant triad. 170, 173, 174, 176, 177, 182, 183, 187, 193, 199, 201.

APPLICATION

Written Materials

Writing the Progression IV-V

The roots of the IV and V triads are a second apart, so the progression IV-V cannot be written with part-writing rules already studied.

Part-Writing Rule 3. In a progression of two triads whose roots in the bass line are a second apart, move the three upper voices to the nearest triad tones in contrary motion to the bass. (See also Figures 10.3-10.4.)

Fig. 10.6.

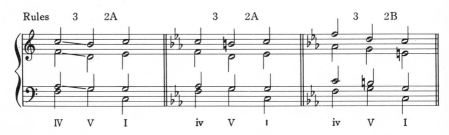

Rules   3   2A   3   2A   3   2B

IV   V   I   iv   V   I   iv   V   I

Violation of this rule is one of the most frequent causes of the appearance of three weaknesses in part-writing most likely to plague the beginning student. They are

a) parallel perfect fifths.
b) parallel octaves.
c) the melodic augmented second.

Fig. 10.7.

The following examples show how violation of Rule 3 can cause the unwanted progressions.

Fig. 10.8.

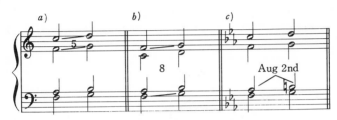

Attempts to avoid parallel octaves by changing the direction of one of the two notes involved do not produce successful results. Figure 10.9 *a* shows a parallel octave between the alto and bass voices. In Figure 10.9 *b*, an attempt was made to avoid the octave by moving the bass down a minor seventh instead of up a major second. These are still parallel octaves but called, in seemingly contradictory language, *parallel octaves by contrary motion.*[2] There are, in our illustration, two *f*'s going to two *g*'s in the same pair of voices. Use of Rule 3 in Figure 10.9 *c* eliminates the offending octaves.

Fig. 10.9.

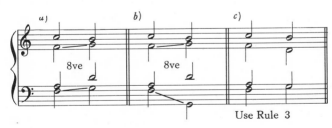

Parallel fifths by contrary motion are likewise to be avoided. Those in Figure 10.10 are caused by violation of Rule 2B.

---

[2]One parallel octave by contrary motion, dominant to tonic, will occasionally be found in the outside voices of the final authentic cadence. See final cadence of "Auld Lang Syne."

Fig. 10.10.

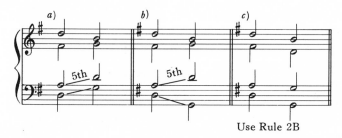

Use Rule 2B

Note, however, that octaves or fifths repeated on the same pitches are *not* considered parallel; the use of these *stationary* octaves or fifths is acceptable.

Fig. 10.11.

Parallel fifths, parallel octaves, and melodic augmented seconds are not wrong or ill-sounding in themselves. Parallel fifths were used in ninth- and tenth-century organum (see Appendix 3, Figure A3.3), and all three are used freely in twentieth-century music. But between these dates, a period of approximately one thousand years, most composers usually considered these sounds undesirable and usually avoided them in their music. In studying the techniques of the seventeenth through nineteenth centuries, it is necessary, therefore, that the student not include them in his writing style.

A typical example of parallel fifths in twentieth-century music is shown in Figure 10.12. The music Figure 10.13, written by the nineteenth-century

Fig. 10.12.

Ravel, *L'enfant et les Sortileges*

Permission for reprint granted by Durand et Cie, Paris, France, Copyright Owners; Elkan-Vogel Co., Inc. of Philadelphia, Pa., Sole Agents.

composer Saint-Saëns, is intended to be suggestive of the Orient, where augmented seconds are found in many scale patterns.

Fig. 10.13.

Saint-Saëns, *Samson and Delilah*

Allegro Moderato

Assignment 10.2.   a) Write cadences as found below. Write chord numbers below the staff.

b) Write, on staff paper, the progression I-IV-V-I or i-iv-V-i, in the following keys, or in other keys as assigned.

E♭ major	A♭ minor
B major	C♯ minor
F♯ major	F minor
D♭ major	D♯ minor

Exceptions to Part-Writing Rule 2

In a few special instances when chords are found with their roots a fifth apart, procedures other than those expressed by Rules 2A and 2B are used.

Part-Writing Rule 2C[3].   In a progression of two triads whose roots in the bass line are a fifth apart, move the third of the first triad up or down the

---

[3]Part-writing rules are not numbered consecutively in the text, but are numbered for ease of reference in Appendix 1; "The Essentials of Part-Writing."

interval of a fourth to the third of the second triad, hold the common tone, and move the other voice by step.

Fig. 10.14.

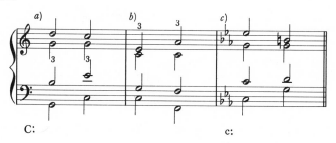

C: c:

The effect of the procedure is the change of position, open to close or close to open, from one triad to the next, as shown in the next two illustrations. This procedure, with the skip of a fourth in the tenor voice, is found in the final cadence of many Bach chorales, such as numbers 9, 27, 41, and 93.

Fig. 10.15.

Brahms, *Die Wollust in den Maien*

Allegretto grazioso

Fig. 10.16.

Hymn: Capetown

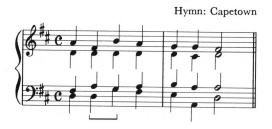

Part-Writing Rule 2D. In an authentic cadence, the root of the tonic triad may be tripled, omitting the fifth of the triad.

Fig. 10.17.

In using Rule 2B in the progression V-I (as might have been done in Figure 10.17*a*), the leading tone always skips down a third to the dominant tone. This descending use of the leading tone, questionable in melodic writing, is satisfactory in an *inner voice*, especially when the leading tone is approached from above. At a cadence, the aural effect of the leading tone proceeding to tonic and the resulting incomplete tonic triad is often preferable to the more conventional procedure of Rule 2B.

Fig. 10.18.

Hymn: Toulon

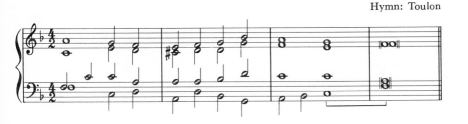

Assignment 10.3. Write cadences, using Rules 2C and 2D as indicated.

Writing Extended Exercises

The triad progressions used in the study of the cadence can also be used in a longer succession of triads to form a phrase. Any pair of triads in the following assignments can be connected with Rules 1, 2A, B, C, D, and 3.

Assignment 10.4.   *a*) Fill in alto and tenor voices using part-writing procedures studied thus far. Make harmonic analysis by placing correct Roman numeral below each bass note.

b) Solve exercises in open score, as assigned, and as explained in Assignment 9.2.

Assignment 10.5. Supply soprano, alto, and tenor lines above a given bass line. In writing a soprano line, observe the rules for melody-writing previously studied, particularly the treatment of the leading tone. The soprano note should be changed when the bass note is repeated. Make harmonic analysis.

Assignment 10.6. Harmonize melodies, supplying alto, tenor, and bass parts. Follow this procedure.

a) Determine the key. Check not only the key signature, but sing melody through, observing the nature of the cadence to determine whether the melody is major or minor.

b) Write in the chord numbers for the cadence below the bass staff.
c) Write in chord numbers leading up to the cadence.
d) Write the bass line, each note being the root of the chosen chord.
e) Fill in inner parts.

Melody-Writing

Assignment 10.7.   Write melodies in phrases or periods, as assigned. Follow previous directions for melody-writing, now including intervals from the subdominant triad.

Ear Training and Music Reading

The Subdominant Triad

Exercise 10.1.   Singing the subdominant triad in any major or minor key.

a) You will hear the tonic note of the key. Sing the tonic triad with letter names. The root of the subdominant triad is found at the interval of a perfect fourth above the tonic. Sing this interval, then sing the subdominant triad with letter names.

b) Sing the subdominant triad immediately after hearing the tonic note.

The Plagal Cadence

Exercise 10.2.   Identifying plagal cadences. Follow directions already given for identifying authentic cadences in Exercises 8.3 and 8.4.

Sight Singing, Subdominant Triad

In *Music for Sight Singing*, study page 53, followed by practice in sight singing from Chapters 6 and 7.

Melodic Dictation, Subdominant Triad

Exercise 10.3.   Melodic Dictation. Listen to melodies containing skips in the subdominant triad. These melodies will also include skips in the tonic and dominant harmonies. Follow directions for melodic dictation outlined in Exercise 5.1.

Harmonic Dictation

In harmonic dictation, the student listens to a series of chords and, without recourse to pitches on the staff, identifies each chord with a Roman numeral symbol. A correct symbol indicates that the student knows (1) upon what scale degree the chord is built and (2) the quality of the sound, which, for the present, will be a major or minor triad. A correct solution, using quality symbols as listed in Figures 2.3 and 2.4, can be accomplished without previous announcement of key; each chord in the solution can be correctly spelled when the name of the key is given.

The ability to write down the soprano and bass lines as in melodic dictation is a valuable addition to exercises in harmonic dictation. Taking down melodic lines first, however, should be avoided, because these lines will often indicate visually the correct harmony, thereby defeating the purpose of harmonic dictation.

Exercise 10.4. Harmonic dictation: tonic, dominant, and subdominant triads.

a) Listen to the entire exercise without writing. At the conclusion of the exercise, sing the tonic note.

b) On the second hearing, sing the root of each triad as the triad is played.

c) On the third hearing, sing the triad roots using the correct chord number for each.

d) Write the chord numbers as the exercise is played.

As progress is made, eliminate steps *b* and *c*. For additional drill, after completion of step *d* the key will be announced. Write the soprano and bass lines on the staff, and fill in inner parts (alto and tenor) by following part-writing rules.

Keyboard Harmony

Plagal Cadences

Exercise 10.5. Playing plagal cadences at the keyboard. Follow directions given in Exercise 8.9 and preceding discussion, substituting the IV or iv triad for the V triad.

a) Play the perfect plagal cadence.

Major	1	1	Minor	1	1
	IV—I			iv—i	

b) Play the imperfect plagal cadences.

Major	6	5	4	3
	IV—I		IV—I	
Minor	6	5	4	3
	iv—i		iv—i	

c) Plagal half cadences are not common; they are shown in Figure 8.4 *e* if practice is desired.

Exercise 10.6. Harmonizing melodic plagal cadences at the keyboard. Following directions given in Exercise 8.10 and preceding discussion, harmonize all cadences, authentic and plagal, in the following melodies from *Music for Sight Singing:* 1, 68, 78, 126, 171.

The Progression I—IV—V—I

Exercise 10.7.[4] Playing the progressions I-IV-V-I and i-iv-V-i at the keyboard. Play the progression with the tonic triad in each of its three possible soprano positions. Play in all major and minor keys. Follow all part-writing rules. In Figures 10.19 *b* and 10.20 *b*, the final tonic triad may be found with its root in the soprano by using Rule 2B from the preceding V triad.

Fig. 10.19. Major Key:

Fig. 10.20. Minor Key:

Melody Harmonization

Exercise 10.8. Melody harmonization at the keyboard. The melodies of Assignment 10.6 may be used at the keyboard. Play appropriate chord for each soprano note. For further practice, copy out each melody in various keys. Using melody (1) from Assignment 10.6 as an example, this can be done as follows:

---

[4]See Chapter 13, "Keyboard Harmony," for discussion of the importance of this exercise.

a) Note the key; in this case, B♭ major.

b) Identify each soprano note by its scale number.

Fig. 10.21.

c) Choose a new key, F for example. Write the melody in the new key by using the same scale numbers.

Fig. 10.22.

d) Harmonize the melody in the key of F major at the piano.

11

The Triad in Inversion

THEORY AND ANALYSIS

A triad (or any chord) is said to be in *inversion* when some note other than the root is in the bass. When the third is in the bass the triad is in *first inversion;* when the fifth is in the bass, the triad is in *second inversion.* Since there are three possible soprano positions and three possible bass positions in a triad, a total of nine combinations of soprano and bass tones exists.

Fig. 11.1.

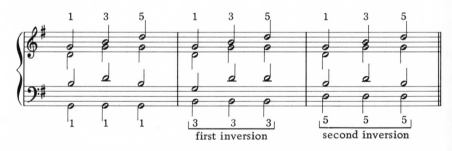

Chords in inversion are found in musical compositions for two reasons.

a) To give variety to the vertical sound. A composition consisting of chords with root in bass only is less interesting musically than alternation of chords with root in bass and chords in inversion.

b) To allow the bass line to be more melodic. When roots in the bass only are used, the bass line will consist mostly of large intervals. Use of inversions allows more step-wise movement and smaller skips in the bass line.

Figure 11.2 *a* displays a bass line in which less than half of the notes are roots of chords. The improvement of the bass as a melodic line can easily be heard by comparing the actual bass line with a bass line consisting only of roots, especially when each is heard against the principal melodic line of the music, as shown in Figure 11.2 *b*. In this example, the "alto" becomes the principal melody when the highest voice, repeating the note *d*, becomes static.

Fig. 11.2.

Beethoven, Sonata for Piano, Op. 28

This excerpt demonstrates one of the most important concepts in the composition of music, the two-part structure existing between the bass line and the melodic line. These two voices, played by themselves, will sound like a good two-voice composition; the judicious use of inversions is the major contributing factor in this effect.[1]

Figured Bass Symbols

When figured bass is required, the symbol 6 is ordinarily used to indicate first inversion. The complete symbol is $\frac{6}{3}$, meaning that there can be found

---

[1]Considered in detail in Chapter 14.

above the bass note an interval of a third and an interval of a sixth (Figure 11.3 *a*). Generally, the 3 is omitted, but understood to be present (Figure 11.3 *b*); if it is necessary to raise or lower the third above the bass, the symbols $\frac{6}{\sharp}$ or $\frac{6}{\flat}$ are used (Figure 11.3 *c, d*).

Fig. 11.3.

The figured bass symbol $\frac{6}{4}$ indicates second inversion. Neither number is omitted.

Fig. 11.4.

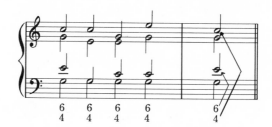

Harmonic Analysis Symbols

Inversion may be indicated in the Roman numeral chord designation by placing a figured bass symbol to the right and a little below the Roman numeral, 6 for first inversion and $\frac{6}{4}$ for second inversion. Examples: IV_6 = IV triad in first inversion; i_6^4 = i triad in second inversion.

Chromatic indications are not ordinarily included when the figured bass symbol is used as part of the Roman numeral designation. When the key is known, the Roman numeral will correctly spell the chord, while the figured bass will indicate the inversion of that spelling.

In Figure 11.8, we find $\flat_4^6$ in the figured bass line and directly below it $i_6^{}\atop 4$ in the harmonic analysis line.

figured bass $\flat_4^6$: $a\flat$ and f are located above c.

harmonic analysis $i_{6\atop 4}$: minor tonic triad (in F minor, $f\ a\flat\ c$) in second inversion.

Use of the First Inversion

The tonic, dominant, and subdominant triads are freely used in first inversion. In any progression already studied, either or both triads may be in first inversion. Use of first inversion also makes possible two chord progressions not previously considered.

1. V_6—IV_6 (major only).[2] The V triad does not ordinarily progress to IV, but as we will study in more detail later, in a series of two or more first inversions, chord progressions that might otherwise be unacceptable become quite usable.

Fig. 11.5.

Mozart, Sonata for Piano in F Major, K.332

2. The IV triad in a minor key. Ordinarily, the subdominant triad in a minor key is a minor triad (iv). The third of this triad is the sixth scale step; when it is found in an ascending melodic line, it is raised one half step, as in the melodic minor scale, causing the triad to become major (IV). For example, in C minor, iv = F A♭ C, IV = F A C, A♭ or A being the sixth scale step. The melodic line 5 ♯6 ♯7 8 from the melodic minor scale is quite commonly found as a bass line carrying the harmony V IV$_6$ V$_6$ i, as shown in Figure 11.6. See also Bach chorale 185, last phrase.

---

[2]v_6—iv_6 can be used in a minor key. The minor dominant triad, v, will be presented in Chapter 18.

Fig. 11.6.

Anon. (c. 1670) *Nun sich der Tag geendet hat*

g: V   IV₆ V₆   i   i₆

Use of the Second Inversion

In contrast to the liberal use of triads in first inversion in the eighteenth and nineteenth centuries, the second inversion is restricted to a limited number of specific musical situations. This is because of the dual nature of the six-four sonority. Upon observing the penultimate chord of Figure 11.2, one clearly sees the triad spelling D F A, i in D minor. Yet, if asked to sing the root of this chord upon hearing it, most persons will respond by singing the bass note A, the root of the V triad in D minor. This contradictory interpretation of the lowest note of the six-four chord is caused by the presence of a perfect fourth above the bass note. From earliest times in the history of Western music, the perfect fourth above the lowest sounding note has been considered a dissonance, requiring a downward resolution to the nearest consonance, a third (major or minor) above this same lowest sounding note (figured bass: 4 3). Therefore, in the penultimate chord of Figure 11.2, if the fourth above the bass is considered a dissonance resolving to a third above the bass (D—C♯), then the A in the bass is considered the root of a V triad, lasting two beats, as in Figure 11.7 *c*.

Fig. 11.7.

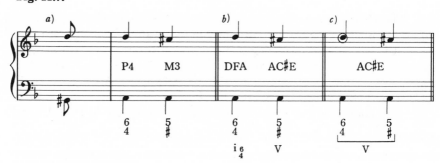

For purposes of instruction, we will consider the six-four sonority as a triad built above its fifth, as in Figure 11.7 *b*, but in writing and listening, the dissonant function of the perfect fourth above the bass should always be kept in mind.

Of the few specific uses of the second inversion, only one, the *cadential six-four*, will be considered in this chapter.[3] This chord is found at the point of a cadence in a phrase of music and is followed by V or V[7]. It usually appears on the strong beat of the measure (Figure 11.8). In triple meter it is often found on the second beat of the measure, allowing the final tonic triad to appear on the strong beat (Figure 11.9).

Fig. 11.8.

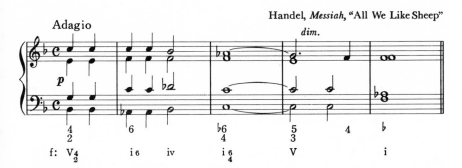

Fig. 11.9.

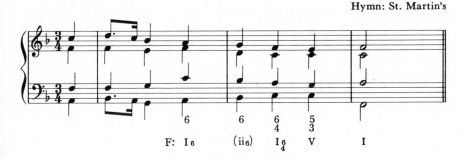

APPLICATION

Written Materials

The Triad in First Inversion

New doubling procedures apply when the triad is found in inversion. In first inversion, normal procedure is to double the soprano note and to retain one each of the remaining triad members.

---

[3]See Chapter 18 for other uses. The tonic six-four chord in measure 3 of Figure 11.2 shows one of these other uses, a *passing six-four* chord.

Fig. 11.10.

Assignment 11.1. *a*) Write single triads in first inversion when soprano and bass note are given.

b) Write single triads when bass note only is given. Write each example in each of the three possible soprano positions.

Writing to or from a Triad in Inversion[4]

When writing a triad in first inversion and connecting it with any triad with its root in the bass, the primary part-writing consideration is the correct approach to the doubled note and the correct resolution of the doubled note. It is possible for each of the two doubled notes to move in three different ways in relation to each other: by contrary motion, by oblique motion, and by similar motion. Figure 11.11 shows these movements in the resolution of the doubled note, while Figure 11.12 shows these movements towards the doubled note of the triad in first inversion.

Fig. 11.11.

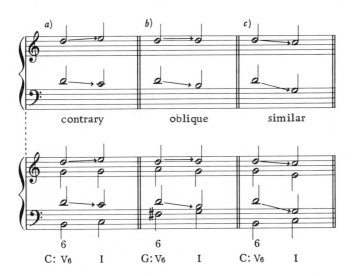

---

[4]The procedures described here and expressed as Rules 6A and 6B (pages 143 and 145) refer to *all* triads in *any* inversion and to any triad containing an unusual doubling, as will be presented later.

Fig. 11.12.

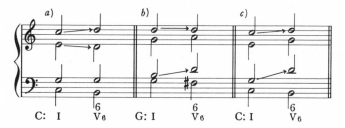

It is always best to use contrary or oblique motion in approaching and leaving the doubled note. In the following excerpt, contrary motion is used exclusively at every occurrence of a triad in first inversion.

Fig. 11.13.

Similar motion is ordinarily necessary only in unusual cases where one voice must be brought into a better range (Figure 11.14) or to effect a change of position (Figures 11.11 *c*, 11.12 *c*).

Fig. 11.14.

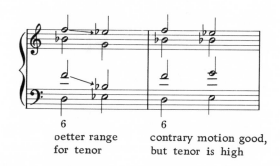

The most efficient procedure for part-writing to or from a triad in first inversion is as follows (Figure 11.15):

Step 1. Write the triad in inversion.

Step 2. Approach or resolve doubled note by contrary or oblique motion if possible.

Step 3. Fill in remaining voice with note necessary to produce normal doubling. When doubled note moves by contrary or oblique motion, the remaining voice usually moves by step or remains stationary, rarely moving by leap.

Fig. 11.15.

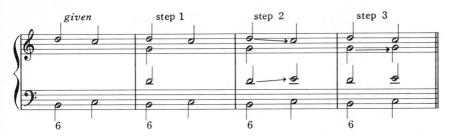

Part-Writing Rule 6A.   When writing to or from a triad in any inversion, write the two voices moving to or from the doubled note *first*, using contrary or oblique motion between the two voices, if possible. When using similar motion, care should be taken to avoid parallel fifths and octaves.

Assignment 11.2.   Write pairs of triads, following Rule 6A. As usual, place chord numbers below each bass tone.

Writing Successive Triads in First Inversion

When triads in first inversion are used in succession, it is impossible for each of these triads to be found with normal doubling in the same pair of voices, since parallel octaves and fifths will result.

Fig. 11.16.

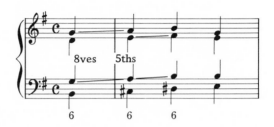

There are two ways to remedy this situation. First, each triad in inversion may have a different doubling, if necessary.

Fig. 11.17.

Bach, *O Herre Gott, dein göttlichs Wort* (♯14)

When using unusual doublings such as these, *avoid doubling the leading tone of the key, or any altered note* (such as the raised sixth scale step in minor). In the example above, Bach has succeeded in resolving each doubled note by contrary motion, has avoided doubling the raised sixth and seventh scale steps, and has moved from triad to triad with a minimum of motion. This example deserves careful study.

Second, it is often possible, especially when there are only two first inversions in succession, to double the soprano note in each triad, but in different pairs of voices (Figure 11.18). Writing IV_6—V_6 or V_6—IV_6 can usually be accomplished by this method.

Fig. 11.18.

Part-Writing Rule 6B. When first inversions of triads are found in *succession*, each succeeding triad must either have a different doubling, or normal soprano doubling may appear in different pairs of voices. Avoid doubling the leading tone or any altered tone.

Assignment 11.3. Write examples of successive first inversions using Rule 6B.

The Triad in Second Inversion

When a triad is found in second inversion, the fifth of the triad (the bass note) is usually doubled. (See Figures 11.8, 11.9, 11.19.)

In writing the cadential six-four chord, the bass note of the I_6^4 is usually approached by step-wise motion. Using triads studied thus far, only the IV or IV_6 will precede the I_6^4. Following the I_6^4, the interval of the sixth above the bass moves to the fifth above the bass, while the fourth above the bass moves to the third above the bass. (Exceptions will be noted in Chapter 18.)

Fig. 11.19.

Assignment 11.4. Write examples of the cadential six-four chord.

Other Part-Writing Considerations

a) The melodic augmented fourth. This interval is usually avoided in melodic writing, and therefore should not appear in any voice line in four-part writing. In the progression IV—V₆, for example (see Figure 11.20 *a*), the bass line may descend by the interval of diminished fifth (inversion of the augmented fourth), making possible a change of direction after the large leap. This necessary change of direction is impossible when using the augmented fourth, since the leading tone should resolve upwards.

b) Overlapping voices. When two adjacent voices (tenor and bass for example) ascend simultaneously, the lower voice should not ascend to a pitch above the higher of the two original tones. This also applies to the upper voice when two tones are descending. See Figure 11.20*b-e*. Although examples may occasionally be found in music (e.g., the last phrases each of Bach chorales 46, 48, and 107), this procedure is comparatively infrequent and should be avoided by the student at this time, unless no other part-writing procedure is effective.

These overlapping voices may often be eliminated simply by changing the direction of one part, as in Figure 11.20 *c*. In other cases, it will usually be necessary to change the position of the first of the two triads, or, if this is impossible, to change the position of a triad appearing before the pair in question.

Part-Writing Rule 7. Triad position may be changed

    a) at a repeated triad

    b) using Rule 2C

    c) at a triad in inversion or a triad with unusual doubling.

In Figure 11.20 *d*, changing the position of the second of the two V triads prevents the overlapping parts. In Figure 11.20 *e*, it is necessary that the IV triad be in close position. This is possible only if the inner voices of the previous I₆ triad are changed.

Many part-writing difficulties other than the above can be solved by going back to a point where Rule 7 may be applied and rewriting the subsequent material.

Fig. 11. 20.

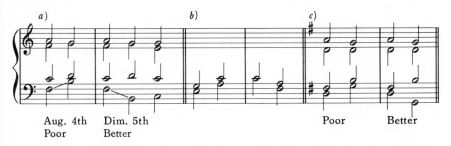

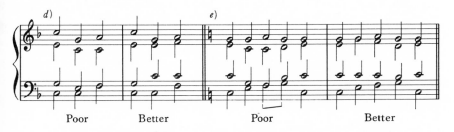

Assignment 11.5. *a*) Write extended exercises, soprano and bass given. Make harmonic analysis.

b) Bass only given. Write soprano line and fill in alto and tenor voices. Make harmonic analysis.

Assignment 11.6. Write on the staff the following progressions based on the given chord symbols. Other keys may be used.

a) D Major $\quad$ V_6 I

b) D♭ Major $\quad$ I V_6 I

c) E Major $\quad$ IV_6 V I

d) G Minor $\quad$ V_6 i

e) B Minor $\quad$ iv_6 V i

f) F Minor $\quad$ i IV_6 V_6 i

g) A Major $\quad$ I IV I_6^4 V I

h) D♭ Major $\quad$ $\frac{3}{4}$ I I_6 I | V V_6 V | I IV V | I ||

i) B Major $\quad$ $\frac{4}{4}$ I | IV_6 V_6 I I | IV V I ||

j) F♯ Minor $\quad$ $\frac{2}{4}$ i V_6 | i i_6 | iv V | i ||

k) D Minor $\quad$ $\frac{4}{4}$ V_6 | i i iv V_6 | i iv i_6^4 V | I ||

l) A♭ Major $\quad$ $\frac{3}{4}$ V | I IV V_6 | I I_6 I | IV_6 I_6^4 V | I ||

Performance of Part-Writing Exercises

Actual performance of part-writing exercises will allow the student to hear the musical effect of his efforts, particularly the effectiveness of the individual parts. Such performance may be accomplished in one of two ways.

As a choral performance. Copy out each of the four parts on separate pieces of paper for distribution to members of the class.

As an instrumental performance. Each of the four parts may be played on such orchestral or band instruments as are available in the theory class. Each of the four parts must be written separately for the use of individual players. Writing for instruments involves technical considerations ordinarily studied as instrumentation. Understanding of the following elementary principles of instrumentation will suffice in writing exercises for performance.

a) Range. Each instrument has one low note below which it cannot play, and an upper range above which its tones are unsatisfactory or difficult. Music written for an instrument must conform to this limitation.

b) Transposition. For some instruments, music is written with pitches differing from the actual sound. A clarinet in B♭, for example, sounds B♭ when the written pitch is C.

c) Clefs. Some instruments use clefs other than the treble and bass clef. The viola uses the alto clef almost exclusively, while other instruments use C clefs as needed.

Details concerning these three principles will be found as Appendix 2. Study these carefully before writing, and consult the player about the problems in playing his particular instrument.

Figure 11.21 illustrates the first few measures of the second exercise in Assignment 11.5 as written for clarinet in B♭, viola, horn in F, and 'cello. Such a combination is not usual, but could occur in a classroom situation, and illustrates use of clefs and transposition.

Fig. 11.21.

Ear Training and Music Reading

Exercise 11.1. Listening to triads in inversion. *a*) Identify the bass note of a major triad as 1. 3, or 5 when the triad is played at the piano. Follow the same procedure used when identifying the soprano note—sing the triad from the root, sing the bass note, and identify the bass note by number.

b) Identify the bass note of a minor triad as 1, 3, or 5. Follow directions outlined in *a*) above.

c) Identify the bass note when major and minor triads are played, as 1M, 5m, 5M, 3m, and so on.

d) Identify both soprano and bass note when major and/or minor triads are played.

e) Spell the triad and the soprano note when the spelling of the bass note is given, or spell the triad and the bass note when the soprano note is given.

Exercise 11.2. Write the triad in inversion from dictation when the bass note is given. Procedure:

a) place given bass note on staff.

b) spell the triad after hearing it played.

c) write soprano note on staff.

Exercise 11.3. Harmonic dictation, first and second inversion of triads. Taking harmonic dictation with inversions follows the basic procedure outlined in Exercise 10.4 with additional steps listed below. This procedure will remain valid for the remaining harmonic dictation exercises in this course of study.

Step 1. Prepare a great staff with treble and bass clefs. Leave space for key signature. Write in time signature as announced.

Step 2. Listen to dictation exercise all the way through without writing. Then sing the tonic key aloud or silently, as instructed. Here is a sample exercise.

Fig. 11.22.

Step 3. Upon the second hearing, sing aloud or silently the root of each triad as it is played, and write its number below the bass staff:

$$V \mid i \; i \; IV \; V \mid i \; iv \; i \; V \mid i \parallel$$

Step 4. As exercise is replayed, listen for the bass note of each triad. If the third is in the bass, add subscript "6" to chord number. If the fifth is in the bass, add "$\frac{6}{4}$".

$$V \mid i_6 \; i \; IV_6 \; V_6 \mid i \; iv \; i_6 \; V \mid i \parallel$$

Step 5. The key signature will be given (in our example, two sharps). Write in the bass line. If chord numbers and inversion symbols are correct, the pitch name of each bass note can be ascertained. Rehearing the exercise at the piano will indicate direction of intervals, up or down. Listening to the bass line as a melodic line will confirm the accuracy of the series of chord numbers or reveal points of error.

Fig. 11.23.

V   i₆   i   IV₆   V₆   i   iv   i₆   V   i
                                          4

Step 6. Listen to the exercise again, this time taking down the soprano line. Optionally, the inner voices may be filled in, either by listening or by following part-writing rules.

As an alternate procedure, the key signature may be given in Step 4. Write the bass line, then indicate inversion in the chord symbols.

Self-Help in Harmonic Dictation

Students desiring to improve their ability in harmonic dictation can do so, working in pairs outside regular classroom instruction. One student will play the selected chord progression as the other writes the chord numbers and the soprano and bass lines according to directions in Exercise 11.3. At this time, material can be derived from two sources.

1. The part-writing exercises of this and preceding chapters make satisfactory harmonic dictation exercises. They may be played as written, or rewritten in other keys before playing (follow directions in Exercise 10.8). In addition, an exercise in a major key can be played in a minor key, or vice versa, by substituting an appropriate key signature.

2. Hymns provide excellent material for harmonic dictation exercises. Hymnbooks are universally procurable, and any hymnbook will furnish examples illustrating most harmonic progressions. In this and following chapters, lists of excerpts from two representative hymnals will be given.

The Hymnal of the Protestant Episcopal Church in the United States of America, hereinafter abbreviated *E.*

The Methodist Hymnal, abbreviated *M.*

The following information will be given.

a) The name of the hymn tune (see footnote, page 19). Many of the hymn tunes listed can be found in other hymnals by consulting the index of tunes. Harmonizations of the same tune in different hymnals occasionally vary.

b) The measure numbers to be used for harmonic dictation drill. In any hymn, measure 1 will be the *first complete* measure. The phrase for dictation may include one or more triads from the previous measure.

c) The number of the hymn (not the page number) in one of the two hymnals listed, for example M-75, means hymn number 75 in *The Methodist Hymnal*.

Since these exercises are excerpts, it can be expected that many will begin and/or end on triads other than the tonic. In a very few cases, an occasional non-harmonic tone, (circled in Figure 11.24), will be found on the weak part of a beat. These can be omitted in playing.

Example: Ellacombe 9-12 M-359. This means measures 9-12 of the hymn tune Ellacombe, to be found in *The Methodist Hymnal* as Number 359.

Fig. 11.24.

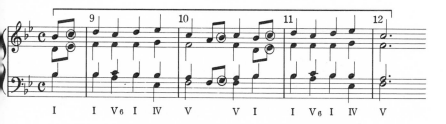

List of hymn tune examples containing I, IV, and V triads only:

Grosser Gott 5–8	M–8
Christus, der ist mein leben 1–2	M–44
Adeste Fidelis 1–4	M–388
	E–12
Davis 8–11	M–129
Horsley 1–2	M–218
Louvan 9–12	M–64
More Love to Thee 1–2	M–185
Tallis' Ordinal 1–2	M–180
	E–298
Webb 1-4	M–248
	E–264
Christe Sanctorum 1–4	E–157(2)
Eudoxia 1–4	E–172
Garden 1–4	E–202

Keyboard Harmony

Exercise 11.4. Play any major or minor triad in first or second inversion, with any member of the triad in the soprano. As in previous keyboard performances of single triads, play each triad in inversion with three notes in the right hand and one in the left, using correct doubling. Example: Play the first inversion of the D major triad, with its fifth in the soprano.

Fig. 11.25.

Silent	find	find	Play
(1) find bass note	(2) soprano note	(3) remaining notes	(4) complete triad

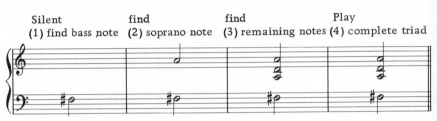

Play these triads, or others as assigned. Soprano note is indicated in parentheses.

First Inversion: Major—C(1), E♭(5), A(3), B(1), D♭(5)
           Minor—D(1), G(5), F♯(3), B♭(1), D♯(5)

Second Inversion: Major—A(3), F(1), G♭(5), E(1), C♯(3)
           Minor—A(1), F♯(5), B(3), G♯(1), E♭(1)

Exercise 11.5. Play exercises from Assignments 11.2—4.

12

Rhythm: Subdivision of the Beat

THEORY AND ANALYSIS

Musical examples studied thus far in rhythmic reading, rhythmic dictation, and sight singing have utilized the divided beat only. By dividing equally each of the divided beats, subdivision of the beat results.

Fig. 12.1.

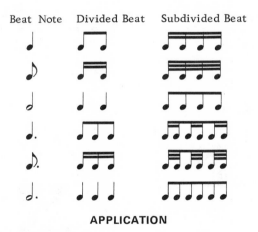

APPLICATION

Ear Training and Music Reading

Exercise 12.1. Reading rhythmic patterns.[1] While making a conductor's beat and tapping the divided beat, read the following examples of sub-

---

[1]Other rhythmic patterns utilizing the subdivided beat will be found in Chapter 19, "Syncopation."

divided beat. Read each line as many times as necessary before proceeding to the next line. Using the guide numbers at the left in Figures 12.2—12.6, read lines in random order as designated by instructor.

It is suggested that the syllable *ta* (*tah*) be used for all notes shorter than the note value receiving one beat.

a) Simple time

Fig. 12.2.

b) Compound time

Fig. 12.5.   **Fig. 12.6.**

Exercise 12.2.   Rhythmic reading. Read the rhythm of melodies from *Music for Sight Singing*, Chapters 11–13. Follow directions for rhythmic reading on page 62.

Exercise 12.3.   Rhythmic dictation. Rhythmic dictation utilizing the subdivided beat will be given at this time. Follow directions given for rhythmic dictation on page 64.

Sight singing. Sing melodies from Chapters 11–12 in *Music for Sight Singing*. These contain the same melodic problems as already studied in Chapters 1–7 of that book. The new problems are rhythmic; all melodies in Part II of *Music for Sight Singing* illustrate the use of the subdivided beat.

Exercise 12.4.   Melodic dictation. Exercises will now contain examples of the subdivided beat as found in Figures 12.2—12.6.

13

Non-harmonic Tones
Harmonizing Melodies at the Keyboard

THEORY AND ANALYSIS

In the study of harmony and part-writing presented thus far, all notes in each of the four voice parts have been members of a triad. Actually, it is not common to find music in which all notes are parts of triads. There are usually other tones present, which sound at the same time as the triad, but are not part of it. These are called *non-harmonic* tones. In Figure 13.1 the circled notes are the non-harmonic tones.

Fig. 13.1.

Bach, *Freuet euch, ihr Christen alle* ($\sharp$8)

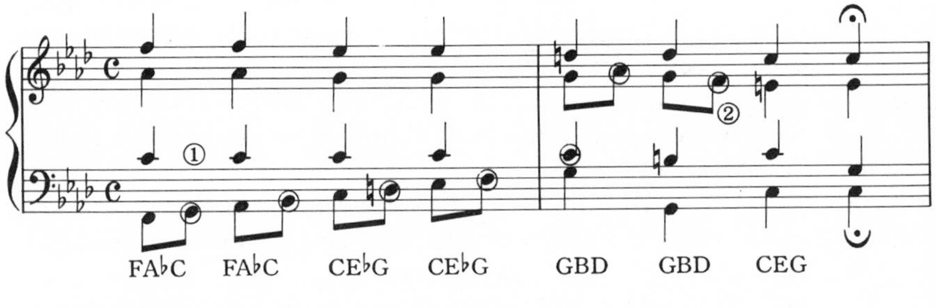

FAbC   FAbC   CEbG   CEbG   GBD   GBD   CEG

Music consisting entirely of pure harmony would become extremely dull to the ear. The addition of the dissonant effect of non-harmonic tones furnishes the necessary contrast to the purity of harmony to make the music more enjoyable. This can be illustrated by playing Figure 13.1, followed by a playing of the same example without its non-harmonic tones.

Fig. 13.2.

It will be observed that the non-harmonic tone is usually found melodically between two harmonic tones. At (1) in Figure 13.1 the non-harmonic tone G is found melodically between the two harmonic tones F and A♭, both harmonic tones belonging to the triad F A♭ C. At (2) the non-harmonic tone F appears between the harmonic tones G of the G B D triad and E of the C E G triad.

Definitions of Non-harmonic Tones[1]

Non-harmonic tones may be identified and classified by the relationship of the dissonance (the non-harmonic tone) to the harmonic tones that precede and follow it. To identify most non-harmonic tones, it is necessary to analyze the *three* notes involved: *a*) the harmonic tone preceding the dissonance, called the note of approach, *b*) the dissonance itself, and *c*) the harmonic tone following the dissonance, called the note of resolution.

There are several classifications into which non-harmonic tones may be placed.

a) *Passing tone.* A non-harmonic tone that is found stepwise between harmonic tones of different pitch is known as a passing tone. See also Figure 13.16 (4), (6), (7), and Figure 13.18, measure 5 (UPT).

Fig. 13.3.

double passing tone

---

[1]There are in current use many names and conflicting definitions for the various non-harmonic tones. For comment on this problem, see "Terminology Variants" on page 163.

Occasionally, passing tones fill in the interval of a fourth between two harmonic tones, necessitating two passing tones adjacent to each other. See also Figure 13.16, (2)–(3) and Figure 13.18, measures 5–6 (APT).

Fig. 13.4.

The second of the two passing tones above occurs on the beat and is known as an accented passing tone, whereas the previous examples have been unaccented passing tones. Any non-harmonic tone occurring in a weak rhythmic position in relation to the note before and after it is designated as unaccented; any non-harmonic tone occurring in a strong rhythmic position in relation to the note before and after it is designated as an accented non-harmonic tone.

Fig. 13.5.

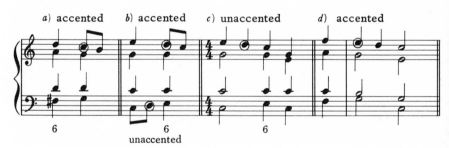

b) *Neighboring tone.* A non-harmonic tone that is found step-wise between two harmonic tones of the same pitch is known as a neighboring tone. When the dissonance is a step above the harmonic tone, it is called an upper neighboring tone; when it is below the harmonic tone, it is called a lower neighboring tone. Neighboring tones, although usually unaccented, may be found accented. See also Figure 13.18, measure 8 (LN).

Fig. 13.6.

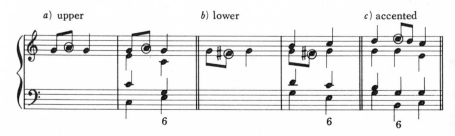

c) Suspension. A non-harmonic tone that is approached by a note of the same pitch and that resolves down by step or halfstep is known as a suspension. The note of approach may be tied into the dissonance, as in Figure 13.7c, d, e, or not, as in Figure 13.7b. See also Fig. 13.18, measure 2 (S), measure 7 (S).

Fig. 13.7.

The dissonance sounds here even though
the note is not actually written at the
point of dissonance.

Less often, the dissonance in a suspension resolves upwards. This figure is sometimes known as a *retardation*.

Fig. 13.8.

d) Anticipation. An anticipation is a non-harmonic tone that sounds the same pitch as the harmonic tone following and is found in a weak rhythmic position. The anticipation is ordinarily found stepwise between two harmonic tones and at the cadence. See also Figure 13.18, measure 6 (A).

Fig. 13.9.

e) *Appoggiatura.* In the appoggiatura figure, the dissonance is approached by leap (interval of a third or larger) and resolves stepwise, usually in a direction opposite to the leap. See also Figure 13.18, measure 9 (App).

Fig. 13.10.

f) *Escaped tone* (also known as *Échappée*). In the escaped tone figure, the dissonance is approached by step and resolves by leap, usually in a direction opposite to that of the note of approach. See also Figure 13.18, measure 4 (ET).

Fig. 13.11.

g) *Changing tone.* This figure involves four notes. The note of approach and the note of resolution are the same pitch. The note of approach proceeds by step up or down to a dissonance. This dissonant note skips an interval of a third in the opposite direction to a second dissonance, which in turn resolves by step to the note of resolution.

Fig. 13.12.

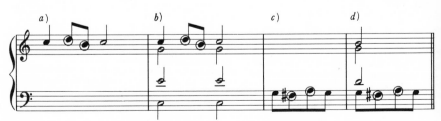

h) Pedal point (or Pedal; Organ point). The pedal point is a note sustained in one voice while in the other voices the harmonies are changing. It often occurs in the bass voice, whence the name pedal, referring to the practice of holding down one note with the foot on the pedal of the organ. When the sustained tone is found as the highest voice, it is known as an *inverted pedal*; when the sustained tone is found in an inner voice, it is known as an *inner pedal* or *internal pedal*. The pedal point is a frequently used device in instrumental music, but is less common in vocal music.

Fig. 13.13.

Table 13.1 (page 164) lists and describes briefly each of these nonharmonic tones. Examples of all types of non-harmonic tones except changing tone and pedal point can be found in Figure 13.18, each identified by a symbol from Table 13.1.

Multiple Non-harmonic Tones

Two or more non-harmonic tones, either of like kinds or of two different kinds, may appear simultaneously. See Figure 13.3*d* and Figure 13.16 (1) and (8) for double passing tones; Figure 13.18, double passing tones in measure 3 and simultaneous passing tone and escaped tone in measure 4.

Terminology Variants

Terminologies for the various non-harmonic tones and the definitions of these terminologies vary widely and have never been standardized. Non-harmonic tones in general are often known as *non-chord tones, foreign tones, accessory tones,* and *bytones.*

Non-harmonic tones are usually classified in one of two ways. In the first system, each non-harmonic tone is named and defined according to the relationship of the dissonance to the harmonic tones that precede and follow it. Non-harmonic tones listed in the previous pages of this chapter have been named and defined according to this principle. Even within this system, other names are often used for terms described earlier in this chapter and as shown in the list of alternate names at the end of this section.

TABLE 13.1.

NON-HARMONIC TONES

Name of non-harmonic tone	Abbreviation	Example	Note of approach	Note of resolution	Direction of resolution
Passing tone, unaccented	UPT		Step-wise	Step-wise	Same direction as approach
Passing tone, accented	APT		Step-wise	Step-wise	Same direction as approach
Neighboring tone, upper	UN		Step-wise	Step-wise	Opposite to approach
Neighboring tone, lower	LN		Step-wise	Step-wise	Opposite to approach
Suspension	S		Same note	Step-wise	Down
Retardation	R		Same note	Step-wise	Up
Anticipation	A		Step-wise	Same note	Same note
Appoggiatura	App		By leap	Step-wise	Opposite to leap
Escaped tone	ET		Step-wise	By leap	Opposite to approach
Changing tones	CT		Step-wise	Step-wise	Same note as note of approach
Pedal Point	P		Held note	--------------------	

In the second system, non-harmonic tones are defined according to rhythmic placement. Any non-harmonic tone that is sounded on an accented beat or part of a beat is known as an *appoggiatura*, this term including the suspension figure (as defined on page 161) when there is no tie into the dissonance. When the tie is present, then the dissonant tone is known as a *suspension*. Unaccented non-harmonic tones carry names similar to those already present or in the list of alternate names below.

Of all the non-harmonic tone designations, only the terms unaccented passing tone, anticipation, and pedal point appear to mean the same thing in all systems of non-harmonic tone terminology. The following list presents some of the more frequently used alternate names for terms listed in Table 13.1.

Neighboring tone: (1) changing tone (when occurring on a weak beat), (2) auxiliary, (3) returning note, (4) turning tone, (5) appoggiatura (when appearing on a strong beat).

Appoggiatura: (1) neighboring tone (when occurring on a strong beat), (2) unprepared neighbor, (3) cambiata, (4) incomplete neighbor, (5) passing tone or turning tone reached by leap.

Escaped tone: (1) neighboring tone (when occurring on a weak beat), (2) incomplete neighbor, (3) passing tone or turning tone left by leap.

Changing tone: (1) double neighbor, (2) cambiata.

Suspension: appoggiatura when not tied to note of approach.

Accented passing tone or *accented neighboring tone:* appoggiatura.

The name *appoggiatura* is also given to a small note appearing before a principal note in a melody. This appoggiatura receives half of the value of the note following, unless the note following is a dotted note, in which case the appoggiatura receives two thirds of the value of the following note.

Fig. 13.14.

Excerpts from Haydn, *The Creation*

This appoggiatura is not to be confused with the *grace note*, a note which looks like an appoggiatura but with a slash across the stem (𝅘𝅥). The grace note is performed without specific time value and as quickly as possible.

Fig. 13.15.

Haydn, *The Creation*

The above is not a complete survey of the appoggiatura. The notation and the use of the appoggiatura, as well as the other non-harmonic tones, is often directly related to the historical period in which the device is used. For complete information, the student is referred to articles on non-harmonic tones in standard musical reference works, such as *Grove's Dictionary of Music and Musicians* and the *Harvard Dictionary of Music* by Willi Apel.

Analysis of Non-harmonic Tones

a) In chorales. The chorales of Johann Sebastian Bach offer unlimited opportunity for study of non-harmonic tones. Each of the four melodic lines in any chorale displays many of them. To identify these non-harmonic tones, it is necessary first to spell the chord; those notes not belonging to the chord will be non-harmonic tones that can be positively identified by relating the dissonant note to its preceding and following notes.

The examples for analysis may contain chords not yet studied. In such cases, merely arrange the notes in a series of thirds to spell the triad or chord; any remaining notes will be non-harmonic.

Fig. 13.16.

Bach, *Ver nur den lieben Gott* (♯146)

   (1)   (2)   (3)   (4)   (5)   (6)   (7)   (8)   (9)

ACE   ACE EG♯B ACE G♯BD   ACE BDF   EG♯B   EG♯B

Note that when an accented non-harmonic tone is used, the chord tone is the note following the accented non-harmonic tone, as in the third chord (E G♯ B) above.

The identification of the note located at the interval of a seventh above the root is sometimes difficult because it often seems to be a chord tone (seventh of a chord) and a non-harmonic tone at the same time. For the present, consider such tones as chord tones when they are accented, and as non-harmonic when they are unaccented.

Fig. 13.17.

Bach, *O Ewigkeit, du Donnerwort* (♯26)

Assignment 13.1. Identify non-harmonic tones circled, but not already labeled, in Figure 13.18. Use abbreviations as given in Table 13.1.

Fig. 13.18.

Bach, *Jesu, Jesu, du bist mein* (♯244)

*⊗ = note held over sounds non - harmonic at this point

Assignment 13.2.   Copy out phrases from Bach chorales listed below. Circle all non-harmonic tones and identify each.

Chorale No.   2, first phrase
5, last phrase
22, first phrase
49, first phrase
111, first phrase
120, first phrase
167, first, second, and third phrases
201, first phrase
219, first phrase
256, first and second phrases
260, entire chorale
280, first and second phrases

b) In instrumental music. Although music in instrumental style may appear different either in whole or in part from music in four-part vocal style, the general principles of composition for each are basically the same, as will be discussed in *Advanced Harmony.*[2] Therefore we will analyze instrumental

---

[2]Robert W. Ottman, *Advanced Harmony: Theory and Practice* (Englewood Cliffs, N 1.: Prentice-Hall, Inc., 1961).

music in the same way as four-part vocal music: locate and identify chord structures and identify remaining tones as non-harmonic tones.

In four-part chorale style, we have found that there is usually a change of harmony on each beat of the measure. Harmonic change in instrumental style is usually less frequent. The piano or instrumental ensemble can, by various devices, prolong a single chord without the resulting monotony of sound produced by the repetition of a single chord in chorale style. For example, in keyboard music, chords are often found "broken," that is, single notes of the chord are played in succession, extending through one or several beats. For purposes of analysis, it is only necessary to reassemble the chord, as in Figure 13.19. Review Figures 2.16—2.18 and 2.22—2.23 for examples of broken chord style.

Fig. 13.19.

Mozart, Sonata for Piano in C Major,
K. 279, first movement

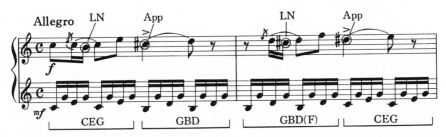

Non-harmonic tones are often chromatically altered—they may be found with an accidental not belonging to the key, as the appoggiatura C♯ in Figure 13.19. Such chromatic alterations do not affect the analysis. Occasionally, two non-harmonic tones will be found in succession, without an intervening harmonic tone.

Block chords are equally useful in instrumental and chorale style. A glance at most any instrumental piece will show changing block chords (Figure 2.24) or repeated block chords (Figure 14.4).

Instrumental writing, as well as vocal writing, may be found in which, at first glance, there seems to be an absence of chords or chord progressions; rather, there seems to be a juxtaposition of two or more different melodic lines. This technique of combining melodic lines, known as *counterpoint*, has been common in Western music since the tenth century (review Chapter 2, "Counterpoint" and Appendix 3, pages 339–341). In the Haydn example that follows, even though four parts rarely sound together, each note in the context of its surrounding notes implies either a specific chord or a non-harmonic tone, as shown in the analysis.

Fig. 13.20.

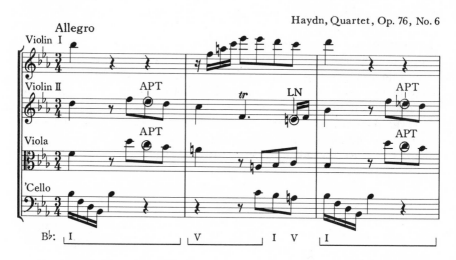

Haydn, Quartet, Op. 76, No. 6

In analyzing instrumental music, look for (1) block chords, (2) broken chords, and (3) two or more melodic lines with or without accompanying chords. Arrange related notes in thirds to determine chord spelling and analysis number; remaining notes will be analyzed as non-harmonic tones.

Assignment 13.3.[3]   From the music scores listed below, copy out the measures indicated. Below the bass line write in chord spellings and the chord numbers (only I, IV, V, and V[7] chords will be found). Circle all non-harmonic tones and identify each with proper abbreviation. These steps are shown in Figure 13.19.

Measure 1 in any composition is the *first complete* measure. Repeats indicated by repeat signs are not numbered. First endings are not numbered. Do not analyze grace notes.

Beethoven, Sonata for Piano No. 5 (Op. 10, No. 1), second movement, measures 1–9.
Chopin, Mazurka No. 16 (Op. 24, No. 3), measures 1–12.
Mendelssohn, *Songs Without Words*
No. 12 (Op. 30, No. 6), measures 15–21
No. 37 (Op. 85, No. 1), measures 1–5

---

[3]Assignments in harmonic analysis in this text will be found in one or more of these sources: Bach, *371 Chorales*, Beethoven, Sonatas for Piano (numbers 1–12 only), Chopin, Mazurkas, Mendelssohn, *Songs Without Words*, Mozart, Sonatas for Piano, and Schumann, *Album for the Young*, Op. 68.

Examples from Murphy and Melcher, *Music for Study* (Englewood Cliffs, N.J.: Prentice-Hall, Inc., 1960) may be used in place of the sources listed. Appropriate chapter numbers from *Music for Study* will be listed in each assignment in harmonic analysis.

Mozart, Sonatas for Piano
   G Major, K. 283, first movement, measures 1–10
   A Major, K. 331, third movement, last 31 measures
Schumann, *Album for the Young*, Op. 68
   No. 8, measures 1–8, 9–16
   No. 11, measures 25–28
   No. 19, measures 1–4

Murphy and Melcher, *Music for Study*: Chapter 1 (I triad), Chapter 2 (V and V⁷, root in bass), Chapter 3 (IV triad), Chapter 4 (Tonic Six-four), Chapter 5 (I, IV, and V in first inversion), and Chapter 7 (V⁷ in inversion).

Determinants of the Harmonic Background of a Melodic Line

In studying the harmonization of a melodic line, we have considered that each note of the melody would bear its own triad. Harmonizing a melody with a chord for each note is common practice in church hymns, but quite uncommon elsewhere, such as in a folk song, an art song, a melody in a symphony, a clarinet solo, and so on. Occasionally, a melody other than a hymn tune may be found in which no non-harmonic tones are implied, such as melody number 41 in *Music for Sight Singing*. Most often, however, the melodic line contains tones implying both harmonic and non-harmonic usages.

In determining whether a note implies a chord tone or a non-harmonic tone, it is necessary to consider one or more of these four factors: *a*) rhythmic placement of melody note, *b*) chord succession, *c*) tempo, and *d*) harmonic rhythm.

a) *Rhythmic placement of melody note.* In most melodies, a note appearing *on the beat* will imply a chord, while a note between beats will imply either another note of the same chord or a non-harmonic tone, as demonstrated in Figure 13.21.

Fig. 13.21.

German Folk Song (MSS 48)

But at times, a note on the beat will imply a non-harmonic tone, as in measures 6 and 7 of Figures 13.22,

Fig. 13.22.

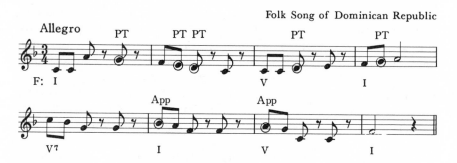

Folk Song of Dominican Republic

or, in a few cases, a note on the beat may imply either a chord tone or a non-harmonic tone, as in Figure 13.23*b.*

Fig. 13.23.

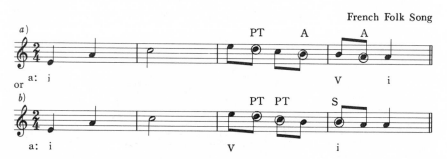

French Folk Song

b) Chord succession. Most folk tunes and the more simple composed melodies can be harmonized using I, IV, and V only. These same tunes can be harmonized with more complex harmonies, as will be done later, but for the present only the three principal triads will be used.

Making use of the three principal triads, the following progressions are possible.

I—V	IV—I	V—I
I—IV	IV—V	V—IV

The V—IV is infrequently found in music and should therefore be used sparingly by the student at this time and only when the melodic line will allow no other progression at that point.

Fig. 13.24.

German Folk Song (MSS 81)

Occasionally, the fourth scale step in the melodic line will imply the seventh of a V^7 chord. In this case, it is only necessary to add a V triad to make a complete V^7 chord.

Fig. 13.25.

German Folk Song (MSS 18)

A IV triad harmonization would be possible in the third full measure of the example above. Since both IV and V^7 are technically correct, the choice will be dictated by the individual student's musical taste.

Care should be taken that each phrase end with some form of cadence, authentic or plagal. In the following example, the end of the phrase could be harmonized with successive I triads, but this is unmusical because of the lack of a cadence.

Fig. 13.26.

French Folk Song (MSS 96)

c) Tempo. As a rule of thumb, it can be said that ordinarily a new chord or a repetition of a previous chord will be placed at each principal beat in the measure, for example, two chords per measure in $\frac{2}{4}$ time, three chords per measure in $\frac{3}{4}$ time, two chords per measure in $\frac{6}{8}$ time, and so on. In a very slow tempo, more chords per measure may be needed, while in a very fast tempo, the call is for fewer chords per measure. In Figure 13.27, the melody to be harmonized has been given three different tempi markings to illustrate the effect on chord selection. If this melody is marked *very slow*, as in *a)*, then the tempo is felt as six beats per measure, indicating the desirability of changing the chord on each of those beats where a change of melody note occurs. In the more common moderate tempo *b)*, the chord changes are more likely to occur on the strong beats of the measure, in this case two beats per measure. When the tempo is rapid, one chord per measure often suffices, as in *c)*.

Fig. 13.27.

It cannot be specifically stated how slow or fast the tempo must be before determining how often a chord change is desirable. This can be determined only by careful study of the melody and applying one's own aesthetic judgment.

d) *Harmonic rhythm.* The rhythmic pattern established by the frequency of chord change is known as harmonic rhythm. In a piece of music, the harmony may change on each beat of the bar.

Fig. 13.28.[4]

Bach, *Du Friedefürst, Herr Jesu Christ* (♯42)

It is also possible that the music may cover several measures with no change of harmony at all.

Fig. 13.29.

Beethoven, Symphony No. 3, first movement

---

[4] $V_{6 \atop 5} = V^7$ in first inversion. See Chapter 19.

These are extremes in the application of harmonic rhythm. More common are patterns in which the harmonic rhythm changes on successive measures or on successive strong beats,

Fig. 13.30.

Beethoven, Sonata for Piano, Op. 2, No. 3, first movement

or in which the harmonic rhythm pattern is more irregular.

Fig. 13.31.

Schumann, *Die Stille*, Op. 39, No. 4

The question arises as to when, rhythmically, a chord change should be made. In general, the strong beats of the harmonic rhythm should coincide with the strong beats of the meter. This statement implies the following observations.

1. Chords may be changed on any beat of the measure.

2. When a change of chord appears on a strong beat of the measure, it may extend into following beats.

3. When a change of chord appears on a weak beat of the measure, it should not be repeated on a following stronger beat. A new chord should appear on the following stronger beat. This also holds true for a bass note; a bass note newly appearing on a weak beat should not be repeated on the following strong beat, even if there is a change in harmony.

4. Exceptions:

The chord appearing on the opening weak beat of a piece of music or of a new phrase may be repeated on the following strong beat. Often, however, no harmony at all is supplied at such points.

Fig. 13.32.

Schubert, *Klage an den Mond* (MSS 348)

A new phrase beginning on a strong beat may repeat the harmony of the previous weak beat.

Fig. 13.33.

Spanish Folk Song (MSS 122)

The following melody is harmonized two different ways to show the effect of incorrect and correct application of the principles of harmonic rhythm. The chord succession in both harmonizations is good. However, beginning in the second measure of the first harmonization a) the chord newly appearing on the second (weak) beat is consistently repeated on the following strong beat, giving an awkward effect of displacement of the natural accent of the melody.

Fig. 13.34.

Examples in which it is possible to interpret the melody in two widely different ways are not common. Most melodies are more likely to follow the example of Figure 13.34*b* where the nature of the melody demands a chord choice in which the harmonic rhythm is correct.

On rare occasions, you may encounter a melody so constructed that only an irregular harmonic rhythm pattern may be possible.

Fig. 13.35.

Assignment 13.4.   Melodic Analysis. Copy out melodies as assigned from Chapters 1–7 and 11–12 in *Music for Sight Singing*. On a bass staff below the melody, write in the implied harmony in block triads with the correct triad number. Circle non-harmonic tones in the melody and identify each by name (abbreviation). Use Figure 13.21 as a guide.

The melodies from *Music for Sight Singing* in the following list offer a minimum of problems and can readily be harmonized using the three principal triads, either for this assignment or for Exercise 13.1. Some melodies in sections 3 and 4 below are in the bass, alto, or tenor clefs; these should be transposed up one or two octaves as necessary and placed in the treble clef.

1. Easy, tonic and dominant triads only: 10, 15, 30, 32, 33, 55, 72, 93, 101, 107.
2. Easy, subdominant triad added: 126, 174, 193, 195, 313.
3. Other melodies requiring two or three principal triads: 34, 51, 52, 55, 57, 66, 70, 78, 90, 111, 147, 160, 165, 193, 195, 203, 327, 330.
4. Melodies in which a fourth scale step will imply (*a*) that the fourth scale step must be combined with the dominant triad to create a V^7 chord, or (*b*) that the fourth scale step may be harmonized either by the dominant seventh chord or by the subdominant triad: 2, 4, 5, 6, 16, 17, 18, 28, 31, 44, 56, 60, 90, 113, 115, 117, 118, 159, 167, 175, 198, 303, 308, 312, 331.

APPLICATION

Written Materials

The principles and techniques of writing non-harmonic tones will be found in later chapters:

Passing tones and neighboring tones, Chapter 15.
Suspensions, Chapter 17.
Appoggiaturas and escaped tones, Chapter 18.

Keyboard Harmony

The abilities to discover the harmonic background implied in a melodic line, to recognize and identify the non-harmonic tones in that line, and to place this information on the staff, as in Assignment 13.4, lead us quite logically to the next step in the practical use of the three principal triads: the harmonization of a melodic line at the keyboard. But while writing on the staff can be done at leisure, harmonizing at the keyboard requires rapid thinking and execution in order to achieve a performance without interruption of the rhythmic patterns of the melody or of the meter established by the time signature. Since chords must be chosen and played quickly, success in melody harmonization at the keyboard will be more assured when there is no question about the ability to spell quickly and accurately the three principal triads of each major and minor key (Assignment 8.1) and to play accurately and without hesitation the chord progression I–IV–V–I or i–iv–V–i in each major and minor key (Exercise 10.7).

Melodies and their harmonizations from Assignment 13.4 may be played at the keyboard as written, with block triads in root position in the left hand and the melody in the right hand. Such a procedure will serve as an introduction to keyboard harmonization; the use of such block triads, however, is unmusical in that it often produces a thick, ugly sound when played in a low register and, of course, always produces parallel fifths.[5]

In all previous keyboard exercises involving single triads and triads in succession, you have been directed to play with three notes in the right and one in the left. In so doing, you have been playing in close position, giving you maximum assurance that part-writing procedures will be correct, particularly since in keyboard playing, vocal range is not a consideration. Keyboard harmonization, then, simply amounts to playing chord progressions already known, but with a melody superimposed, as shown in Figure 13.36. Note that it is not necessary to repeat the triad on every beat. The triad once played need not be repeated until a change of triad, though often, as in our figure, if a single triad lasts more than one measure, it may be repeated on the next down beat. Use the sustaining pedal on the piano to keep the harmonic sound alive between actual playing of the triads.

Fig. 13.36.

German Folk Song (MSS 48)

---

[5]In another common practice, the left hand plays a chord selected from the progression I—IV$_6$—V$_6$—I, producing the aural effect of the desired chord progression with a minimum
of finger movement. This also produces all the undesirable musical effects described above, plus frequent doubled leading tones that usually resolve to tonic by parallel octaves, as well

Other styles of playing as shown in Figure 13.37 *a* and *b* may be attempted by those with more keyboard proficiency. The left hand accompaniment figure of *b* can be adapted to any meter scheme, as shown in *c*.

Fig. 13.37.

a) open position

b) rhythmic accompaniment in left hand

c) left hand in various meters

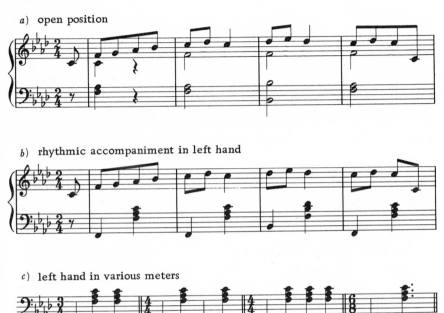

It will often be found useful to harmonize a cadence with the tonic six-four chord, especially with a soprano line 3–2–1 or 1–7–1. The tonic six-four can be preceded by the tonic or subdominant triad, but should not be preceded by the dominant triad. It must appear on a strong beat of the measure, or may appear on the second beat in triple time, and is followed by the dominant triad.

as frequent occurrences of other parallel octaves and fifths. While this procedure may suffice for amateurs or for avocational interest, professional musicians should be satisfied only with a performance that is technically correct and aesthetically pleasing, especially when this skill is to be used in the teaching of other persons. The methods of keyboard harmonization described in this chapter are admittedly a little more difficult than the two "short cut" methods described. But students who have practiced keyboard exercises in previous chapters to the point of playing with ease and accuracy should experience little difficulty in learning to harmonize a melody so that it sounds professionally competent and pleasing to the ear.

Fig. 13.38.

a)

i   i   i $_{4}^{6}$ V   i

b)

German Folk Song (MSS 317)

I   I   IV   I $_{4}^{6}$ V   I

Students working in pairs can practice keyboard harmonization and sight singing simultaneously. While òne student sings the melody (or plays it on an instrument), the other will accompany him. In this procedure, the melody need not be played by the keyboard player; instead, he may divide the accompaniment figure between the two hands. A few such methods of accompaniment are shown in Figure 13.39.

Fig. 13.39.

English Folk Song (MSS 10)

a)

b)

Exercise 13.1. Play melodies with accompaniment of tonic, dominant, and subdominant triads at the keyboard, using piano accompaniment styles shown in Figures 13.36—13.39. Practice first the melodies listed in Assignment 13.4, followed by other melodies from *Music for Sight Singing*, Chapters 1–7 and 11–12, as assigned.

14

Secondary Triads
Principles of Chord Progression
The Diminished Triad
The Leading Tone Triad

THEORY AND ANALYSIS

The Secondary Triads

The secondary triads in a key are those built on scale steps other than I, IV, and V. In a major key, these triads are:

Fig. 14.1.

In a minor key, alternate forms of the triads appear because of the use of different forms of the minor scale.

Fig. 14.2.

Of the triads listed in Figure 14.2, III+ and vi° are less frequently used. Note also in this figure that on the sixth and seventh scale steps, the root of each of the two triads is a different note (A♭, A♮; B♭, B♮). For chords built on the sixth and seventh scale steps, the triad number always indicates whether the lowered or raised tone is the root:

VI always refers to a triad built on the lowered sixth scale step.
vi° always refers to a triad built on the raised sixth scale step.
VII always refers to a triad built on the lowered seventh scale step.
vii° always refers to a triad built on the raised seventh scale step.

No other chord spellings are to be found (except as rarities) on the sixth and seventh scale steps in a minor key; therefore, the chord number will specify whether the chord is built upon the raised or lowered scale step.

Principles of Harmonic Progression[1]

In studying the three principal triads, there has been little difficulty in determining the progression of one triad to the next. We found that both the dominant and subdominant triads can progress directly to the tonic of the key, the goal of the harmonic progression, and the tonic, in turn, may progress to either. The subdominant also progresses easily to the dominant; only the reverse of this progression was found to be infrequently used.

With the addition of the secondary triads, making a total of seven diatonic triads, we find it theoretically possible for any one triad to progress to any one of six other triads. It might seem that we should be at liberty to follow any triad by any other triad. But before making such an assumption, we should ask, "Are there any restrictions governing the choice of chord succession?" If we should attempt to answer this question by looking in composed music for an example of each possible chord progression, the answer would be "No," since diligent search would certainly and eventually reveal an example of any possible succession of two chords. But by the time we had located every possible chord progression, we would have noted that certain chord progressions appear over and over again, while others appear infrequently or rarely. Composers have not chosen to utilize all possible chord progressions equally; an understanding of the style of the "common practice" period is dependent in part on knowledge of the relative frequency of use of the various and numerous chord progressions available, and the reasons for variance in frequency.

Progression of chords, one to another, is always described in terms of root

---

[1]This survey treats the subject of triads to be studied in this and following chapters. It should be reviewed periodically during the remainder of the course.

movements, that is, the intervallic distance between the roots of the two successive chords in question, regardless of the actual bass notes (inversions) used. These intervallic distances can only be three: the fifth, the third, and the second. The fourth, the sixth, and the seventh are merely the inversions of these (a root movement C up to G, a fifth, is the same as a root movement C down to G, a fourth), while progression by the same root note or its octave is static.

Root movement *down by fifth* accounts for a large percentage and often a majority of the chord progressions in the music of most composers. This is the movement of the authentic cadence (V–I), which is so effective in establishing a sense of key. It has been surmised by many theoreticians that the basic quality of the downward fifth lies in its relationship to the first interval (other than the octave) in the overtone series: a fifth, 3 down to 2 (Figure A3.12 in Appendix 3). Should we start with the tonic note of the key and progress down by fifths (or up by fourths), the following progression would result.[2] The brackets, above or below, indicate progressions commonly used.

$$\text{I—IV—vii}°\text{—iii—vi—ii—V—I}$$

Progressing *up by fifth* (down by fourth) produces another series:

$$\text{I—V—ii—vi—iii—vii}°\text{—IV—I}$$

Progressing *down by second* produces the series:

$$\text{I—vii}°\text{—vi—V—IV—iii—ii—I}$$

while progressing *up by seconds* produces:

$$\text{I—ii—iii—IV—V—vi—vii}°\text{—I}$$

The series produced in progressing *down by thirds* is

$$\text{I—vi—IV—ii—vii}°\text{—V—iii—I}$$

and *up by thirds* is

$$\text{I—iii—V—vii}°\text{—ii—IV—vi—I}$$

The commonly used progressions can be extracted from the six series listed above and tabulated as shown in Table 14.1.

---

[2]Chord numbers for major keys are used throughout this discussion and in Tables 14.1 and 14.2, but refer equally to minor keys unless otherwise noted.

TABLE 14.1.

THE COMMONLY USED CHORD PROGRESSIONS

I: I may progress to any other chord.
Any chord may progress to I when I interrupts a progression listed in this table (e.g., ii—I—V)

ii: ii—V, ii—vii°

iii: iii—IV, iii—vi

IV: IV—ii, IV—V, IV—vii°, IV—I

V: V—vi, V—I.

vi: vi—ii, vi—iii—IV, vi—IV, vi—V

vii°:   vii°—I, VII—III in minor.

With only a few exceptions, as will be noted at appropriate times, this table is valid for seventh chords and altered chords as well as for the diatonic triads listed.

The tonic triad at the cadence is the goal of any harmonic progression, though the finality of the cadence is often modified as a half cadence or a deceptive cadence. The tonic triad is also most often the beginning point of a harmonic progression, although a different chord (often V) may initiate the harmonic movement at the beginning of a phrase or section of music. To reach the goal at the cadence, a composer has many choices, even when restricting himself to diatonic triads and the progressions listed in Table 14.1. Since progression by downward fifth is most common, we can plot a progression from any triad to its goal, the tonic, as shown in the left-hand column of Table 14.2. And, in turn, we can delay or hasten progress towards the ultimate tonic by interpolating root movements of seconds, thirds, or upward fifths, as shown in the right-hand column of Table 14.2. In the progression I–vi–V–I, for example, vi, going down by root movement of a second to V, hastens movement to the tonic by replacing two downward fifths, vi–ii–V.

Both columns of Table 14.2 contain all the chord progressions from Table 14.1, used in all possible combinations. In interpreting this table, special note should be made concerning the use of vii°: (1)vii°–iii (major only)[3] is ordinarily used only when the series continues to tonic by downward fifths (see "Harmonic Sequence" later in this chapter) and (2) vii° may be substituted for V in any progression listed except vi–V or V–vi (explained under "Leading Tone Triad" later in this chapter).

Although we have placed the possible chord successions into two groups,

---

[3]VII-III in minor is regularly used without restriction. See Chapter 18.

TABLE 14.2.

ROOT MOVEMENTS
TO A CADENCE
ON THE TONIC

Roots Progressing *by Downward Fifths*	*Other Combinations of* *Common Root Movements*
I IV vii° iii vi ii V I	I IV ii V I
	I IV V I
I vii° iii vi ii V I	I vii° I
I iii vi ii V I	I iii vi IV ii V I
	I iii IV ii V I
	I iii vi IV V I
	I iii IV V I
I vi ii V I	I vi iii IV ii V I
	I vi iii IV V I
	I vi IV ii V I
	I vi IV V I
	I vi V I
I ii V I	
I V I	I V vi ———— to I

the common progressions of Table 14.1 and the less common progressions (those not appearing in Table 14.1), there is actually a third classification; these are certain progressions that, standing alone, are infrequently used, but in special situations can be considered equal in frequency of use and desirability as the common progressions. There are three such situations:

1. *First inversions in succession.* When a bass line moves by step and each note is the third of a chord, any resulting succession of chords is acceptable. Review Figure 11.5 and accompanying discussion.

2. *Harmonic sequence.* A harmonic sequence is a series of chords with a regularly recurring pattern of root movements, a series in which any resulting pair of triads or chords is acceptable. Each series of chords in the left-hand column of Table 14.2 is a harmonic sequence, since the roots are always a fifth apart, usually written with the chord roots describing the pattern fifth down, fourth up, fifth down, etc. (or its inversion, fourth up, fifth down), as shown in Figure 14.3, which also shows the VII chord in a minor key.

Fig. 14.3.

Allegro con brio   Haydn, Sonata in G Major for Piano

Any other regular pattern of root movements can be used, such as third down, second up, third down, etc. or, as in Figure 14.4, the pattern fourth down and fifth up, I–V–ii–VI, the latter chord being altered.

Fig. 14.4.

Schubert, *Valses nobles*, Op. 77

3. *Chromatic bass line.* When the bass line ascends or descends by a series of half steps, any chord succession resulting is usually satisfactory. Further discussion and illustration of this type of chord movement will be presented during the study of altered chords in *Advanced Harmony.*

A survey such as this serves merely to show all the possibilities from which a composer may choose and to provide a source for a list of those progressions that composers of the seventeenth-nineteenth centuries used with any degree of frequency. At the present time, our study of harmony will concern itself principally with those progressions indicated in Tables 14.1 and 14.2 as commonly used progressions, while study of the remainder will be considered in later chapters and in *Advanced Harmony.*

By restricting yourself at present to these progressions, you will be able to make immediate and effective use of harmonic materials with a minimum chance of error in chord choice, whether it be in melody harmonization at the keyboard or on paper, or in original composition. Knowledge of the commonly used progressions will be found valuable in taking harmonic dictation; knowing what to listen for and what to expect next after a given chord will be found most helpful in developing your harmonic listening ability. A complete understanding of this and following chapters will be made easier and clearer if Table 14.1 is memorized now.

The Diminished Triad

The diminished triad is composed of two minor thirds. The resulting distance between the root and the fifth of the diminished triad is the interval of a diminished fifth (one half step smaller than a perfect fifth); the interval of the diminished fifth when inverted becomes an augmented fourth.

Fig. 14.5.

Because of the interval of the diminished fifth, the diminished triad is classified as one of the dissonant triads.[4] Both the interval of the diminished fifth and its inversion, the augmented fourth, are known commonly as a *tritone,* referring to the fact that the interval is composed of three whole steps (six half steps). The interval equally divides the octave.

---

[4]Consonant triads are defined (in the historical period under study) as those containing consonant intervals: the octave, perfect fifth, perfect fourth, major and minor thirds, major and minor sixths. Triads or chords containing other intervals are dissonant.

Fig. 14.6.

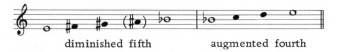

diminished fifth   augmented fourth

The diminished triad is most frequently used in first inversion. Typical examples of its use are seen in Figures 14.7 and 14.8.

Fig. 14.7.

Bach, *O Welt, sieh hier dein Leben* (♯117)

A♭:   I   IV   vii°₆   I

Fig. 14.8.

Mozart, Sonata in D Major for Piano, K. 284,
third movement

i   i   ii°₆   V⁷   i

The diminished triad, either vii° or ii°, may appear with its root in the bass when it occurs during the course of a harmonic sequence, as shown in Figure 14.3, where the ii° triad is seen with its root in the bass.

The Leading Tone Triad

The triad on the leading tone is a diminished triad in both major and minor keys. Its symbol is vii°, and it is ordinarily found in first inversion, vii°₆, as in Figure 14.7.

Assignment 14.1. Spell the vii° triad in each major and minor key.

The vii° triad bears a striking resemblance, both in sight and sound, to the V⁷ chord. The vii° triad looks like the upper three notes of the V⁷ chord and

is often symbolized as V_0^7, meaning a V^7 with its root missing (in C: vii°
or $V_0^7 = B\ D\ F$; $V^7 = G\ B\ D\ F$). In progressing to the tonic, the vii° triad
has the aural effect of a dominant chord and for this reason can be used
freely as a substitute for V with few exceptions, as noted in the discussion of
Table 14.2. Two specific uses of this triad, however, far outnumber any
other usages:

1. Between the tonic triad and its first inversion (Figure 14.9) or reverse
(Figure 14.10).

Fig. 14.9.

Bach, *Schau, lieber Gott, wie meine Feind* (♯3)

a: V   i   vii°$_6$ i^6 V$_4^3$ i   V$_6$ i   V

2. After the IV triad when the soprano note of the IV triad ascends, as in
Figures 14.7 and 11.13.

Assignment 14.2.   Harmonic analysis. In each of the following phrases from
Bach chorales, find the vii°$_6$ triad and describe its use. Phrases marked * contain only triads studied thus far; make complete analysis of triads and non-
harmonic tones.

*26, first phrase	*267, first phrase
*47, first phrase	273, fourth phrase
*53, first phrase	289, first phrase
*244, first phrase	363, first phrase

See also Murphy and Melcher, *Music for Study*, Chapter 13. (These contain
triads not yet studied.)

APPLICATION

Written Materials

Writing the Diminished Triad

Only the use of the first inversion of the diminished triad will be considered at this time.

The normal voice distribution for any diminished triad in first inversion is two thirds, one root and one fifth (bass note doubled), except that when the triad is found with the fifth in the soprano, the fifth is usually doubled (two fifths, one root, one third).

Fig. 14.10.

Bach, *Zeuch uns nach dir*

I₆   vii°₆   I   V   V   I

Fig. 14.11.

Bach, *Aus meines Herzens Grunde* (♯1)

I   V₆   I   vii°₆   I₆   I

Assignment 14.3.   Writing diminished triads. Double the third when the root or third is in the soprano; double the fifth an octave lower when the fifth is in the soprano.

Writing the Leading Tone Triad

Although the vii° triad sounds like an incomplete dominant seventh (V_0^7), the fifth of the triad (in C major, F of B D F) ascends, whereas the same note of the dominant seventh chord (in C major, F of G B D F) always descends. In this respect the vii° triad differs completely from the V^7. When the fifth of vii° is in the soprano, it is doubled, the upper fifth resolving down and the lower fifth resolving up.

a) Use of Rule 6. Since this triad is used almost exclusively in first inversion, part-writing Rule 6 may be used in approaching and leaving the triad. See progression i vii°₆ i₆ in Figure 14.9.

b) IV—vii°₆. Use of the vii°₆ instead of V following the IV triad when the melody ascends (as in Figures 14.7 and 11.13) is necessary to prevent parallel fifths and octaves. Should the progression IV–V be used with an ascending melody line, it would be impossible to follow part-writing Rule 3 (triads with roots in the bass a second apart).[5] When the root of the IV triad is in the soprano, this tone is held over as the soprano note of the following vii° triad.

Fig. 14.12.

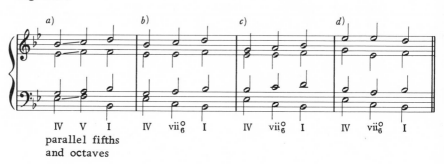

Were Figure 14.12 in the parallel minor key (Bb minor), the subdominant triad in examples *b* and *c* would be major (IV) to allow use of the melodic minor scale in the tenor and soprano voices, respectively, while in example *d*, the subdominant triad would be minor (iv) because of the descending sixth scale step.

c) Unequal fifths. The interval of the diminished fifth in the vii° triad is often preceded and/or followed by a perfect fifth in the same pair of voices. The visual effect is that of parallel fifths; these fifths, however, are called *unequal fifths* and their use is perfectly acceptable.

---

[5]For an example of such a IV-V progression, see Bach chorale number 177, first phrase. This procedure is little used.

Fig. 14.13.

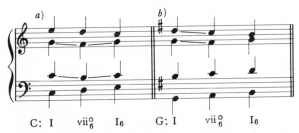

C: I   vii°₆   I₆   G: I   vii°₆   I₆

d) vii°₆ with the fifth in the soprano. As a melody tone, the fifth of the vii°₆ triad (or any diminished triad) normally descends, as in Figure 14.11. It may progress upwards when found in a melody line moving in similar motion with the bass at the interval of a tenth (an octave plus a third).

Fig. 14.14.

Bach, *Vater unser im Himmelreich* (♯47)

vii°₆   i₆

Assignment 14.4. Part writing. Fill in alto and tenor voices. Be particularly careful of the approach and resolution of all doubled notes in triads in first inversion. As usual, write in triad numbers below the bass part.

Assignment 14.5. Part-writing, bass line only given. Supply melody line and fill in alto and tenor parts.

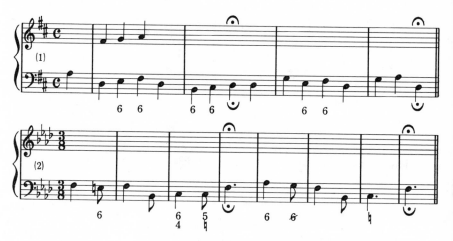

Assignment 14.6. Write in four voices the following progressions.

a) D Major $\quad \frac{3}{4}$ V $\Big|$ I$_6$ vii$^\circ_6$ I $\Big|$ IV$_6$ I$_6$ $_4$ V $\Big|$ I $\Big\|$

b) G♭ Major $\quad \frac{4}{4}$ I $\Big|$ IV vii$^\circ_6$ I I$_6$ $\Big|$ IV V I $\Big\|$

c) G minor $\quad \frac{2}{4}$ V $\Big|$ i i$_6$ $\Big|$ vii$^\circ_6$ i $\Big|$ iv V $\Big|$ i $\Big\|$

d) B♭ minor $\quad \frac{4}{4}$ V $\Big|$ i i IV* vii$^\circ_6$ $\Big|$ i iv i$_6$ $_4$ V $\Big|$ i $\Big\|$

*Third or fifth of triad in soprano.

Melody Harmonization

The Triad in Inversion. In harmonizing melodies from previous chapters, we have always placed the root of the triad in the bass. The result has usually been a series of large skips in the bass voice. Though it is more acceptable to have such skips in the bass than in the other voices, it is preferable that the bass line be made more melodic, either by reducing the number of large leaps or the size of these leaps. This can be accomplished by the use of triads in inversion. Compare the bass lines of the two examples below, the first of which is a Bach chorale and the second the same harmonization with the root of each chord in the bass part.

Fig. 14.15.

Bach, *Was Gott tut, das ist wohlgetan* (♯293)

The triad to be used for each melody note should be chosen first when harmonizing a melody. With the use of inversions, it now becomes necessary to decide which triads will be in inversion and which will have the root in the bass, so the bass line should be written *before* the alto and tenor. The soprano and bass together should make a good two-part composition.

When the bass line moves with the soprano, their related movements can be in any one of four directions.

    a) contrary motion to each other

    b) oblique motion—soprano stays on same tone while bass moves, or soprano moves while bass maintains the same tone

    c) similar motion to each other

    d) stationary motion—both soprano and bass repeat their tones.

Fig. 14.16.

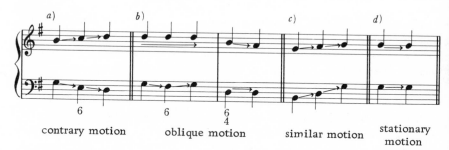

contrary motion	oblique motion	similar motion	stationary motion

By extracting the soprano and bass only from Figure 14.15 we can find the following types of motion.

Fig. 14.17.

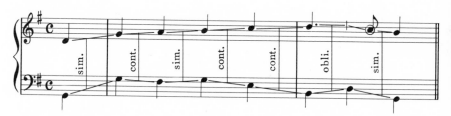

Of the four types of motion, contrary and oblique are the most frequently used, although similar motion is good when found as intervals of thirds or sixths between soprano and bass.[6] (See Figures 14.15 and 14.17, progression

---

[6]At this point, consideration should be given to the "hidden octave" and the "hidden fifth" (sometimes called "direct octave" and "direct fifth"). A hidden octave occurs when two voices progress in similar motion to a perfect octave; a hidden fifth occurs when two voices progress in similar motion to a perfect fifth.

hidden 8ves	hidden 5ths

These need concern the student *only* when they occur between the two outer voices of a composition. Even then they are acceptable when *a*) the chord is repeated (Figure 14.17, first two chords) or *b*) when the triad roots are a fifth apart (Figure 14.10, progression I-V at the fermata). In other circumstances hidden octaves and fifths between outer voices often do not sound well. Any such octave or fifth should be used only after careful consideration of its aural effect.

from third to fourth chord.) Inversions should be chosen to make the bass line progress more by intervals of seconds and thirds rather than by larger leaps. Note, however, that cadences are usually more effective when their triads have roots in the bass. For the present, the first inversion only will be used, except that the I_6^4 may be used at a cadence.

By following the above directions, several possible bass lines can be found to fit a given melody, final choice to be dictated by musical taste. The following examples show how each of two melodies could be harmonized in a number of different ways.

Fig. 14.18.   **Fig. 14.19.**

Assignment 14.7. Melody harmonization. Supply harmony and three lower voice parts when melody only is given. As this is a problem in diminished triads, use the vii$_6^{\circ}$ triad wherever practicable.

Assignment 14.8. Write original exercises using the four triads studied to date. Write four-measure phrases or periods, as assigned. Write for voices or instruments, as assigned. Pay particular attention to *a*) chord choice, *b*) harmonic rhythm, *c*) melodic writing, and *d*) the bass line. In addition, indicate the tempo of your composition and include dynamic markings.

Ear Training and Music Reading

The Diminished Triad

Exercise 14.1. Singing diminished triads. From a given pitch, sing a diminished triad, calling the given pitch 1, 3, or 5, as directed, or sing with pitch names when the name of the given pitch is supplied.

Fig. 14.20.

Exercise 14.2. Identifying the soprano when the diminished triad is played. For this ear training exercise, the diminished triad will be played in first inversion only. Follow this procedure.

a) Listen to triad.

b) Sing triad from root, bearing in mind that the bass tone heard is always "3."

c) Sing the soprano note.

d) Identify the soprano note as 1, 3, or 5.

e) Spell the triad when the name of the soprano note is given.

Exercise 14.3. Identifying the tritone by ear. Since the diminished fifth and the augmented fourth are exactly the same size, it is impossible to differentiate between them unless a chord is sounded at the same time.

Fig. 14.21.

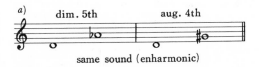

Procedure:

a) Listen to interval; listen to triad, played in first inversion, from which interval is taken.

b) Sing triad from root, singing 1–3–5–3–1.

c) Sing interval with correct numbers.

d) Identify interval by name; if numbers are 1 up to 5 or 5 down to 1, it is a diminished fifth; if numbers are 5 up to 1 or 1 down to 5, it is an augmented fourth.

Fig. 14.22.

or

a) listen   b) sing   c) sing

Spell the interval or write interval on the staff when the name of the first note is given.

The Leading Tone Triad

Exercise 14.4.   *a*) Singing the leading tone triad. In the given key (major or minor) sing the progression I–vii°–I or i–vii°–i. Sing each triad from its root with letter names.

b) Sing the progression I–IV–vii°–I or i–IV–vii°–i in the given key.

Exercise 14.5.   Harmonic dictation. The vii° can easily be identified, because it is a diminished triad and generally progresses directly to the tonic triad. Any or all of the following steps will be helpful in distinguishing the various triads studied thus far.

a) After listening to dictation exercise, write down the *type* of each triad, using the symbol *M* for major, *m* for minor, and *d* for diminished.

b) Sing with scale numbers or with letter names as directed, the root of each triad as the progression is played.

c) Sing each triad with the numbers 1–3–5, or sing each triad with correct spelling in the given key, as directed.

Self-Help in Harmonic Dictation

Excerpts from hymns listed below contain examples of tonic, subdominant, dominant and leading tone triads only.

Gräfenberg 7–9	M–134
Olivet 7–10	M–143
Schumann 1–2	M–181
Ratisbon	M–401
	E–153
Petra 9–10	E–70
Doncaster 1–4	E–293
Spanish Chant 5–6	E–332
Silver Street 11–12	E–552

Upon completion of Assignment 14.8, each of two students working together may use his original composition as a harmonic dictation exercise by playing his composition while the other student takes down the triad numbers and the soprano and bass lines. This procedure should be continued in each subsequent chapter.

Keyboard Harmony

Exercise 14.6. Play cadences in Figure 14.23 in any major or minor key.

Fig. 14.23.

Exercise 14.7. Play examples from Assignments 14.4 and 14.7 at the keyboard.

15

The Supertonic Triad

In a major key, the supertonic triad is a minor triad (ii). In a minor key it is a diminished triad (ii°) or a minor triad (ii) when used in conjunction with the melodic minor scale.

Fig. 15.1.

Assignment 15.1. Spelling the supertonic triad.

a) Spell the ii triad in each major key.
b) Spell the ii° triad in each minor key.
c) Spell the ii triad in each minor key.

Use of the Supertonic Triad

Unlike each of the three principal triads, the supertonic triad is most frequently found in first inversion. The progressions $ii_6-V-(I)$ or $ii_6-I_6^4-(V-I)$, or in minor with ii_6°, are among the most commonly used progressions in all music. They are particularly useful at cadence points, even more so than IV–V–I.

Fig. 15.2. ii⁰₆-V¹

Bach, *Wo soll ich fliehen hin* (♯281)

g: i   ii⁰₆   V

Fig. 15.3. ii₆-I₆
                    ⁴

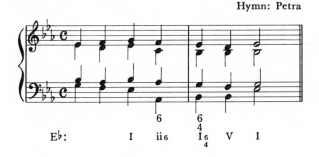

Hymn: Petra

E♭:   I   ii₆   I₆   V   I
                                    ⁴

The supertonic triad with its root in the bass, though much less common than in first inversion, is useful in a major key (ii° in minor, being a diminished triad, is rarely found with its root in the bass²) and regularly progresses to V (Figure 15.4) or to I₆ (Figure 15.5). In progressing to the tonic six-four chord, the bass note of ii leaps up a fourth to the bass note of I₆, the only regular exception to the principle that the bass tone of the cadential six-four chord is approached by step.

Of the triads studied thus far, the supertonic triad is preceded by IV (Figure 15.4) or by I (Figure 15.6).

---

¹The progression ii⁰₆-V is used here as a half cadence, one of a number of half cadences discussed in full in Chapter 18.

²A common exception is ii⁰ in a harmonic sequence. See Figure 14.3.

Fig. 15.4.   IV-ii-V

Hymn: Hanover

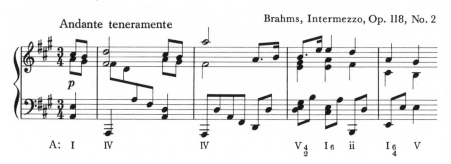

G: IV   ii   V   I

Fig. 15.5.   ii-I$_6^4$

Andante teneramente

Brahms, Intermezzo, Op. 118, No. 2

A: I   IV   IV   V$_2^4$ I 6 ii   I$_6^4$ V

Fig. 15.6.   I-ii-V

Beethoven, Sonata in C Minor, for Violin and Piano
Op. 30, No. 2

Adagio cantabile

A♭: I   ii   V   V$_2^4$ I 6   I

ii 6   ii   ii 6 I$_6^4$ V

In progressing from ii to vii$^{o}_{6}$, there are two notes in common while the remaining voice moves step-wise. This step-wise motion usually gives the aural impression of a passing tone figure at the point of the vii$^{o}_{6}$ in the progression I$_{6}$–vii$^{o}_{6}$–I (or reverse[3]), as in the alto line D♯—E♯ in Figure 15.7. In the first analysis there is no supertonic triad; D♯ is an accented passing tone.[4] Only when the tempo is very slow might two separate triads be considered in analysis. If this were the case in Figure 15.7, the supertonic triad would be the minor ii triad in a minor key, the triad's fifth being raised by the demands of the ascending alto line.

Fig. 15.7.

Bach, *Wo soll ich fliehen hin* (♯25)

Passages that include non-harmonic tones and in which two or even more analyses are possible are fairly frequent. When encountering such "ambiguous non-harmonic tones," the choice of one analysis is often difficult and is usually dependent upon the tempo of the composition and upon the aural impression of the passage upon the individual listener.

Characteristics of the Supertonic Triad

The supertonic triad displays a striking resemblance to the subdominant triad, both in function and in sound. Both progress naturally and easily to the V or vii° triads. When the supertonic triad is used in first inversion, as it is most commonly, its bass note is the subdominant note of the key, causing the ii$_{6}$ and IV triads to sound very much like each other (Fig. 15.8).

The progression ii–V displays the commonly used root movement, the downward fifth; on the other hand, the commonly used progression IV–V displays root movement of a second up. Yet IV is actually the furthest root from the tonic when its distance is measured in downward fifths, as shown

---

[3]See Bach chorale 44, first phrase.
[4]This D♯ is *not* dissonant with the other tones that sound simultaneously; the dissonance is heard against the E♯ G♯ B triad.

Fig. 15.8.

C: IV   V   I   ii₆   V   I

in Table 14.2. So we have two chords similar in sound and in function, each with a totally different relationship to the tonic in terms of root movements.

A possible explanation may be found in the concept of the "missing root" presented in the previous chapter, where vii° appeared to be a V^7 with its root missing, thereby explaining why each moved easily to the tonic. In the same way it could be conjectured that IV is really a ii^7 with its root missing; the three upper notes of ii^7 (C: D F A C) are the same as the IV triad (C: F A C).

Fig. 15.9.

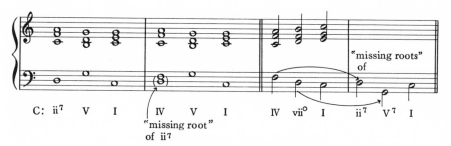

C: ii^7 V   I   IV   V   I   IV   vii°   I ii^7 V^7 I

"missing root" of ii^7

"missing roots" of

Assignment 15.2. Harmonic analysis. The following excerpts contain examples of the supertonic triad and triads previously studied. Spell each chord, identify it by number and inversion, and identify non-harmonic tones.

Beethoven: Sonata for Piano, No. 1 (Op. 2, No. 1), fourth movement, measures 59–68.
Chopin: Mazurka No. 23 (Op. 33, No. 2), measures 1–8.
Mendelssohn: *Songs Without Words*
   No. 8 (Op. 30, No. 2), measures 5–8
   No. 39 (Op. 85), No. 3), measures 1–3
Mozart: Sonatas for Piano
   G Major, K. 283, first movement, measures 36–38 (in D major)
   C Major, K. 279, first movement, measures 1–4, 31–33 (in G major)

D Major, K. 284, third movement, variation 7, measures 1-3
Schumann: *Album for the Young*, Op. 68
  No. 20, last 8 measures
  No. 22, measures 1-4
Murphy and Melcher, *Music for Study*, Chapter 6

APPLICATION

Written Materials

Alternate Doubling in Minor Triads

In addition to the normal doublings already studied, any minor triad may be commonly found with its third doubled, regardless of soprano note. This is particularly true when the third of the minor triad is one of the three primary scale tones of the key: tonic, subdominant, or dominant. In the case of the supertonic triad, the third of the triad is the subdominant note of the key, so it is commonly doubled. See also Figures 2.9, 11.9, and 15.3.

Fig. 15.10.

Writing the Supertonic Triad

Most progressions in which the supertonic triad is found can be written with part-writing procedures already presented.

Rule 2A or 2B: ii–V.   See Figure 15.11 *a* and *b*. See also Figures 15.4 and 15.6.

Rule 3:   I–ii.   See Figure 15.11 *a* and *b*. See also Figure 15.6.

Rule 6A, 6B: Any progression to or from ii$_6$ or ii$^{\circ}_6$. See Figure 15.11 *c*. See also Figures 15.2, 15.3, and 15.6. When used in first inversion, the supertonic triad is only rarely found with its fifth as a soprano note.

Procedures for connecting triads whose roots in the bass are a third apart, as in the progression IV–ii (Figure 15.4), will be considered in Chapter 17.

Fig. 15.11.

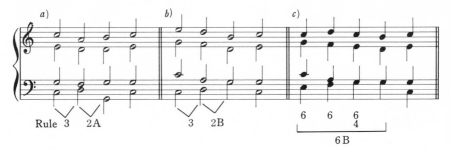

Writing Passing Tones and Neighboring Tones[5]

The writing of any type of non-harmonic tone can be accomplished by the observance of one general procedure:

Part-Writing Rule No. 8: When a non-harmonic tone is used, it temporarily replaces a harmonic tone. Write the triad with normal doubling if possible and substitute the non-harmonic tone for one of the triad tones. Introduce and leave the non-harmonic tone according to the definition of the particular non-harmonic tone being used.

Application of this procedure to the unaccented passing tone and unaccented neighboring tones is very simple. A triad tone progresses by step to the dissonance and continues by step to the next harmonic tone. The dissonance is a substitute for the harmonic tone just left.

Fig. 15.12.

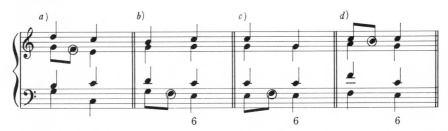

Passing tones are extremely common in all forms and styles of music and can be located in almost all music examples presented to this point. Review in particular Figure 13.18. Neighboring tones are also common, especially the lower variety. See Figure 13.18, measures 8 and 9 for lower neighboring tones and chorale number 200, fifth phrase, for an upper neighboring tone.

---

[5]Review Chapter 13 "Definitions of Non-harmonic Tones."

The importance of Rule 8 is more obvious in writing the accented non-harmonic tones. The dissonance and the accompanying chord are sounded simultaneously, with the dissonance then resolving to a chord tone. In establishing the doubling at the point of dissonance, the dissonant note should be considered a temporary substitute for the note that follows. In Figure 15.13 *a*, the triad containing the dissonance would ordinarily include only one third. Since the resolution of the dissonance *is* the third, the dissonance represents the third temporarily; therefore, the third will not be doubled in another voice as in Figure 15.13 *b*.

Fig. 15.13.

In context, this can be seen in the tenor voice at (3) in Figure 13.16, where A temporarily substitutes for the third of the triad, G♯. Note also here the two passing tones in succession to fill in the interval between the harmonic tones C and G♯.

If, on the other hand, the note of resolution is ordinarily doubled, the dissonance and note of resolution may sound simultaneously. In Figure 15.13 *c*, the root G is normally doubled, so the dissonance A temporarily substitues for one of the two G's at the same time the other G is sounding. This example can be seen in context in Figure 2.10; on the fourth beat of this same figure another similar accented passing tone occurs.

Care must be exercised when writing a non-harmonic tone at the interval of a seventh above the root of a chord, even if the root is not in the bass. This dissonance creates the aural effect of a seventh chord; therefore, this dissonance must resolve downwards.

Fig. 15.14.

Passing tones and neighboring tones, as well as other non-harmonic tones, are commonly found as double or triple dissonances (two or three dissonances sounding simultaneously) or in combination with each other. Figure 15.15 shows at (1) and (2) double passing tones, at (3) a lower neighbor sounding together with two passing tones in contrary motion, and at (4) an upper neighbor and a passing tone sounding together.

Fig. 15.15.

Bach, *Ver Gott vertraut, hat wohl gebaut* (♯137)

For further study, the following figures and chorales contain many combinations of these multiple dissonances: Figures 2.17, 8.3, 13.20, 13.30, 15.6; chorales 17, 100, 102, 119, 121[6], 122, 209, and 335.

Figured Bass Symbols for Non-harmonic Tones

There are no standard figured bass symbols for non-harmonic tones; symbols are used that will best express the particular musical situation at the time. Very often, two or more figures will be found under a single bass note.

Fig. 15.16.

---

[6]The second cadence includes parallel fifths, produced by the simultaneous sounding of an anticipation and a passing tone.

These will be read in the same manner as the figuration for second inversion,
$\begin{smallmatrix} 6 & 5 \\ 4 & 3 \end{smallmatrix}$. Each horizontal line of figuration is read from left to right, indicating
a melodic progression at the given interval above the bass. When the bass
note changes, the number or numbers under the new bass note have no
connection with the numbers under the previous bass note. The figured bass
of Figure 15.16 is read as follows:

8 7   octave above bass (in tenor) moves to seventh above bass;
6 5   at same time, sixth above bass (in soprano) moves to fifth above bass.

5 – 8 7   third above bass (in soprano) moves to fourth, then to fifth above
3 4 5 –   bass; dash (—) indicates previous number is held; at the same time,
       fifth above bass (in tenor) is held, then leaps to the octave and pro-
       ceeds to seventh above bass.

Assignment 15.3.   Writing the supertonic triad. Fill in alto and tenor voices.
Supply harmonic analysis below the staff. Continue to write some exercises,
as assigned, in open score, as described in Assignment 9.2.

Assignment 15.4. Add soprano, alto, and tenor voices when bass line only is given. Do not add non-harmonic tones at this time (see Chapter 17). Make harmonic analysis.

Assignment 15.5. Write the following harmonic progressions in four parts. Choose a time signature and write a progression that is rhythmically interesting and displays acceptable harmonic rhythm.

a) E♭ Major   I ii₆ I₆ vii°₆ I IV V I

b) F minor   V i i₆ vii°₆ i ii°₆ V i

c) B Major   V I₆ V₆ I I ii₆ V I I IV vii°₆ I ii₆ I₆⁴ V I

In the following progressions, no inversions are indicated. Choose inversions that will make a good bass line.

    d) A Major   I I IV vii° I vii° I ii I V I
    e) B minor   i iv V i vii° i i V V i ii° i V I
    f) D♭ Major   V V I IV vii° I ii vii° I ii I V I

Melody Harmonization Using the Supertonic Triad

The supertonic triad is useful in harmonizing the second and fourth scale steps of the key. The sixth scale step harmonized with the supertonic triad (fifth of the triad as soprano note) is much less common in major; in minor it is rare: the normal soprano doubling of the fifth of a diminished triad means that the lowered sixth scale step is doubled, making resolution awkward if not impossible. Any other doubling in minor emphasizes the tritone too strongly.

Of the triads studied so far, the supertonic triad may be preceded by the tonic and followed by the dominant or leading tone triads. Review Tables 14.1 and 14.2. Review "Melody Harmonization" in Chapter 14.

Assignment 15.6. Harmonize these melodies, using the supertonic triad where appropriate. Use either two staves, two voices on each staff, or open score with C clefs, as assigned.

Assignment 15.7. Write original exercises including examples of the supertonic triad. Follow directions in Assignment 14.8.

Ear Training and Music Reading

Exercise 15.1. Singing the supertonic triad.

a) In a major key: Sing the tonic triad of the given key; sing the supertonic note and sing the ii triad with letter names.

b) In a minor key: Sing the tonic triad of the given key; sing the supertonic note and the ii° triad with letter names.

c) Same as *b)* but sing the ii triad.

Exercise 15.2. Sing with letter names each of the following chord progressions in the given key.

Major key: I ii V I; I ii vii° I

Minor key: i ii° V i; i ii vii° i

Example: i–ii°–V–i in F minor

Fig. 15.17.

F A♭ C A♭ F   G B♭ D♭ B♭ G   C E G E C   F A♭ C A♭ F

Exercise 15.3. Harmonic dictation exercises will now include the supertonic triads studied in this chapter. Caution should be taken not to confuse the first inversion of the supertonic triad with the subdominant triad, root in bass. Review "Characteristics of the Supertonic Triad" in the early pages of this chapter.

Self-Help in Harmonic Dictation

The following excerpts from hymns contain only triads studied thus far.

Italian Hymn	1–3	M–3
Creation	1–4	M–43
		E–309
Louvan	13–16	M–64
Spanish Hymn	1–4	M–77
St. Agnes	1–4	M–82
		E–24
Tallis' Canon	5–6	M–180
		E–165

Pleyel's Hymn	1–8	M–300
Pleyel's Hymn	1–2	E–578
Dort	10–13	M–480
Bristol	1–2	E–7
Yorkshire	21–24	E–16
Spanish Chant	13–16	E–332

Keyboard Harmony

Exercise 15.4. Playing the supertonic triad at the keyboard.

a) Play the progression I–ii$_6$–V–I in all major keys.

b) Play the progression i–ii$_6^o$–V–i in all minor keys.

c) Play the progression I–ii$_6$–I$_6^4$–V–I in all major keys.

d) Play the progression i–ii$_6^o$–i$_6^4$–V–i in all minor keys.

Fig. 15.18.

$$\text{I} \quad \text{ii}_6 \quad \text{V} \quad \text{I} \qquad \text{i} \quad \text{ii}_6^o \quad \text{V} \quad \text{i} \qquad \text{i} \quad \text{ii}_6^o \quad \text{i}_6^4 \quad \text{V} \quad \text{i}$$

Harmonizing a melody at the keyboard. The vii° triad and the ii or ii° triad can be found useful in harmonizing a melody at the keyboard in two different ways.

1. Although most melodies can be harmonized with I, IV, and V, portions of some melodies are better harmonized with other triads.

a) When the melody ascends by step after a IV triad, the vii$_6^o$ is ordinarily used.

Fig. 15.19.

Russian Folk Song (MSS 58)

$$\text{I} \qquad \text{IV} \qquad \text{vii}_6^o \qquad \text{I} \qquad \text{etc.}$$

b) When the melody outlines a supertonic triad, the same triad is ordinarily found in the harmonization.

Fig. 15.20.

Haydn, Symphony in G Major, No. 100 (MSS 206)

In the above example, the melody at "ii" outlines a ii triad and therefore cannot be harmonized by I, IV, or V.

2. The vii° and ii (or ii°) triads can often be used to give variety to a harmonization, instead of using only I, IV, and V.

Fig. 15.21.

German Folk Song (MSS 93)

Harmonizations can also be made more interesting through use of inversions—the first inversion during the course of the phrase and the I_6^4 at the cadence.

Exercise 15.5. Harmonizing melodies at the keyboard. Harmonize these melodies from *Music for Sight Singing*, occasionally using vii°, ii, or ii° in place of one of the three principal triads. Numbers marked * contain appropriate places for the leading tone triad. 2, 5, 7*, 58*, 65, 71*, 87, 107*, 124, 173, 204, 205, 206, 208, 313, 317, 320*, 353*, 368, 373.

16

The Melodic Line (II)

THEORY AND ANALYSIS

Form

Although the regular four-measure phrase and the eight-measure period appear frequently in music, phrases and periods of shorter and greater length are also of common occurrence. These often will be found to be extensions or contractions of the four-measure and eight-measure groupings studied in Chapter 5. Use of extended or contracted phrases, along with regular phrase lengths, helps to avoid the monotony of a constant succession of regular phrase lengths. There are many ways of modifying the regular phrase length; some of the more important ways are shown below. The illustrations of extended phrases are parts of complete periods. The student should study the entire melody in each instance and note particularly that the other phrase of the period is often regular.

a) Repeating a part of a phrase.

Fig. 16.1.

French Folk Song (MSS 126)

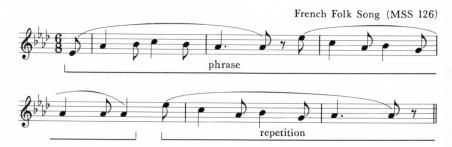

Exact repetition of an *entire* phrase is not extension. Since a phrase and its repetition are considered a single phrase, they cannot be considered as a period.

b) Evading the cadence at the end of the phrase, allowing the melody to continue further to the ultimate cadence.

Fig. 16.2.

French Folk Song (MSS 63)

Without the evasion and extension, the phrase might have appeared as a normal four-measure phrase.

Fig. 16.3.

c) Using a sequential pattern during the course of the phrase.

Fig. 16.4.

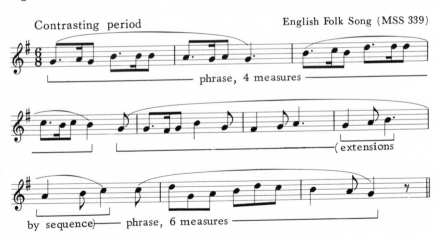

Without the two measures of sequence, the consequent phrase would be a normal four-measure phrase.

Fig. 16.5.

Observe, however, that a sequence in itself does not necessarily indicate the presence of an extension. A normal four-measure phrase may contain a sequence, as shown in Figure 5.12.

d) Lengthening a motive.

Fig. 16.6.

German Folk Song (MSS 54)

one measure extra length

e) Adding an additional motive to the phrase.

Fig. 16.7.

German Folk Song (MSS 82)

(phrase composed of three motives)

f) Occasionally phrases may be more or less than four measures in length. The following is a six-measure phrase, made up of two three-measure motives.

Fig. 16.8.

Russian Folk Song (MSS 107)

In some instances, a two-measure phrase or an eight-measure phrase may be considered a regular phrase length.

a) When the tempo is very fast or when each measure contains only a few notes, an eight-measure phrase may be considered regular. The extremely rapid tempo of Figure 16.9 (one beat to the measure) produces a phrase of only eight beats in eight measures, comparable in sound to four measures of two beats each.

Fig. 16.9.

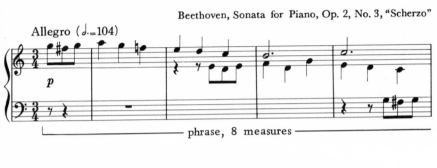

b) When the tempo is very slow or when each measure contains many notes, a two-measure phrase may be considered regular. In melody 219 from *Music for Sight Singing*, two measures of $\frac{12}{4}$ meter suffice to constitute a phrase. In Figure 16.10, the extremely slow tempo allows the completion of a phrase in a two-measure span.

Fig. 16.10.

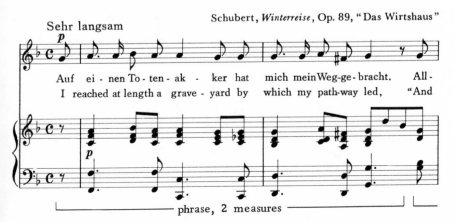

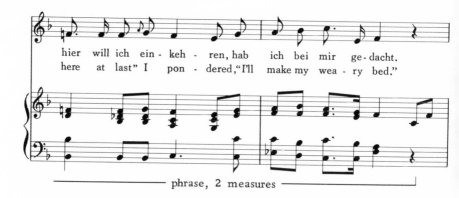

hier   will   ich   ein - keh - ren, hab   ich   bei   mir   ge - dacht.
here   at   last"   I   pon - dered,"I'll   make my   wea - ry   bed."

phrase, 2 measures

Two additional forms, each larger than the period, can be constructed by the addition of phrase lengths.

a) The *phrase group* consists of three or more phrases (very often three) each of which differs melodically from the others. Usually, each of the first two phrases ends with a half cadence or an imperfect cadence and the last phrase ends with a perfect cadence.

Fig. 16.11.

Mendelssohn, *Das Schifflein* (MSS 211)

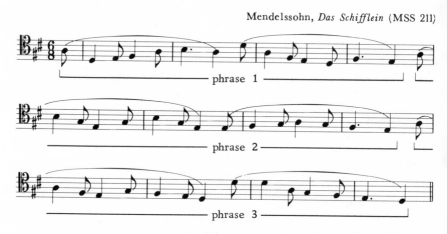

phrase 1

phrase 2

phrase 3

Any or all phrases of a phrase group may be lengthened by extension.

b) The *double period* consists of four phrases. Each of the first three phrases ends with a half cadence or an imperfect cadence, the last with a perfect cadence. Phrases one and three are usually similar to each other and very often identical, or nearly so, as in Figure 16.12. A form consisting of four different phrases (quite common in folk music) is usually considered a phrase group but could be identified as a double period.

Fig. 16.12.

Mendelssohn, *Venetianisches Gondellied,*
Op. 57, No. 5

This example can be analyzed conveniently by assigning alphabet letters to each of the four phrases, the same letter for identical or nearly identical phrases and different letters for differing phrases. Thus the melody can be analyzed as *a b a c* since the first and third phrases are identical, and the second and fourth phrases differ from *a* and from each other. In cases where phrases are nearly alike, the prime symbol (') is used with the repeated letter. For example, see *Music for Sight Singing*, melody 85, which is a double period *a b a b'*; the first and third phrases are identical while the second and fourth phrases are nearly identical. Review also Figure 2.26.

No two successive phrases are identical in the double period, since simple phrase repetition would result. A melody analyzed as *a a b c* would be a phrase group, since *a* is simply a repeated phrase and not a period. (See *Music for Sight Singing*, melody 367.)

Any or all phrases of the double period may be found with extensions or in irregular lengths, as described previously.

Assignment 16.1. Copy out melodies from *Music for Sight Singing* and analyze the form of each. Indicate the following, using Figure 16.4 as a guide.

a) The beginning and ending of each phrase

b) The form of the entire melody (contrasting period, phrase, group, and so on)

c) The location of any extensions and a description of each

d) The location of any phrases other than of four-measure length

Extensions: 5, 47, 71, 124, 161.

Phrase groups or double periods: 25, 103, 134, 196, 249.

Any of above, not identified: 17, 22, 51, 56, 79, 80, 91, 101, 143, 149, 164, 171, 180, 200, 231, 244, 314, 354, 384, 385, 387, 393.

APPLICATION

Written Materials

Melody-Writing

In previous melodic study, all melodic intervals have been part of specific tonic, dominant, or subdominant triads. Melodic intervals may have several other implications, as follows.

a) The interval or intervals may outline a chord other than tonic, dominant, or subdominant.

Fig. 16.13.

German Folk Song (MSS 204)

b) Each note of the interval represents a different chord (a chord change occurs as the interval is sounded).

Fig. 16.14.

Mexican Folk Song (MSS 362)

Two such leaps in the same direction are ordinarily not written (but see melody 359 in *Music for Sight Singing*).

c) The interval is a leap from a chord tone to a non-harmonic tone (or, less often, in the case of an escaped tone, a leap from a non-harmonic tone to a chord tone).

Fig. 16.15.

English Folk Song (MSS 370)

d) The interval is found in a melodic sequence.

Fig. 16.16.

Brahms, *Vergebliches Ständchen* (MSS 232)

See also melodies 210, 212, 363, and 373.

Assignment 16.2. Write original melodies in various forms as assigned. Use extensions as studied in this chapter. Make a *complete analysis* of each melody you write. This will include *a*) an analysis of the form, as in Figure 16.4 and *b*) an analysis of the implied harmony and the non-harmonic tones, as shown in Figures 16.15 and 16.16.

Ear Training and Music Reading

Sight singing and melodic dictation materials presented up to this point have included only those intervals found in the three principal triads. These intervals are the ones most often used in melodic writing, but often found in contexts other than the three principal triads.

Chapters 8a and 13a in *Music for Sight Singing* present examples of such melodic writing. Study the prefatory material to Chapter 8.

The following exercises will aid in singing these intervals in their new contexts.

Exercise 16.1. Singing individual scale tones. No note of the scale is more than a whole step away from one of the notes of the tonic triad (Figure 16.17 *a*). Choose a note of the scale, play the tonic note of the key, sing the tonic triad, and finally sing the chosen note. Example (Figure 16.17 *b*): Sing A in the key of C.

Fig. 16.17.

Exercise 16.2.   Singing intervals. Figure 16.18 lists all the possible diatonic intervals (thirds through sevenths) in the key of C. Select the interval to be sung. Play the tonic note of the key, find the first note of the interval as in Exercise 16.1 and sing the interval.

For adequate practice, Figure 16.18 should be copied in several other keys. In minor keys, use the lowered sixth and raised seventh scale steps.

Fig. 16.18.

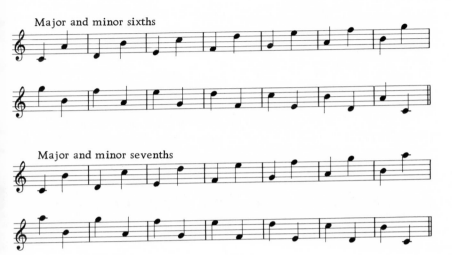

Exercise 16.3. Melodic dictation. After having practiced sight singing as outlined above, take comparable melodies from dictation, paying particular attention to those intervals not found in the three principal triads.

17

The Submediant and Mediant Triads

THEORY AND ANALYSIS

The two remaining secondary triads are built on the submediant and mediant tones of the scale; both are minor triads (vi and iii) when found in a major key (Figure 17.1 *a*) and both are major triads (VI and III) when found in a minor key (Figure 17.1 *b*). Because of the altered sixth and seventh degrees in the minor scale, two additional triads are possible in a minor key. These are the vi° and the III+, diminished and augmented triads (Figure 17.1 *c*). Because of the infrequent use of the two latter triads, they will not be considered in this chapter.

The submediant and mediant triads are used almost exclusively with their roots in the bass. In the following discussion of these triads, root position only is meant unless otherwise indicated.

Fig. 17.1.

Assignment 17.1. Spelling the submediant and mediant triads.
a) Spell the submediant triad in each major and minor key.
b) Spell the mediant triad in each major and minor key.

In terms of resolution, the submediant triad is one of the most versatile of triads (as shown in Table 14.1, Table of Commonly Used Chord Progressions), resolving regularly to the supertonic, subdominant, and dominant triads, as well as to the mediant when the mediant is followed by the sub-dominant. Only the progression to the leading tone triad is little used. The submediant triad is usually preceded by the tonic or dominant triad or, less often, by the mediant triad.

The mediant triad has less opportunity for display, its resolution being limited usually to the submediant and subdominant triads, and preceded only by the tonic except in the special progression vi–iii–IV (VI–III–iv).[1]

Root Movement by Downward Thirds

With the inclusion of the submediant triad, it is possible to construct a harmonic pattern based on root movement by thirds.[2] Of all the possible root movements by thirds, the progression I–vi–IV–ii (in whole or in part) is of most common occurrence.

Fig. 17.2. I-vi-IV-ii

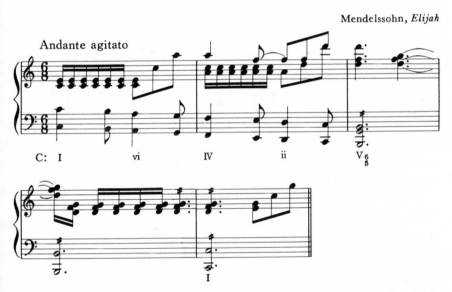

Mendelssohn, *Elijah*

In the progression I–vi–ii$_6$, the impression of root movement by thirds is maintained because of the similarity of IV and ii$_6$.[3]

---

[1]Although the mediant triad in major may also on occasion proceed directly to the dominant, the progression is rare enough to be considered later in the study of less common progressions.

[2]Review Chapter 14, "Principles of Harmonic Progression."

[3]Review Chapter 15, "Characteristics of the Supertonic Triad."

Fig. 17.3. i-VI-iv

C. H. Graun (1701-1759) *Der Tod Jesu*

i   VI   iv

Fig. 17.4. I-vi-ii$_6$

Etwas bewegt   Schubert, *Die Winterreise* "Frühlingstraum"

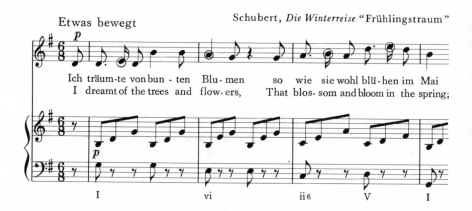

Ich träum-te von bun - ten Blu- men   so wie sie wohl blü-hen im Mai
I dreamt of the trees and flow- ers,   That blos- som and bloom in the spring;

I   vi   ii 6   V   I

Root Movement by Downward Fifths

Progression by downward fifth from the submediant is common in both major and minor, while that from the mediant is comparatively uncommon in minor. See also Figure 17.4, vi–ii$_6$.

Fig. 17.5. iii-vi

Mässig bewegt   Wagner, *Lohengrin* (Act III)

Bb: I   iii   vi   ii 6   V7   I

Fig. 17.6.   vi-ii

Johann Schein (1586-1630), *Ach lob den Herrn*

Eb: I   vi   ii

Root Movement by Seconds; The Deceptive Cadence

Both the submediant and mediant triads are commonly found in an upward progression by second: V–vi and iii–IV and the comparable progressions in minor. The only progression by downward second used with any degree of frequency, other than I–vii°, is found at this point, the progression vi–V (VI–V).

When the progression V–vi or V–VI occurs at a cadence point, it is known as a *deceptive cadence*. The reason for the name becomes obvious from study of Figure 17.7. In each cadence, the V triad seems to demand resolution to the tonic triad, but instead the submediant triad is found as the resolution. (Note carefully that the first phrase of Figure 17.7 is in the key of F, while the second phrase is in the key of C.)

Fig. 17.7.   V-vi

Bach, *Heilig, heilig* (♯235)

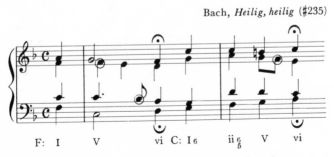

F: I   V   vi C: I 6   ii 6/5   V   vi

This progression may appear equally as well within the phrase.

Fig. 17.8.   V-VI

Bach, *Wer weiss, wie nahe mir* (♯204)

By resolving down by step, the submediant triad immediately reaches the dominant, thereby bypassing the intermediate resolution of IV and/or ii.

Fig. 17.9.   VI-V

Andante moderato

Brahms, *Ein deutches Requiem*, Op. 45

The resolution of the mediant to the subdominant is much more widely used than the resolution by downward fifth to the submediant. This progression, preceded by either I or vi (I–iii–IV, vi–iii–IV, and comparable progression in minor) is particularly useful in harmonizing the descending scale, where the mediant triad is used to harmonize the descending leading tone. Figure 17.10 shows the complete E♭ major scale harmonized, including the iii–IV progression. The first note of the scale could just as easily been harmonized with the tonic triad, as shown in Figure 17.10 *b*.

Fig. 17.10.

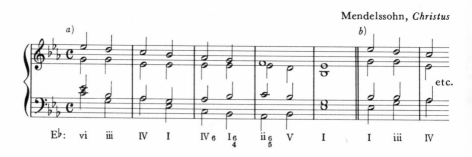

Mendelssohn, *Christus*

The progression vi–iii–IV is unique in that the vi–iii is ordinarily found *only* when followed by IV.

Triads Incorporating the Ambiguous Non-harmonic Tone

In Chapter 15, we observed that a passing tone in the vii° triad seemingly created a ii triad on the first half of the beat. A similar situation exists in the submediant triad, where a passing tone on the second half of the beat apparently produces a IV₆ triad. In Figure 17.11, the vi triad is found with a doubled third, allowing the IV₆ triad to be found with normal doubling (soprano doubled in first inversion).

Fig. 17.11.

Bach, *Alle Menschen müssen sterben* (♯153)

D: I   vi(IV₆) I₆

Another frequent device is a vertical sonority that can be spelled as a mediant triad and occurs immediately preceding the tonic triad, often at the cadence. In reality, it is a dominant triad with a non-harmonic tone in the soprano voice (or, more rarely, in an inner voice).

Fig. 17.12.

Hymn: Hamburg

F: I   V   vi   ii ⁶₅   V   I

At the * the triad can be spelled A C E, which would be iii in F major. But because of the cadence, it is more logical to consider the A to be an upper neighbor to the V triad. The aural effect, at this point, is certainly that of an authentic cadence.

In a similar situation in a minor key (Figure 17.13), the sonority at the *
is spelled A♭ C E, an augmented triad, III+ in the key of F minor. Again
the aural effect of the authentic cadence indicates that the A♭ in the soprano
is a non-harmonic tone, this time an appoggiatura.

Fig. 17.13.

Melchior Vulpius (1560-1616) *Der Tag bricht an*

f: i   v₆   VI   III   iv   V
                                        i

Special Use of the Tonic Triad in a Chord Progression

The tonic triad is often found between the two triads of a commonly used
progression. In Figure 17.14, placing the tonic triad between vi and IV only
temporarily interrupts a normal chord progression. Such placement of a tonic
chord can be made between the two triads of any progression studied thus
far, for example, ii–I–V, iii–I–IV, and so on. See also Figure 17.16, I–vi–
I–V–I.

Fig. 17.14.

Bach, *Wie schön leuchtet der Morgenstern* (♯323)

vi   I₆   IV

The Submediant and Mediant Triads in Inversion

There are three specific situations in which the submediant and mediant
triads may appear in first inversion. Otherwise, the occurrence of these triads
in any inversion is quite rare.

1. In a harmonic sequence.

Fig. 17.15.

Bach, *French Suite V,* "Gavotte"

G: I   V₆   vi   iii₆   iv ii   V   I

2. In a series of first inversions. See Bach Chorale 106, third phrase.

3. When the bass tone of the previous chord is held over to become the third of the submediant or mediant: I–vi₆, V–iii₆.

Fig. 17.16.

Schubert, *Du bist die Ruh*, Op, 59, No. 3

Langsam

pp

Du bist die Ruh,   der   Frie - de mild,
You are my joy,   my   peace in grief,

pp

E♭: I   vi₆   I₆   V⁷   I

Assignment 17.2. Analyze the harmony and the non-harmonic tones of the following excerpts.

Mozart, Sonatas for Piano
   C Major, K. 545, second movement, measures 12–16,
               third movement, measures 1–8
   B♭ Major, K. 333, third movement, measures 13–16
   D Major, K. 284, third movement, variation 11, measures 1–3
   D Major, K. 311, second movement, last 8 measures
Schumann, *Album for the Young*, Op. 68
   No. 9, measures 1–4; No. 37, measures 9–16
Mendelssohn, *Songs Without Words*, No. 7 (Op. 30, No. 1), measures 1–6
Murphy and Melcher, *Music for Study*, Chapters 11, 12, 14.

APPLICATION

Written Materials

The Submediant Triad

Part-writing procedures previously presented can be used in these progressions.

Rule 2 (A, B, C)   vi–ii   Figure 17.17 *a, b*
                             Figure 17.6

Rule 3   V–vi   Figure 17.17 *c*
                             Figure 17.7

                    vi-V   Figure 17.17 *d*
                             Figure 17.20

Rule 6 (A, B)   Any progression in which one or both triads are in inversion

                    vi–ii₆   Figure 17.17 *e*
                             Figure 17.5

                    VI–ii°₆ Figure 17.8

Rule 8   vi–(IV₆) Figure 17.11

Fig. 17.17.

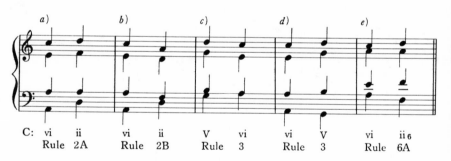

The following progressions require new part-writing procedures:
  a) I–vi or i–VI
        vi–IV or VI–iv
        IV–ii

In these progressions, the roots of the two triads are in the bass and these roots are at the interval of a *third* apart.

Part-Writing Rule 4A. When the bass notes of two successive triads are roots of the triads and these triad roots are a third apart, hold the two common tones and move the other voice step-wise.

Fig. 17.18.

See also Figure 17.3, i–VI–iv and Figure 17.6, I–vi.

Part-Writing Rule 4B. When the bass notes of two successive triads are roots of triads and these triad roots are a third apart, and when the soprano voice moves by leap, the second triad may be in either close or open position.

Rule 4B applies, of course, only when it is desirable that both triads display normal doubling: two roots, one third and one fifth. Choice of open or close position in the second triad is determined by the necessity to avoid poor voice range, parallel octaves, or parallel fifths. It will often be more desirable to double the third in one of the triads, as described under Part-Writing Rule 5 below.

Fig. 17.19.

See also Figure 15.4, IV–ii.

    b)   V–vi or V–VI, soprano ascending
           vi–V, soprano descending
           VI–V, either soprano motion
           I–ii, soprano ascending

In these progressions, the roots of the two triads are a second apart. When the melody progresses in the same direction as the bass, Rule 3 cannot be used; in the other progressions, an attempted use of Rule 3 will cause one or more of these faults: parallel fifths, parallel octaves, doubled leading tone, or melodic augmented second.

Part-Writing Rule 5. When it is impossible or undesirable to follow normal rules for triads with roots in bass, double the third in the *second* of the two triads. But if this third is the leading tone or any altered tone, double the third in the *first* of the two triads.

Fig. 17.20.

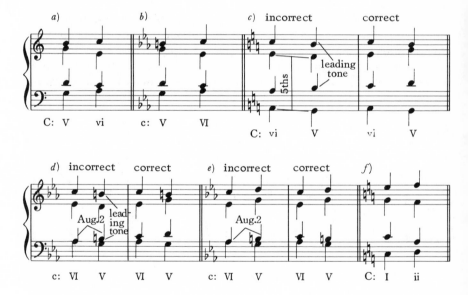

See also Figure 17.7, second V–vi, Figure 17.8, V–VI, and Figure 17.9, VI–V.

When the triad with the doubled third is a minor triad, note that the normal alternate doubling in the minor triad results.[4] In the case of the VI triad in a minor key, more often than not it is desirable that the third of this major triad be doubled; since this third is the tonic note of the key, it is a very effective doubling.

---

[4]Review Chapter 15, "Alternate Doubling in Minor Triads."

The procedure expressed by Rule 5 will be found useful in many situations in which the regular rule does not produce the best results. For example, in Figure 17.21, opening progression I–vi, Rule 4A cannot be used. Rule 4B is possible, but doubling the third in the vi triad keeps both the alto and tenor voices in better range, as is true in the other I–vi progression of this figure.

Fig. 17.21.

Mendelssohn, *Elijah*

Assignment 17.3.   Part-Writing. Write exercises showing various uses of the submediant triad. Fill in inner voices and make a harmonic analysis of each example.

(Exercises 7–12: last triad is submediant)

The Mediant Triad

Part-writing procedures previously presented can be used in these progressions.

Rule 2 (A, B, C)	iii–vi, III–VI	Figure 17.22 *a*
		Figure 17.5
	vi–iii, VI–III	Figure 17.22 *b*
		Figure 17.10
		Figure 17.13
Rule 3	iii–IV, III–iv	Figure 17.22 *b*
		Figure 17.10
		Figure 17.13
Rule 4 (A, B)	I–iii, i–III	Figure 17.22 *c*
Rule 5		Any progression in which a doubled third is required (Figure 17.22 *d*).
Rule 6 (A, B)		Any progression in which one or both triads are in inversion (Figure 17.22 *e*).

The "mediant" triad created by the presence of a non-harmonic tone (review Figures 17.12, 17.13 and accompanying discussion) is indicated by the figured bass symbol 65. The sixth above the bass is treated as a non-harmonic tone in the V triad, temporarily substituting for the fifth of the triad to which it resolves (Figure 17.22 *f, g*).

Fig. 17.22.

Assignment 17.4. Part-Writing. Write exercises showing use of the mediant triad. Fill in inner voices and make a harmonic analysis of each example.

Writing Suspensions

The use of Rule 8, presented in Chapter 15 in relation to passing tones and neighboring tones, is equally applicable to the writing of suspensions. The dissonance, the suspended note, temporarily replaces a chord tone and resolves down by step to that chord tone. Suspensions are of several varieties, each identified by the figured bass symbol usually associated with it.

    a) The 4 3 suspension.

Fig. 17.23.

Bach, *Du Lebensfürst, Herr Jesu Christ* (♯102)

The suspended note G in the tenor temporarily replaces the following note F♯. At the resolution, the triad has normal doubling—two roots, one third, one fifth.

    b) The 7 6 suspension.

Fig. 17.24.

Bach, *Auf meinen lieben Gott* (♯304)

As its figuration indicates, the 7 6 suspension occurs in a first inversion, as in this figure where it is found in the vii°₆ triad. With the fifth in the soprano, the normal doubling in vii°₆ is two fifths. Here, the suspended note temporarily replaces the root, F♯, and normal doubling is found at the point of resolution.

    c) The 9 8 suspension.

Fig. 17.25.

Haydn, *Missa Sanctae Caecilae*

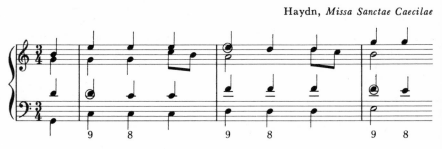

In the 9 8 suspension, the dissonance is usually sounded simultaneously with its resolution since the note of resolution is a doubled note.

    When this suspension is found in the tenor voice at an interval of a second above the bass voice, it is known as a 2 1 suspension. It is not commonly used.

Fig. 17.26.

Bach, *Jesu, geh voram*

d) The 5 suspension (sometimes known as the 2 3 suspension).
  2

This suspension is always found in the bass voice, the necessary figuration 5
                                                                              2

giving its name. Since the suspended note in the bass temporarily replaces the third of the triad, the upper voices show normal doubling for first inversion. The alternate name 2 3 derives from the fact that the interval of a second at the point of suspension resolves to the interval of a third. See also Figure 2.10.

Fig. 17.27.

Bach, *Aus meines Herzens Grunde* (♮1)

e) Suspensions in the tonic six-four chord. When figured above the *actual* root of the tonic triad, the 5 4 suspension of Figure 17.28 is the same as a 9 8 suspension, while the 7 6 suspension of Figure 17.29 is the same as a 4 3 suspension.

Fig. 17.28.

Bach, *Als der gütige Gott* (♮159)

Fig. 17.29.

Berlioz, *La Damnation de Faust*

f) The 9, 7, and 4 suspensions

These suspensions are identical with the 9 8, 7 6 and 4 3 suspensions, except that at the moment of resolution of the suspended note, there is a change of structure in the harmony—either another inversion of the chord, or a different chord. The 9 suspension is the most common of the three.

Change of inversion

Fig. 17.30.

Bach, *Befiehl du deine Wege* (♯367)

Change of harmony

Fig. 17.31.

Bach, *Meinen Jesum lass ich nicht* (♯152)

g) Suspensions with ornamental resolutions. These are of two varieties. First are those in which the note or notes of ornamentation are found below the pitch of the dissonance. Figure 17.32 *a* shows a skip of a third down to another dissonance preceding the resolution, while *b* of the same figure shows the note of resolution ornamented by a lower neighboring tone.

Fig. 17.32.

a) Bach, *Liebster Jesu, wir sind hier* (♯328)
b) Bach, *Heilig bist du Herr, Gott Zaboath*

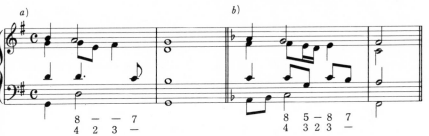

Second are those in which a note of ornamentation is higher than the suspended dissonance, with an eventual normal downward resolution.

Fig. 17.33.

Mozart, *Die Zauberflöte*, K. 620

h) Chain suspensions. A chain suspension occurs when two or more suspensions follow each other in succession, the note of resolution of one suspension becoming the note of approach for the next suspension. In the Bach chorales, see number 237, first phrase, for a chain of two suspensions; number 168, second phrase for a chain of five suspensions.

Fig. 17.34.

Allegro moderato　　　　　　　　　Mozart, *Mass in C Minor,* K. 427

i) The double suspension. The sounding of two suspensions simultaneously produces a very effective dissonance, as shown at the beginning of the third full measure of Figure 15.6, where Beethoven combines a 9 8 and a 7 6 suspension over the ii₆ triad. In the Bach chorales, see number 41, last phrase, and number 166, fourth phrase.

The *rhythmic factor* in the writing of suspensions is of particular importance. In all the examples just cited, you will observe that the note of approach is the same length or longer than the suspended note. This is invariably true in four-part vocal style; instrumental style, particularly keyboard, allows the note of approach to be shorter than the dissonance.

Fig. 17.35.

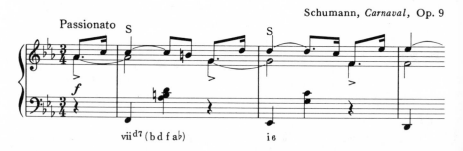

Schumann, *Carnaval,* Op. 9

Passionato

vii^{d7} (b d f a♭)　　i₆

You have also probably observed that the suspension always occurs at a strong rhythmic position in relation to the note of resolution. When the suspension and note of resolution each occupy a half beat, the suspension may appear on any beat of the measure, resolving on the weak half of the beat, as in Figures 17.24, 17.26, 17.28, and 17.33. When the resolution occurs on the following beat, the suspension occurs on a strong beat of the measure, as in Figures 17.25, 17.27, 17.29, 17.30, 17.31, and 17.32. In triple time, the suspension and resolution may occur on the second and third beats respectively when the tonic chord appears on the next strong beat, as in Figure 17.23.[5]

Assignment 17.5. Writing suspensions. Complete each exercise by filling in alto and tenor voices. Make harmonic analysis. Circle each suspended note.

---

[5]Compare this rhythmic placement with that of the tonic six-four chord in triple meter. Review Chapter 11, "Use of the Second Inversion."

Assignment 17.6. Extended exercises in part-writing. Complete each exercise by filling in alto and tenor voices. Solve some of these exercises using open score with C clefs, as assigned. Make harmonic analysis and identify all non-harmonic tones.

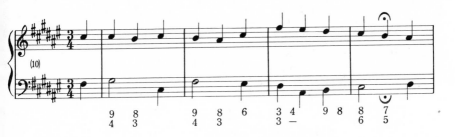

Ear Training and Music Reading

Exercise 17.1 Singing the submediant triad. Sing with letter names the tonic triad of the given key. Find the submediant note by singing a minor third below the tonic in a major key, or by singing a major third below the tonic in a minor key. Sing the submediant triad with letter names. (See Figure 17.36 *a, b*).

Exercise 17.2. Singing the mediant triad. Follow directions given in Exercise 17.1 but find the mediant note by singing a major third above the tonic in a major key, or a minor third above the tonic in a minor key. (See Figure 17.36 *c, d*.)

Fig. 17.36.

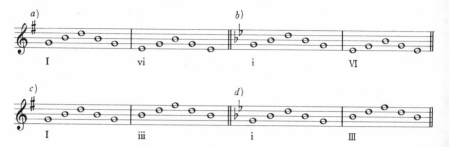

Exercise 17.3.   Sing with letter names each of the following chord progressions in keys given by instructor.

Major key: I vi ii V I	I iii IV V I
I vi V I	I vi iii IV V I
I vi IV V I	I iii vi ii V I
I V vi	
Minor key: i VI iv V i	i III iv V i
i VI ii° V i	i VI III iv V I
i VI V i	i III VI ii° V i
i V VI	

Follow example as given in Figure 15.17.

Exercise 17.4.   Harmonic dictation. Harmonic dictation will now include the submediant and mediant triads. The most common uses of these triads, and therefore the ones to be found most often in the dictation exercises, will be those in the progressions in Exercise 17.3. Other uses of these triads may be added as the progressions are studied in part-writing.

Self-Help in Harmonic Dictation

The Submediant Triad

St. Denio	9–16	M–27
		E–301
St. Bride	1–2	M–51
Irish	1–7	M–56
		E–444
Herr Jesu Christ	7–10	M–124
St. Dunstan's	1–4	M–155
Orientis Partibus	1–4	M–162
Dundee (French)	1–4	M–215

Liebster Jesu	1–2	M–257
Ratisbon	1–4	M–401
		E–153
Hanover	1–4	M–409
		E–288
Weimar	1–4	E–37
Jervaulx Abbey	1–3	E–128
All Saints	1–2	E–130
Riley	1–4	E–292
Deus Tuorum Militum	1–4	E–344

The Mediant Triad

Lenox	11–15	M–100
Warum sollt ich	4–7	M–379
Gelobt sei Gott	1–4	M–449
St. Matthew	1–4	M–457
St. Magnus	5–8	M–458
		E–106
Knickerbocker	1–3	E–207
Riley	13–16	E–292

Keyboard Harmony

Exercise 17.5. Play the deceptive cadence in each major and minor key. In major, when the melody line between V and vi descends, use part-writing Rule 3; when melody line ascends, use Rule 5. In minor, always use Rule 5.

Fig. 17.37.

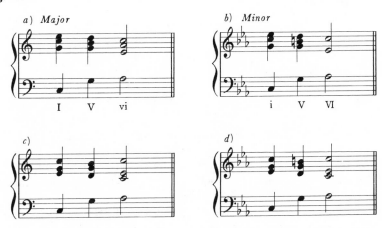

Exercise 17.6.   Play chord progressions using the submediant and mediant triads. As with previous keyboard exercises, all the following progressions can be played in close position, using three notes in the right hand and one in the left, and following correct part-writing procedure from triad to triad. Although illustration of all possible progressions would consume too much space, two typical examples follow.

Fig. 17.38.

a) Play the following progressions in any or all keys, as assigned.

Major keys

I vi ii V I	I iii IV V (or vii°₆) I
I vi IV V (or vii°₆) I	I iii vi ii V I
I vi V I	I iii vi IV V (or vii°₆) I
I vi ii₆ V I	I V vi iii IV V (or vii°₆) I
I IV V vi	(opening tonic chord with
I ii₆ V vi	third in soprano)

Minor keys

i VI iv V i	i III iv V i
i VI ii°₆ V i	i III VI iv V i
i VI V i	i III VI ii°₆ V i
i iv V VI	i V VI III iv V i
i ii°₆ V VI	(opening tonic chord with
	third in soprano)

b) Play part-writing exercises in Assignments 17.3 and 17.4.

Harmonizing the Scale at the Keyboard. Enough harmonic vocabulary has now been acquired to harmonize major and minor scales, both ascending and descending. More than one harmonization is possible in each case. Examples of major and minor scales, using triads with roots in the bass, are written out. Other harmonizations are suggested by chord numbers.

Fig. 17.39. Major.

I   V   I   IV   I   IV   vii°₆   I   I   iii   IV   I   IV   I   V   I

* inversion necessary here

Fig. 17.40. Minor.

i   V   i   iv   i   IV   vii°₆   i   i   III   iv   i   iv   i   V   i

* inversion necessary here

Major, ascending

(Scale steps)	1	2	3	4	5	6	7	8
	I	V(V₆)*	I	IV	I	IV	vii°₆	I
	I	V(V₆)	I	IV	I₆	ii	V	I

Major, descending

	8	7	6	5	4	3	2	1
	I	iii	IV	I	ii₆	I₆₄	V	I
	I	V	vi	iii	IV	I₆₄	V	I

Minor melodic, ascending

	1	2	3	4	5	6	7	8
	i	V(V₆)	i	iv	i₆	IV	vii°₆	i
	i	V(V₆)	i	iv	i₆	ii	V	i

Minor melodic, descending

	8	7	6	5	4	3	2	1
	i	III	iv	i	ii°₆	i₆₄	V	i
	i	III	iv	V	iv₆	i₆₄	V	i

*Triads in parenthesis are alternate harmonizations.

Exercise 17.7. Play harmonized major and minor scales, ascending and descending, and with various triad progressions, as assigned.

Exercise 17.8. Play assignments 17.3–17.6 at the keyboard.

18

Miscellaneous Triad Usages

THEORY AND ANALYSIS

The v Triad in a Minor Key

The v (minor) triad is used instead of the V (major) triad when one of the melodic lines descends through the seventh scale step at the time a dominant triad is used. Observe the alto line in Figure 18.1 and the bass line in Figure 18.2.

Fig. 18.1.

Fig. 18.2.

The VII Triad in a Minor Key

The VII (major) triad in a minor key ordinarily is preceded by the tonic and progresses to III. The lowered seventh scale step (the root of the triad) does not in this instance continue down by step to the sixth scale step. Rather, this lowered seventh scale degree functions as a dominant to the mediant triad, its root being a perfect fourth below that of the mediant.

Fig. 18.3.

Handel, Suite X, "Air"

The VII and III triads in minor are the only diatonic major triads in either a major or minor key that can function as a dominant to another diatonic triad. When a chord functions as a dominant to another chord not actually the tonic of the key, it is known as a *secondary dominant chord.* The aural effect of any secondary dominant chord progression, including VII-III, is often that of a temporary change of key; in Figure 18.3, VII-III sounds much like V-I in the key of F major. Use of secondary dominant chords in harmony is very common, but usually an altered tone is required in the secondary dominant chord, for example in C major: II-V, D F♯ A-G B D, as will be explained further in Chapter 20.

Assignment 18.1.   Spell the v triad and the VII triad in each minor key.

Half Cadences

The V triad of the authentic half cadence may be preceded by triads other than I. These half cadences are commonly used.

Major key:	ii–V	*Minor key:*	ii°₆–V
	IV–V		iv–V
	vi–V		

The half cadence iv-V in a minor key is often known as a *Phrygian cadence.* It is so named because in the progression iv₆-V the bass descends one half step while an upper voice ascends one whole step (Figures 18.4a, 18.5). This is characteristic of the Phrygian mode,[1] a medieval scale in which 1-2 is a half step and 7-8 is a whole step (Figure 18.4c). In the cadence iv-V (Figure 18.4b), the characteristic half step and whole step relationship is reversed.

Fig. 18.4.

Fig. 18.5.

The Six-Four Chords (Triads in Second Inversion)

The *cadential six-four* chord, the most frequently used of all six-four chords, has already been studied.[2] In its most common form, the moving voices above the bass proceed downward. But occasionally the upper voices ascend after the cadential six-four.

Fig. 18.6.

[1]Mode is a term applied to various orderly arrangements of the diatonic scale (c d e f g a b c), particularly to scales of the medieval European era (see page 346 ff). Major and minor scales are sometimes known as major and minor modes.

[2]Review Chapter 11, "Use of Second Inversion."

The normal resolution of the cadential six-four is occasionally interrupted by another sonority whose bass note is a step above or below the bass note of the cadential six-four. An example of such an interruption can be seen in Figure 18.20, I_6-ii$_6^4$-V-I.

There are three other uses of the six-four chord.

a) The Passing Six-Four. This six-four chord occurs ordinarily between a triad with root in bass and its first inversion, or vice versa. Usually the three-note scale line in the bass is countered by the same three-note line, but in the opposite direction, in an upper voice, as in Figure 18.7 and in measure 2 of Figure 18.8, though at times the three-note pattern in the upper voice may be missing, as in Figure 18.8, measure 3 and Figure 18.11, measure 3.

Most common of the passing six-four chords is the passing V_4^6 found between two positions of the tonic triad.

Fig. 18.7.

Fig. 18.8.[3]

Brahms, Trio, Op. 8

Passing six-four chords other than those on V and I are uncommon,[4] though theoretically any triad can be found in second inversion as a passing chord. Sometimes these passing six-four chords are found between two different chord numbers, both of which normally progress to the same chord.

---

[3]The two outside voices of this excerpt form a canon.
[4]The passing I_6 is commonly used in the progression IV_6-I_4^6-ii$_5^6$ and will be considered in the study of seventh chords.

In Figure 18.9, the vi_6 is found between V_4^2 and vii°_6, both of which normally resolve to I.

Fig. 18.9.

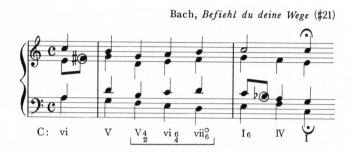

Bach, *Befiehl du deine Wege* (♯21)

b) The Pedal Six-Four[5]. Here the chord preceding the six-four has the same bass note as the six-four; the six-four usually resolves to the same triad which preceded it. The name derives from the pedal point effect in the bass. The pedal 6 is most commonly found in the pattern I-IV_6^4-I.

Fig. 18.10.

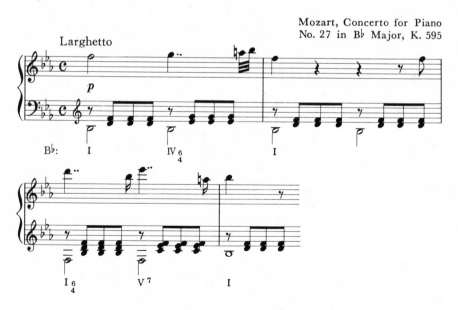

Mozart, Concerto for Piano No. 27 in B♭ Major, K. 595

Larghetto

---

[5]Also known as an auxiliary six-four or an embellishing six-four.

c) The Arpeggiated Six-Four. Preceding this six-four chord is the same chord with root or third in the bass. The bass line shows an arpeggio effect.

Fig. 18.11.

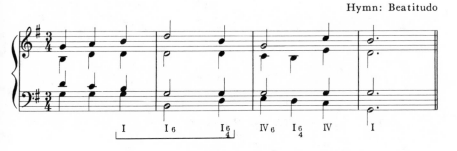

Hymn: Beatitudo

I   I 6   I 6/4   IV 6   I 6/4   IV   I

The tonic six-four chord in Figure 18.10 could be described as an arpeggiated six-four since it follows a tonic triad with root in bass; it is also a cadential six-four chord because of its location in the phrase.

Chromatic Non-harmonic Tones

Notes in music are often chromatically altered by placing an accidental before the note. This is done for one of five reasons.

a) To notate the various forms of the minor scale (raised seventh degree in harmonic minor; raised sixth and seventh degrees in melodic minor).

b) To alter a non-harmonic tone.

c) To alter a chord, for example, in F major, to alter the ii triad (G Bb D) to a II triad (G B D).

d) To indicate diatonic tones of the scale when the music is written in a key other than that of the key signature.

e) To remind the performer of the proper accidental, even when not actually necessary.

All the above uses are illustrated in the following excerpt.

Fig. 18.12.

Mozart, Sonata in F Major, K. 332

Allegro assai

Measure 1. The key signature indicates F major, but the music is in the key of C minor. Therefore, E♭ and A♭ will need to be added. The E♭ appears in this measure.

Measure 2. The F♯ is an altered non-harmonic tone. It is an appoggiatura, altered from F to F♯. The B natural is raised from B♭ because of the use of the harmonic minor scale.

Measure 3. The natural sign before the F is not required, but is placed as a reminder to the performer because F♯ has been sounded in the previous measure.

Measure 7. The F♯ is part of an altered chord, D F♯ A♭ C (a French sixth, to be studied later).

Of these five uses of altered tones, the second will be the concern of the following material.

Fig. 18.13.

At the *, the altered upper neighboring tone, C♭, sounds simultaneously with the suspension E♭ in the alto. This complex combination of tones results in a vertical structure, F A♭, C♭ E♭, at the point of the altered non-harmonic tone.

Fig. 18.14.

Semplice   Chopin, Mazurka, Op. 33, No. 3

At the *, the single chromatic non-harmonic tone E♮ and the double chromatic non-harmonic tones B♮ and D♮ create no new chord structures. Note that the E♮ is a passing tone between E♭ and its upper neighboring tone, F.

Spelling the altered non-harmonic tone. Altered non-harmonic tones are usually spelled according to the direction in which the non-harmonic tone resolves. When the non-harmonic tone resolves *upwards*, it takes the letter name *below* the note of resolution. In Figure 18.14, the non-harmonic tone resolving up to F is spelled E♮ rather than F♭. When the non-harmonic tone resolves *downwards*, it often takes the letter name *above* the note of resolution, as at the * in Figure 18.13 and at (1) in Figure 18.15. There is considerable latitude, however, in a descending series of half steps, when the chromatically altered note is often the same letter name as the note of resolution, as at (2) in Figure 18.15.

Fig. 18.15.

Più lento   Chopin, *Waltz*, Op. 64, No. 2

Other Non-harmonic Usages

The *pedal point* is relatively infrequent in four-part vocal style, found mostly in large sections of extended choral works. The following short excerpt shows a pedal point above which is a series of first inversions with non-harmonic tones in the soprano lines.

Fig. 18.16.

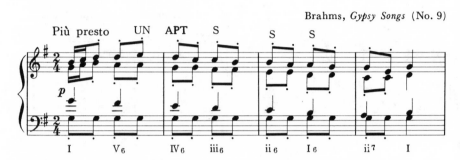

Brahms, *Gypsy Songs* (No. 9)

The *appoggiatura chord* is a name often given to a group of tones forming a chord but sounding over a bass note from a different chord. It is often found in keyboard music at a final cadence.

Fig. 18.17.

Beethoven, Sonata for Piano in A Major, Op. 2, No. 2, third movement

APPLICATION

Written Materials

Writing the v and VII Triads in a Minor Key

No new part-writing procedures are required for writing either of these triads.

The third of the v triad (the lowered seventh scale step) must descend. It is always found as part of a descending melodic minor scale line.[6]

---

[6]A dominant triad in which the minor third ascends indicates that the music is written in a mode other than major or minor.

The secondary dominant function of VII negates the necessity of resolving the lowered seventh scale step downwards. The VII triad and the VII-III progression is written using the same procedures as for the V triad and the V-I progression.

Fig. 18.18.

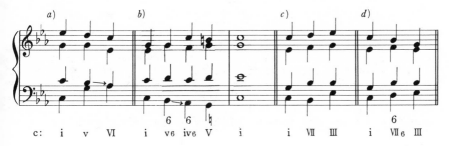

Assignment 18.2. Part-writing, v and VII triads. Fill in alto and tenor voices. Make harmonic analysis.

Writing the Phrygian Cadence

In the Phrygian cadence, the iv_6 triad can be written with any doubling.

Fig. 18.19.

Examples of cadences in Figure 18.19 may be found as follows:
  a) Figure 18.5
  b) Bach chorale No. 292, second phrase
  c) Figure 15.7

Assignment 18.3. Write examples of Phrygian cadences.

Writing Six-Four Chords

In writing any of the six-four chords, these two part-writing procedures usually apply.

  a) *Approach and Departure.* The bass note of the six-four is preceded and followed only by
      (1) the same bass note
      (2) a note a step above or below
      (3) a skip in the *same* chord
      (4) a skip from the supertonic note in the progression $ii(ii^7)\text{-}I_6^4$.

  b) *Doubling.* The bass note, fifth of the triad, is always doubled. Use Rule 6A to approach and leave the doubled note.

Assignment 18.4. Write examples of the various uses of the six-four chord. Fill in inner voices and make harmonic analysis. In addition, identify each six-four chord as cadential, passing, pedal, or arpeggiated.

Writing Anticipations, Escaped Tones, and Appoggiaturas

Rule 8, "Writing Non-harmonic Tones," continues to be applicable in writing these three varieties of non-harmonic tones. At (1) in Figure 18.20, the appoggiatura D temporarily replaces its resolution, C. At the point of resolution, normal doubling is found.

Fig. 18.20.

Bach, *Jesu, nun sei gepreiset* (♯252)

App

There is less concern with voice distribution in writing the anticipation and escaped tone, since these usually appear on the weak part of the beat, after the chord structure has already been established.

Anticipations are fairly common, particularly when used at the cadence in the soprano or tenor voice. Use of the appoggiatura and escaped tone is minimal in four-voice texture; these two dissonances will be found more useful in instrumental style of writing. Examples of anticipations may be seen in Figure 13.18, measures 6 and 16, and in Figures 7.2 and 7.3. The escaped tone is shown in Figure 8.5, measure 1, and Figure 13.18, measure 4.

Assignment 18.5.   Part-writing. These exercises contain examples of most chord progression and part-writing procedures studied to date. Fill in inner voices and make harmonic analysis. Solve exercises in open score, as assigned.

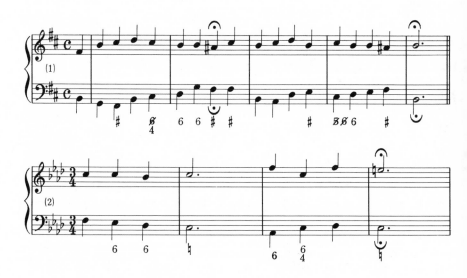

Assignment 18.6. Part-writing. The bass voice only is given. Add soprano, alto, and tenor lines. Make harmonic analysis.

Assignment 18.7.   Part-writing an unfigured bass. In this type of problem, the bass line only is given, and without figuration. It must be determined which triads are in inversion and which have the root in the bass. Many solutions are possible for each exercise, so try several and compare them with each other, finally selecting the most musical. Below are three of the possible figurations for the first two measures of the first exercise.

Fig. 18.21.

Melody Harmonization

In four-part vocal style, non-harmonic tones may be used very sparingly, as in a simple church hymn where perhaps only a single passing tone is found at the final cadence. At the other extreme, they may be used to make each of the four vocal parts a truly melodic line, as in the chorales of Johann Sebastian Bach. In these chorales the use of non-harmonic tones allows almost continual melodic movement from one chord to the next, in contrast to the "block chord" effect of the usual church hymn.

The use of non-harmonic tones to create the effect of continual melodic movement can be supplemented by two other devices.

a) By changing the structure of the chord, or by changing the inversion of the chord on the weak half of the beat (for example, on the second eighth note when a quarter note receives one beat).

Fig. 18.22.

Bach, *O Gott, du frommer Gott* (♯337)

b) By changing chords within the beat duration.

Fig. 18.23.

Bach, *Alles ist an Gottes Segen* (#128)

I 6   vi   I 6   vii°₆   I   IV6

When harmonizing a melody line, care must be exercised not to create parallel fifths and octaves through the use of non-harmonic tones.

Fig. 18.24.

Assignment 18.8.   Music examples in four voice parts are furnished. Add passing tones at appropriate places. Any given note may be placed on the weak half of the beat to make a place for an accented passing tone.

Assignment 18.9. Add suspensions and passing tones to the examples given. Given notes may be changed rhythmically to make suspensions possible.

With all the diatonic triads now available in melody harmonization, it is theoretically possible that each scale step can be a member of three different triads. Therefore, it is not enough simply to match a given triad to a given melody tone. A second and equally important consideration in chord choice is the relation of the chosen chord to those that immediately precede and follow it. Use Tables 14.1 and 14.2 as a guide to this aspect of chord choice.

Assignment 18.10. Melody harmonization. Harmonize the following melodies, as assigned, from hymn, chorale, and folk sources. Review Chapter 14, "Melody Harmonization," for basic procedures. Use the submediant and mediant triads, the v and VII triads in a minor key, and any nonharmonic tones. Include harmonic analysis and tempo and dynamic markings.

When a melody begins on a tonic or dominant pickup, all four voices may carry this note, regardless of relationship of these notes to the next chord.

Assignment 18.11. Write original exercises for voices or instruments in forms assigned by the instructor. Make harmonic analysis. Indicate tempo and dynamics.

Ear Training and Music Reading

Exercise 18.1. a) Listen to the tonic note of a minor key. Sing the v triad with letter names.

b) Listen to the tonic note of a minor key. Sing the VII triad with letter names.

Exercise 18.2. a) Sing with letter names the progression i-v-VI-iv-V-i in each minor key.

b) Sing with letter names the progression i-VII-III-iv-V-i in each minor key.

Exercise 18.3. Harmonic dictation exercises will now include the chords and progressions studied in this chapter.

Self-Help in Harmonic Dictation

Phrygian Cadence

Leoni	1–2	M–30
		E–285
Aus der Tiefe	1–2	M–95
Heinlein	1–2	E–55
Babylon's Streams	1–2	E–60

v Triad

Wer nur den lieben Gott	1–4	M–210

St. Bride   1   M–339
Old Hundred Twelfth   1–6   E–225

VII Triad

Bryn Calfaria   1–2   M–314

Keyboard Harmony

Exercise 18.4. Play each of the following progressions in each major and minor key.

$$I-V_6^4-I_6-IV-V\ (vii_6^o)-I$$

$$I-IV_6^4-I-V-I$$

$$i-V_6^4-i_6-iv-V(vii_6^o)-i$$

$$i-iv_6^4-i-V-i$$

$$i-v-VI-iv(ii_6^o)-V-i$$

$$i-v_6-iv_6-V-i$$

$$i-VII-III-iv-V(vii_6^o)-i$$

Exercise 18.5. *a*) Play this ascending minor scale:

1 2 3 4   5 6 7 8
i—V—i—VII—III—ii—V—i

(III-ii is an irregular progression)

b) Play this descending minor scale:

8 7 6   5 4 3   2   1
i—v—VI—III—iv—i$_6^4$—V—i

Melody Harmonization at the Keyboard. Using keyboard procedures previously learned, melodies may be harmonized using the harmonic materials learned in Chapters 17 and 18. The following example shows a keyboard harmonization using vi and at the cadence the V triad with the 6 5 melody line.

Fig. 18.25.

French Folk Song (MSS 72)

I   I   vi   ii 6   V 6 5   I

Exercise 18.6.   Harmonize melodies at the keyboard. In these melodies from *Music for Sight Singing*, the indicated triads or progressions can be used effectively. Be sure the indicated triad is so placed that a good progression results in relation to its preceding and following triads.

a) The vi triad (major keys). 27, 44, 65, 66, 72, 97, 109, 126, 137, 144, 173, 179, 221, 320, 343.

b) The VI triad (minor keys). 54, 79, 141, 151, 312, 326.

c) The iii triad (major keys). 3, 26, 66, 72, 132, 139, 165, 307, 320, 328.

d) The III triad (minor keys). 80, 316.

e) The progression vi-iii-IV or VI-III-iv. 5, 26, 82, 125, 127, 182.

f) The Phrygian cadence. 46, 47, 52, 76, 80, 88, 91, 314.

g) The v triad. 75, 125, 151, 326.

h) The VII triad. 47, 74, 75, 88.

19

The Dominant Seventh
and Supertonic Seventh Chords
Rhythm: Syncopation

THEORY AND ANALYSIS

Interplay between consonance and dissonance has been one of the principal features of Western music since the development of free organum in the eleventh century (review Appendix 3). By the fourteenth century it was well established that the consonant intervals consisted of the major and minor thirds, the major and minor sixths, the perfect fifth, and the perfect octave. A vertical sonority was consonant when each of the notes in the upper voices formed a consonant interval with the lowest sounding note.[1] Up to and throughout the sixteenth century, consonances could be used freely, but dissonances could be used only in certain well-defined situations comparable to some of the non-harmonic tone usages already described in the present course of study. Use of any dissonance that would create what we today would call a complete seventh chord was limited to the weak part of the beat. Dissonances on the strong part of the beat could create the impression of an incomplete seventh chord, the fifth of which was always missing. In Figure 19.1, at (1) the passing tone F in the alto voice appears on the weak part of the beat and momentarily creates a vertical sonority G B D F and at (2), in a similar situation, the vertical sonority F A C E. At (3) the suspension D

---

[1]The perfect fourth, though consonant when used between any two upper voices, was considered dissonant when found above the lowest sounding voice. Review Chapter 11, "Use of the Second Inversion."

creates an incomplete vertical sonority of E G (B) D at the point of resolution of the soprano suspension.

Fig. 19.1.

Palestrina (1525-1594), Mass *Ad Fugam*, " Kyrie "

Not until the seventeenth century did the dissonant seventh appear simultaneously with a complete triad to form a complete seventh chord, early examples of which are shown in Figure 19.2 at *. Here, as another author has so colorfully described it,[2] the non-harmonic tone is "frozen" to the triad to create the seventh chord.

Fig. 19.2.

Franz Tunder (1614-1667), *Wachet auf* (Cantata)

But in these four-note structures, the seventh still obeys the traditional laws of dissonance in that the seventh must be properly approached and resolved, a practice that remained standard for seventh chord usage through the late nineteenth century.[3]

Terminology for Seventh Chords

A seventh chord, consisting of a triad plus the interval of a seventh above the root of the triad, may be built upon any scale degree. The harmonic

---

[2] Roger Sessions, *Harmonic Practice* (New York: Harcourt, Brace & World, Inc., 1951).

[3] Chords built in thirds but larger than a triad are still known as dissonant sonorities, though to the modern ear these rarely fit the definition of a dissonance as a harsh or unpleasant sound.

analysis symbol for a seventh chord consists simply of the usual Roman numeral for the triad with a superscript ^{7} added: V^7, ii^7, $ii°^7$, etc. A seventh chord may also be identified by the quality of its sound, describing first the quality of the triad (major, minor, diminished) and secondly the quality of the interval of the seventh, which, for purposes of this chapter, will always be a minor seventh. The chord types to be considered in this chapter are:

Major-minor seventh chord: a *major* triad plus a *minor* seventh. Example, G B D F: G B D = major triad, G up to F = minor seventh; G B D F is a major-minor seventh chord.

Minor-minor seventh chord: a *minor* triad plus a *minor* seventh. Example, D F A C: D F A = minor triad, D up to C = minor seventh; D F A C is a minor-minor seventh chord. The term *minor seventh chord* may be used.

Diminished-minor seventh chord: a *diminished* triad plus a *minor* seventh. Example: D F A♭ C: D F A♭ = diminished triad, D up to C = minor seventh; D F A♭ C is a diminished minor seventh chord. The term *half diminished seventh chord* may be used, a term that differentiates this sound from the diminished-diminished (fully diminished) seventh chord (example, D F A♭ C♭) to be studied in *Advanced Harmony.*

Any seventh chord is commonly used with its root in the bass and in each of its three inversions. The list of figured bass symbols for these is illustrated in Figure 19.3 by the V^7 chord, but is applicable to any seventh chord.

Root in bass: 7, usually reduced to 7 only unless 5 and 3 are altered.
    5
    3

First inversion: 6, usually reduced to 6 only.
    5   5
    3

Second inversion: 6, usually reduced to 4 only.
    4   3
    3

Third inversion: 6, usually reduced to either 4 or 2.
    4   2
    2

Fig. 19.3.

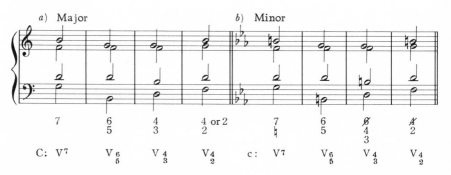

The Dominant Seventh Chord

The seventh chord build upon the dominant scale degree $(V^7)^4$ is by far the most commonly used of all seventh chords, and it is more frequently used, at least in instrumental style, than the dominant triad (V). The definition, construction, spelling, and melodic use of the dominant seventh chord has already been presented in Chapter 8, which should be reviewed at this time. With the intervening study of non-harmonic tones completed, it is now possible to consider the harmonic uses of the dominant seventh chord.

The treatment of the seventh of the seventh chord has much in common with the treatment of the non-harmonic tone. Both are dissonant; both must be carefully approached and resolved. In actual seventh chord usage, the three-note figure, consisting of approach, dissonance, and resolution, is similar to certain non-harmonic tone figures. In each case, the seventh resolves down by step. This principle applies not only to the V^7 chord, as shown in Figure 19.4, but to *all* other seventh chords as well.

Fig. 19.4.

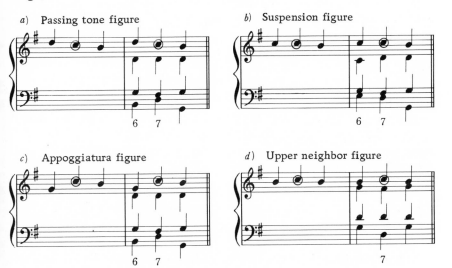

In a chord progression, the choice of chords to precede and follow the seventh chord is limited by the strictness of the approach to and departure from the seventh. Ordinarily, the V^7 is followed by the tonic or submediant triads only.

---

[4] V^7 refers to the major-minor seventh chord on the dominant in both major and minor keys. The v^7 (minor-minor seventh) in minor keys is rarely used.

The Supertonic Seventh Chords

The supertonic seventh chord is built upon the second tone of the scale. In a major key, it is a minor seventh chord. In a minor key, it is a diminished-minor seventh chord. The supertonic seventh chord with the raised fifth (raised sixth scale degree), a minor seventh chord, is theoretically possible; it is rarely used[5] and will not be considered here.

Fig. 19.5.

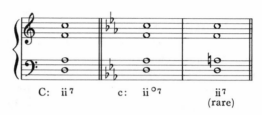

C: ii^7 c: ii$^{\circ 7}$ ii^7
                                        (rare)

Like the supertonic triad, the supertonic seventh chord is used most frequently in first inversion, particularly at a cadence point. In Chapter 15, we noted the resemblance in sound and in function between the subdominant triad and the supertonic triad in first inversion. The same resemblance is to be found in the ii$_6^5$ (ii$_6^{\circ 5}$); to some theoreticians this chord is known as a subdominant triad with an added sixth (in Figure 19.6, B♭ D F plus a sixth above the bass, G).[6]

Fig. 19.6.

Hymn: Hesperus

ii $_6^5$

Another common use of the ii$_6$ is in conjunction with the passing six-four chord in the progression IV$_6$–I$_6^4$–ii$_6^5$ (or, in minor, iv$_6$–i$_6^4$–ii$_6^{\circ5}$). This progression can be seen in Figure 17.10. Also, review Chapter 18, "The Passing Six-Four."

---

[5]When the fifth of the chord (raised sixth scale degree) resolves upwards, and the seventh of the chord resolves downwards, both meet on the same note, resulting in a doubled leading tone.

[6]This vertical sonority was possible in pre-seventeenth-century writing because each interval above the bass was consonant with the bass, for example, above B♭, a third D, a fifth F, and a sixth G.

The supertonic seventh chord can regularly be found with any other member in the bass voice, though their occurrences are less frequent than the first inversion. The function of the supertonic seventh in a chord progression is the same as for the supertonic triad, therefore the progressions from Table 14.1 will apply here.

Assignment 19.1. Spell the supertonic seventh chord in each major and minor key.

Assignment 19.2. Analysis of seventh chords. In each of the figures from previous chapters and in the figures listed below can be found one or more examples of a dominant seventh chord or a supertonic seventh chord. Spell each of these seventh chords, identify each by chord number and by quality of sound, and indicate the method of approach and departure from the seventh of the chord.

Example: Figure 15.6, the chord on the fourth beat of the first full measure.

Eb G Bb Db: major-minor seventh chord

V_2^4 in the key of Ab major

The seventh, Db, is in the bass voice. It is approached by step from above and resolves down by step (passing tone figure).

Sources: Figures 2.13, 2.15, 2.17, 2.18, 2.19, 11.2, 14.8, 15.5, 17.2, 17.7, 17.10, 17.12, 17.16, plus all figures in Chapter 19.

Assignment 19.3. Harmonic analysis. Indicate chord numbers and non-harmonic tones from the following excerpts.

Beethoven, Sonata for Piano, No. 3 (Op. 2, No. 3), first movement, measures 5–8
Chopin, Mazurka No. 18 (Op. 30, No. 1), measures 5–8 (G minor)
Mendelssohn, *Songs Without Words*
    No. 6 (Op. 19, No. 6), measures 28–29
    No. 16 (Op. 38, No. 4), measures 4–5
    No. 41 (Op. 85, No. 5), measures 6–9
    No. 43 (Op. 102, No. 1), measures 25–26
Mozart, Sonata for Piano in D Major, K. 311, third movement, measures 23–26
Schumann, *Album for the Young*, Op. 68
    No. 19, measures 17–20
    No. 28, measures 1–4
Murphy and Melcher, *Music for Study*, Chapter 15

APPLICATION

Written Materials

General Procedure for Writing Seventh Chords

In *all* seventh chords, the seventh, being a dissonance, must be treated carefully. Part-writing Rule 9 will suffice in most instances; certain exceptions to the usual resolution of the seventh will be noted as individual seventh chords are presented.

Part-Writing Rule 9. The seventh of a seventh chord, its note of approach, and its note of resolution comprise a three-note figure similar to certain non-harmonic tone figures: the passing tone figure, the suspension figure, the appoggiatura figure, and the upper neighboring figure. The resolution of the seventh is usually down by step.

Writing Seventh Chords, Root in Bass

The dominant seventh chord with its root in the bass may be found complete (all four chord tones present) or incomplete (fifth missing and root doubled). The complete V^7 is often followed by an incomplete tonic triad, the incomplete V^7 by a complete tonic triad.

Fig. 19.7. Incomplete V^7

Nicht schnell   Schumann, *Das Schifflein*, Op. 146, No. 5

Fig. 19.8. Complete V^7

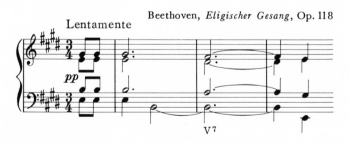

Lentamente   Beethoven, *Eligischer Gesang*, Op. 118

The infrequent supertonic seventh with root in bass is usually found with all four members present. When followed by V^7, the V^7 is usually incomplete, as in Figure 19.9.

Fig. 19.9.

Moderato

Haydn, Mass in B♭ Major

ii 7

Writing Seventh Chords in Inversion

When writing a seventh chord in inversion, all four notes of the chord are usually present. The bass note should be approached by the same note, by step, or by leap from a direction opposite to its resolution. In the following figures, observe the approach and resolution both of the seventh of the chord and of the bass note. Review also the ii$_6^5$ chord in Figure 19.6.

Fig. 19.10.

Hymn: Greenland

Fig. 19.11.

Hymn: Dix

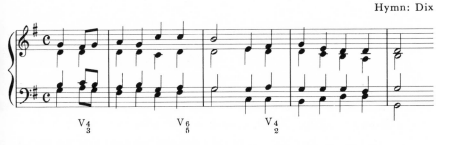

Fig. 19.12.

Hiller, Johann Adam (1792)
Was sorgst du ängstlich für dein Leben

ii °$^4_2$ V$^6_5$

Exceptional Practices

In common with any other theoretical device used in music composition, exceptions can be found in the use of the seventh chord. One such exception is unique with the V^7 chord, the *passing five four-three* (V$^4_3$). This chord is found between two positions of the tonic triad, similar to the passing V$^6_4$ (review Chapter 18). When used with an ascending bass line, the seventh of the V^7 ascends, as in Figure 19.13. The descending variety is seen in Figure 19.10.

Fig. 19.13.

Hymn: Duke Street

I   V$^4_3$ I$_6$

The descriptions of other exceptional practices that follow apply to both the dominant seventh and the supertonic seventh chords.

a) Transfer of seventh. The seventh chord may be repeated with the seventh occurring in a different voice part. The seventh in the last of such a series resolves normally. (See Fig. 19.14)

b) Irregular or ornamental resolutions. The seventh may be found ornamented, as in the ormamental resolution of the suspension (Figure 19.15). The resolution of the seventh may be delayed when it is held over into the next chord (Figure 19.16).

Fig. 19.14.

Allegro

Weber, *Mass in G*

ff

Fig. 19.15.

Bach, *Wenn wir in höchsten Nöten sein* (♯247)

V⁷

Fig. 19.16.

Bach, *Von Gott will ich nicht lassen* (♯191)

C: vi   ii₆   ii⁷

In Figure 19.17, the seventh of the ii⁷ is held into the next chord and at the same time is transferred to another voice.

Fig. 19.17.

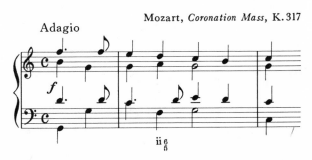

Mozart, *Coronation Mass*, K.317

Adagio

f

ii ⁶₅

c) Double dissonance. Although a seventh chord already includes one dissonance (the seventh), a second dissonance may be sounded when its use conforms to the general rule for writing non-harmonic tones. In Figure 19.18, the accented passing tone, D, temporarily replaces C♯ in the dominant seventh chord A C♯ E G. This figure also demonstrates the passing five four-three chord.

Fig. 19.18.

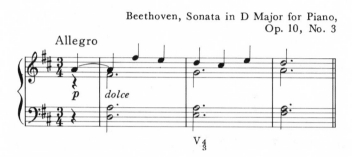

Beethoven, Sonata in D Major for Piano,
Op. 10, No. 3

Assignment 19.4. Write dominant seventh chords with root in bass. Indicate below each example the non-harmonic tone usage represented by the seventh of the chord.

Assignment 19.5. Write dominant seventh chords in inversion. Indicate below each example the non-harmonic usage represented by the seventh of the chord.

Assignment 19.6. Write examples of the supertonic seventh chord. Write harmonic analysis below each exercise. Solve some of the exercises in open score.

Assignment 19.7. Write extended exercises using both dominant seventh and supertonic seventh chords. Exercises 4 and 5 are unfigured. Supply a figured bass before adding alto and tenor voices. Make harmonic analysis of all work.

Assignment 19.8. Melody harmonization. Harmonize melodies using dominant seventh and supertonic seventh chords. Half notes in the melody can often be harmonized using two chords, one on each quarter note. Use non-harmonic tones where appropriate. Melodies from Assignment 18.10 may also be used at this time. Make harmonic analysis of all work.

Assignment 19.9. Write original exercises demonstrating various uses of the dominant seventh and supertonic seventh chords.

Writing Melody Harmonizations for Keyboard Performance

Even a brief glance at any piece of music for keyboard will reveal a style of writing that seems quite unrelated to the four-voice choral style we have been studying. But close examination will show a more direct relationship between the two styles than might be expected upon casual observation. In fact, all styles of writing in the historical period under study follow all the basic harmonic and melodic principles set forth in preceding chapters. The application of these principles to writing for various instruments or instrumental combinations varies according to the physical construction and capabilities of the particular instrument or combination. The keyboard, for example, has a range of eighty-eight notes compared to the limited range of a human voice, and it can perform many notes simultaneously compared to the single tone of the human voice.

The principles of music composition first developed during the Medieval and Renaissance eras, a time when instruments were in rudimentary stages of their development. Originally, instruments played individual lines of vocal compositions.[7] The earliest original compositions for keyboard instruments or instrumental ensemble were virtually indistinguishable from choral music, except for the lack of words. From this point on, instrumental music developed with less dependence on the vocal style and, for each instrument, according to its own capabilities and limitations. But even through the nineteenth century, instrumental music still displays the influence of vocal style of writing. We will approach our study of the instrumental style of writing by showing (1) the similarity between four-part vocal style and instrumental style and (2) the differences made possible by the unique character and capabilities of the particular instrument or combination of instruments. More specifically, we will investigate piano keyboard style, limiting ourselves at present to the use of block chords and arpeggiated chords and non-harmonic tones in harmonizing given melodies. Figures 19.19— 19.23, and other earlier figures as designated, illustrate the features of keyboard style discussed in the following paragraphs.

1. Part-writing procedures, principles of doubling and of resolution, principles of non-harmonic tone usage and principles of harmonic progression, as already studied, apply to all styles of piano writing listed in this

---

[7]Most of the so-called *a cappella* music of this era was intended for voices accompanied by instruments or for instruments alone, as well as for voices alone.

discussion. Two exceptions to the principles of doubling in choral style apply to writing for the piano:

a) One or more voice lines may be doubled in octaves. Called *sonority doubling,* it is found most frquently in the bass voice and can be seen in Figures 2.19, 2.23, and 17.33, where the sonority doubling is an octave lower than the normal bass line, and in Figure 19.19, where the sonority doubling in measures 1 and 2 is above the tenor and an octave above the normal bass line, and in measures 5 and 6 where the sonority doubling of the soprano is found an octave lower and below the alto line. These octaves are not considered parallel because they simply reinforce a single voice line, whereas two different voices in octaves do constitute actual parallel octaves.

b) Tones that ordinarily demand specific resolutions, such as leading tones, altered tones, and sevenths of seventh chords, may be doubled, one in each hand, but only when one of these tones continues on to a different tone before the other doubled note resolves. In Figure 18.10, in the V^7–I cadence, the seventh E♭ sounds in both hands simultaneously, but the upper E♭ skips to the third, A, before the lower seventh resolves. See also Figure 18.14. Though acceptable, this procedure should be used sparingly.

2. Block chords may be used in the right hand, with the soprano notes of the chord succession forming the melodic line. This procedure is similar to keyboard harmonization of melodic lines as first presented in Chapter 13, "Keyboard Harmony." For examples in written piano music, see Figures 10.2 and 17.33.

3. Block chords may be found in the left hand. This treatment is less common. Avoid placing chords so low as to create a thick, muddy sound, and be particularly careful to avoid parallel fifths and octaves in the left-hand chord progression or between notes in the left hand and the right hand (review Chapter 13, footnote 5). See Figures 14.8 and 19.23.

4. Chords may be found in open structure. Here, care must be taken that adjacent voices in each clef are close enough together, usually an octave or less, so that the hand can play both notes at the same time. See Figures 13.30 and 19.19. Changes from open position to close position, or vice versa, or to block chords in the left hand may be made during the course of the piece.

5. Chords in the accompaniment may be arpeggiated (usually left hand) by sounding a single low note followed by one or more block chords, usually repeated. This is familiarly known as the "oom-pah" style and was first presented in Figure 13.37 as one way of harmonizing melodies at the keyboard. In this style the V^7 is by far more frequent than the V triad. See Figures 14.4, 18.10, 18.14, 18.15, and 19.20. In the latter figure, note the care shown by Schubert in the doubling of the leading tone in the V^7 chord, F A C E♭. In measure 2, the leading tone is in the right hand, so is omitted in the left hand; in measure 3, the leading tone is in the left hand as it is not

found at that point or later in the right hand; in measure 7, the leading tone in the first V⁷ moves to C on the third beat to avoid doubling the leading tone in the melody line.

6. Chords in the accompaniment may be arpeggiated, one note at a time, a device known as an *Alberti bass* when found in the left hand (review Chapter 2, footnote 8). This is one of the more common methods of presenting chords in keyboard style and may be seen in almost any composition for piano. See Figures 2.17, 2.18 (note omission of third in arpeggiated V⁷ chord to allow for its presence in the melody), 2.19, 2.23, 11.2 (in measures 2–3, arpeggiated sonority doubling), 11.5, 13.19, 14.3, 15.5, 17.4, 17.16 (arpeggios in right hand), 18.12 and 19.22.

7. The number of notes sounding simultaneously is not limited to four as in choral style, but may range from a single tone to as many as eight or more. Three-voice texture is quite common, as in Figure 2.17 where the arpeggiated left hand represents two voices. In Figure 19.22, measures 5–6, the left-hand intervals omit the third of each triad since these are represented by non-harmonic tones in the right hand, each appearing on the first beat of successive measures. In three-voice texture, the third of the chord or its representative should always be present. The music of Figure 19.19 is primarily in four voices with a fifth note as sonority doubling; in measures 5–6, the number of voices increases to six and then to eight notes by increasing the number of voices with sonority doubling.

8. A piece of music, or even a phrase within a piece of music, does not have to remain in one style, but can change from one to another, as in Figures 15.5 and 19.22, which change from arpeggiated chords to block style. Two styles may be found simultaneously: in Figure 11.2, close position and arpeggiation are found together; in Figure 14.4, the "oom-pah" style is found with complete added sonority doubling; and in Figure 2.23, we find block chords in the left hand plus arpeggiation and melodic line in the right hand. Various combinations of these features are too numerous to mention, but they can easily be studied by reference to any standard piano works. The student may even wish to attempt a little elementary counterpoint, such as in Figure 19.21 where the simple triadic melody in measure 1 is imitated in the left hand of the piano in measure 2. See also Figure 19.24(8).

Assignment 19.10. Writing a melody harmonization in keyboard style. Choose a melody from *Music for Sight Singing*, Chapters 1–8 or 11–13, or from any other source, particularly a folksong collection. Harmonize the melody in keyboard style as discussed in the preceding eight points. Any given melody can be harmonized in countless ways. In Figure 19.24, the first phrase of melody number 102 from *Music for Sight Singing* has been set in eight different ways to show you just a few of the possibilities. Do not be satisfied with your first attempt but write several versions in order to arrive at the best possible harmonization.

Fig. 19.19.

Beethoven, Sonata for Piano, Op. 10, No. 1

Fig. 19.20.

Schubert, *Valse sentimentale*, Op. 50, No. 5

Fig. 19.21.

Schumann, *Erstes Grün*, Op. 35, No. 4

Einfach

Du   Jun - ges Grün, du   fri - sches Gras! wie

man - ches Herz durch dich ge - nas,

Fig. 19.22.

Mozart, Sonata in G Major, for Piano
K. 283

Allegro

Fig. 19.23.

Mozart, Sonata in C Major for Piano
K. 309

Allegro con spirito

Fig. 19.24.

German Folk Song   (MSS 102)

Assignment 19.11. Melody-writing. After studying syncopation from the latter part of this chapter, write melodies in forms as assigned, using patterns of syncopation in Figures 19.25–26 or other patterns as found in Chapters 9 and 14 of *Music for Sight Singing.*

Ear Training and Music Reading

Exercise 19.1. Sing the progression I–ii⁷–V–I in major keys and i–ii°⁷–V–i in minor keys, using letter names.

Exercise 19.2. Harmonic dictation will now include examples of dominant seventh and supertonic seventh chords.

Self-Help in Harmonic Dictation

V^7			ii^7 *or* $ii^{\circ 7}$		
Cambridge	1–4	M–24	Forest Green	1–4	M–33
Irish	8–14	M–56	Nun freut euch	1–4	M–58
		E–444	Morecambe	1–4	M–138
Evan	all	M–68	Ellers	9–16	M–236
St. Peter	1–4	M–81	Barnabas	1–4	M–332
		E–455	St. Theodolph	1–4	M–424

V^7

Faithful Guide	all	M–106
Arfon	5–8	M–112
Munich	1–4	M–167
		E–114
Arlington	all	M–239
		E–325
Salzburg	1–7	M–295
Halifax	13–16	M–456
Arfon (Major)	5–8	M–464
Lyons	1–8	M–473
		E–260
Claudius	9–12	E–138
Wigan	1–4	E–338

ii^7 or $ii^{\circ 7}$

Ballerma	5–8	M–461
Tantum Ergo	1–4	M–546
Arsberg	17–20	M–788
St. Phillip	9–12	E–57
Swedish Litany	1–2	E–82
Winkworth	1–2	E–226
Capetown	1–4	E–275
Leoni	5–8	E–286

Syncopation

Syncopation occurs when the normal or expected pattern of rhythm, accent, or meter is deliberately upset. This effect is frequently created by tying a weak beat or a weak part of a beat into the next strong beat or part of a beat. The following are some of the basic patterns of syncopation.

Fig. 19.25.

Pattern	Example in *Music for Sight Singing*
	245
	246
	252
	402
	405
	251
	263

Syncopation may also be created by accenting a weak beat or part of a beat when there is no tie into the next strong beat or part of a beat.

Fig. 19.26.

Pattern	Example in *Music for Sight Singing*
	397
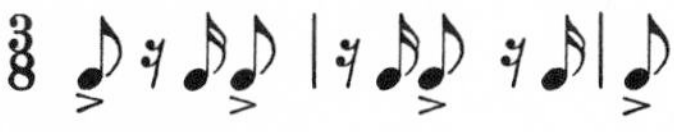	266
	413

Exercise 19.3. Rhythmic reading. Read the patterns in Figures 19.25 and 19.26, using the conductor's beat and background tap. Repeat each pattern as many times as necessary before going on to the next pattern.

Exercise 19.4. Rhythmic reading. Read the rhythm in melodies from Chapters 9 and 14 from *Music for Sight Singing.*

Exercise 19.5. Rhythmic dictation. Exercises will now contain examples of syncopation.

Sight Singing: Sing melodies from Chapter 9 and 14 from *Music for Sight Singing.*

Keyboard Harmony

Exercise 19.6. Play the following progressions in any major or minor key. Opening triad may be in any soprano position.

a) I–V^7–I

b) I–V_5^6–I

c) IV–V_2^4–I_6

d) I–V_3^4–I_6

e) vi–V^7–I

f) i–V^7–i

g) i–V_5^6–i

h) iv–V_2^4–i

i) i–V_3^4–I_6

j) VI–V^7–i (VI: third in soprano and doubled)

Exercise 19.7.   Play the following progressions in any major or minor key. Opening triad may be in any soprano position.

a) $I-ii_6^5-V-I$

b) $I-ii_4^3-V-I$

c) $I-ii_4^2-V_6^5-I$

d) $I-IV_6-I_6^4-ii_6^5-V-I$

e) $i-ii_6^{o5}-V-i$

f) $i-ii_4^{o3}-V-i$

g) $i-ii_4^{o2}-V_6^5-i$

h) $i-iv_6-i_6^4-ii_6^{o5}-V-i$

Exercise 19.8.   Melody harmonization. In the following melodies, use the cadence formula ii_6^5-V-I or $ii_6^{o5}-V-i$ when the penultimate melody note allows the use of two chords, as shown in Figure 19.27. Harmonize melodies 30, 114, 134, 174, 212, 309, 351, 367, and 373.

Fig. 19.27.

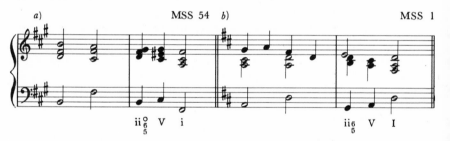

20

Elementary Modulation
Secondary Dominant Chords:
The Dominant of the Dominant

THEORY AND ANALYSIS

Modulation

Our study of harmony this far has been concerned with the use of chords and chord progressions within a given key. A music composition usually makes use of more than just its beginning key; it may progress to and through one or more other keys before returning to the original key at the end of the piece.

Modulation is the term used to describe the process of going from one key to another. From a given key, modulation to *any* other major or minor key is possible. For our elementary study, we will consider the two most commonly used modulations: (1) from a major key to its dominant key (example: C major to G major) and (2) from a minor key to its relative major key (example: C minor to Eb major). The change from one key to another is usually accomplished through a device known as a "common chord" or a "pivot chord."[1] This is a chord that has a spelling common to both keys but at the same time has a separate function in each key.

In Figure 20.1, phrases 1 and 2 are in G minor. The chord common to both keys, and around which the modulation pivots occurs at the *. Play the chorale up to and including the pivot chord. Note that the pivot chord

---

[1]Other means of modulation and modulation to all other keys will be presented in *Advanced Harmony*.

309

sounds like the tonic chord in G minor. Now play beginning with the pivot chord; the pivot chord sounds as vi in B♭ major.

Fig. 20.1.

Bach, *Wo soll ich fliehen hin* (♯281)

The pivot chord is usually located *before* the first appearance of a dominant-tonic progression, (I_6)-V-I or vii°₆-I, in the new key. It is very often the chord immediately preceding this cadential progression, as in Figure 20.1, where the pivot i = vi immediately precedes the first V-I of the new key of B♭. Only infrequently is any dominant or leading tone chord in either key found as a pivot; dominant function is so strong in one key that it is improbable that it will be heard as a different function in another key. Eliminating dominant harmonies in both keys, there are four possible pivots between a minor key and its relative major, spelled here in the keys of Figure 20.1, G minor to B♭ major.

$$i = vi \ (G \ B♭ \ D)$$
$$III = I \ (B♭ \ D \ F)$$
$$iv = ii \ (C \ E♭ \ G)$$
$$VI = IV \ (E♭ \ G \ B♭)$$

Modulation from a major key to its dominant can be accomplished in the same manner. There are three possible pivots, spelled here in the keys of Figure 20.2, A major to E major.

$$I = IV \ (A \ C\sharp \ E)$$
$$iii = vi \ (C\sharp \ E \ G\sharp)$$
$$vi = ii \ (F\sharp \ A \ C\sharp)$$

In Figure 20.2, the pivot is $vi = ii$, this being the first chord preceding the new dominant function, I_6^4 in E major.

Fig. 20.2.

Beethoven, Symphony, No. 2, Op. 36

Occasionally, a chord appearing earlier than that immediately preceding the new V-I will act as the pivot, or, each of two or more different chords immediately preceding the new V-I can assume the function of a pivot chord. In Figure 20.3, $i = vi$ in measure 5 or $iv = ii$ in measure 6 will serve equally as a pivot. Any choice of pivot is usually correct when the resulting harmonic progression in *both* keys is a normal chord progression, as defined in Table 14.1. Measures 5 and 6 together produce in E minor the progression i-iv or in G major the progression vi-ii, both regular progressions.

Fig. 20.3.

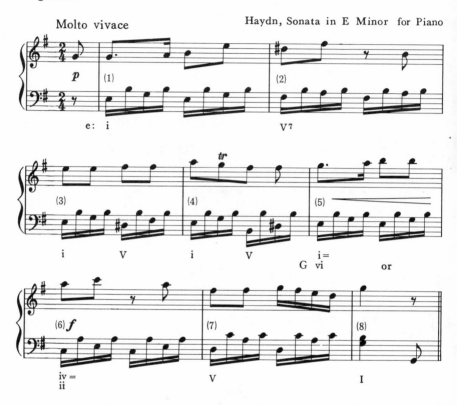

Return to the Original Tonic Key

Once a new key is achieved, there may be an immediate return to the old key, a very common occurrence, or the music may continue for a variable length of time in the new key or in other keys before making the return. For our purposes at present, we will consider only the *direct return* to the original key. After a modulation to a new key, return to the original tonic is accomplished simply by beginning the next phrase with I, V-I, or some other basic progression in the original key. In the final cadence of Figure 20.2 (modulation to the dominant), a minor seventh (D) is added to the E major triad, allowing the next phrase to begin with the tonic triad in the original key of A major. Figure 20.1 ends with a cadence in B♭ major. The complete chorale shows two more phrases in B♭ major, while the final phrase begins with iv$_6$-V-I in the original key of G minor.[2]

---

[2]The first phrase of Figure 20.9, when analyzed as a modulation, is followed by a direct return to the original key.

Other methods of return exist, of course, but these involve study of other modulatory processes, included in *Advanced Harmony*.

Secondary Dominant Chords: The Dominant of the Dominant

Secondary dominant chords were first mentioned in Chapter 18 and illustrated in Figure 18.3 where we saw a secondary dominant progression in D minor, VII-III (C E G—F A C). Played alone, these two triads sound like V—I in F major; the VII triad stands in dominant relationship to III and is therefore called a secondary dominant.

How do we know that this VII—III progression from Figure 18.3 is not really V—I in F major? To demonstrate the difference between a secondary dominant progression and a modulation we will look at the first three triads from Figure 18.3, shown below as Figure 20.4 *a*, and the three triads starting at the * from Figure 20.1, shown below as Figure 20.4 *b*. The root movement in the two excerpts is identical, but in *a*, the analysis indicates a secondary dominant progression, while at *b*, the analysis is V—I in a new key. The difference in analyses lies in the cadential goals of the respective harmonic progressions, shown also in Figure 20.4 *a* and *b*. In *a*, the phrase very clearly concludes with a half cadence (i–V) in its original key, D minor. There is no change of key, but the F major (III) triad is given a temporary feeling of tonic by the dominant relationship of its preceding triad C E G (VII).[3] In

Fig. 20.4.

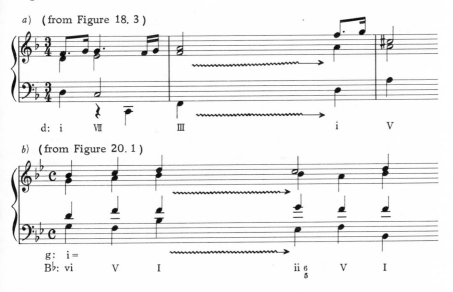

a) (from Figure 18. 3)

d: i   VII   III   i   V

b) (from Figure 20. 1)

g: i =
B♭: vi   V   I   ii 6   V   I
                          5

---

[3]Giving a non-tonic chord the temporary feeling of tonic is also known as *tonicization*.

b on the other hand, the phrase displays an unmistakable cadence in B♭ major, therefore, the second and third triads (FAC—B♭DF) are analyzed as V—I in the new key of B♭.

In theory, any chord may be preceded by a major triad or major-minor seventh chord standing in dominant relationship to it. The spelling of this secondary dominant chord usually includes a chromatically altered tone, VII—III in minor being an exception. At present, we will consider the most common secondary dominant chord, that built upon the second scale step and which functions as the *dominant of the dominant*.[4] Figure 20.5 illustrates this triad in major and in minor and identifies it by two widely used but different systems of Roman numeral analysis, II and V of V. II indicates a major triad and the scale step location of its root (C: II = D F♯ A); V of V indicates that the triad stands in a dominant relationship to V (C: V of V = a dominant function of V, therefore, D F♯ A). Either terminology is acceptable and both will be used in this text.

Fig. 20.5.

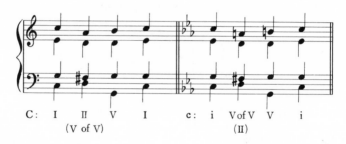

```
C:   I    II    V     I        c:   i   V of V   V    i
         (V of V)                        (II)
```

Fig. 20.6.

Adagio   Mozart, Sonata in F Major for Piano, K 280

```
A♭:   I 6        V              I 6        IV6    I 6     V6 of V
        4                         4               4
```

---

[4]The dominant of the dominant function can be expressed by other chords, as will be presented in *Advanced Harmony*. In C major, F♯ A C is the leading tone triad of V (G B D), a secondary vii°-I progression. Two different seventh chords can be built above this root, F♯ A C E and F♯ A C E♭.

Any secondary dominant may be found as a seventh chord (II^7 or V^7ofV) as shown in the following two figures, or may precede a V^7 chord, as shown in Figure 20.8.

Fig. 20.7.

Gluck, *Alceste*, "Ah! malgré moi"

Lentemente

Vos ten - dres pleurs, vos re-grets si tous chants;

F: I   vi 6 V_2^4ofV   V 6 V^7 I

(II_2^4)

Fig. 20.8.

Tempo giusto   Chopin, Waltz, Op. 64, No. 2

c♯:   i II^7 V^7 i

($V^7$of V)

The three preceding examples show the dominant of the dominant during the course of the phrase. Very common also is the use of this function at the cadence.

Fig. 20.9.

Bach, *Du Lebensfürst, Herr Jesu Christ* (♯102)

The first cadence of Figure 20.9 can easily be analyzed as a half cadence, VofV—V (II–V), particularly because the V triad progresses directly to I at the beginning of the second phrase. But this cadence also displays all the chracteristics of a modulation, where the tonic triad in measure 3 can be considered the pivot chord I = IV followed by a V–I cadence in D major. If, in a passage such as this, the progression is analyzed as a modulation, it is at best a "transient modulation" because of the indefinite establishment of a change of key and the quick return to the original tonic.

Again we have the question, what is the correct analysis, secondary dominant or modulation? In Figure 20.9, the D major triad at the first cadence, appearing only once, maintains a strong feeling of dominant (wanting to resolve to the original tonic) in spite of its two preceding chords. Only as the new tonic is given more emphasis, by repeating chords of the dominant key, as in Figure 20.10, or by other devices, does the impression of a definite modulation take place.

There is no strict dividing line in differentiating a secondary dominant progression from a modulation. A choice can only be made through subjective evaluation by the individual listener, which, of course, will vary from person to person. Figure 20.2, the example first used to illustrate modulation to the dominant will sound to some as a real modulation, to others as a transient modulation, and to still others as a half cadence in the original key. In Figure 20.10, where the tonic triad of the dominant key is approached three times, the impression of a real modulation to the dominant is consider-

Fig. 20.10.

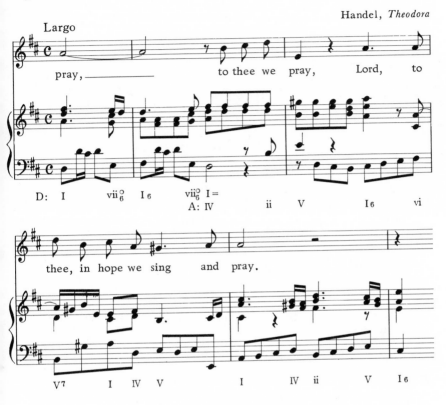

Handel, *Theodora*

ably stronger. As a help in making a choice of analysis, we can say that as a rule of thumb, a *single* occurrence of a pivot plus V–I, as in measure 3 of Figure 20.9, is not sufficient to establish clearly a new key. A modulation is more certain when a cadence in a new key is approached through a tonic six-four chord, as in Figure 20.2, or when the cadence formula in the new key is reiterated as in Figure 20.10. In any event, no attempt at identification should be made without *hearing* the passage in question and deciding for yourself whether the cadence is stable in the key of the dominant or simply a half cadence in the old key.

Fortunately, choice of analysis is much less of a problem when modulating to keys other than the dominant of a major key. In any other modulation, such as that to the relative major (Figure 20.1) or to the minor dominant of a minor key (Figure 20.11, E minor to B minor), the new tonic triad usually possesses stability as a key center, lacking as it does the urgency and insistence of a major dominant triad to return immediately to the original tonic.

Fig. 20.11.

Beethoven, Sonata for Piano, Op. 10, No. 3

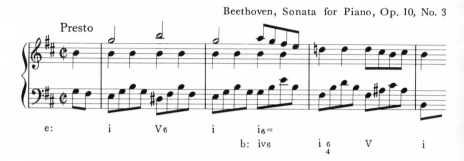

Presto

e: i   V₆   i   i₆=
                                b: iv₆   i ⁶₄   V   i

Terminology Variants

In addition to II and VofV, many other symbols identifying the dominant of the dominant chord are in current usage. They can be classified in three groups:

a) $\dfrac{\text{V}}{\text{V}}$, V/V, V $\searrow$ V

b)   [V], X. The symbol is placed below the chord preceding the diatonic V chord.

c)   II (third of the triad is raised)
       ♯
       3
       II (fourth scale step is raised)
       ♯
       4

Assignment 20.1.   Spell the three pivot chords that can be used to modulate from each major key to its dominant. (Note: The dominant key of C♯ major is G♯ major, for which there is no key signature. In this key, new accidentals are shown as ✗'s in the music, or the enharmonic key of A♭ major may be used. The excerpt from Chopin, Mazurka Op. 6, No. 2 from Assignment 20.4 contains a phrase in G♯ major.)

Example: Modulate from C major to G major.

   I = IV, C E G; iii = vi, E G B, vi = ii, A C E.

Assignment 20.2.   Spell the four pivot chords that can be used to modulate from each minor key to its relative major.

Example: Modulate from C minor to E♭ major.

i = vi, C Eb G
III = I, Eb G Bb
iv = ii, F Ab C
VI = IV, Ab C Eb

Assignment 20.3. a) Spell the dominant of the dominant triad (II or VofV) in each major and minor key.

b) Spell the dominant seventh of the dominant triad (II⁷ or V⁷ofV) in each major and minor key.

Assignment 20.4. Harmonic analysis. Indicate chord numbers, non-harmonic tones and location of the pivot and its function in each key when a modulation occurs. These music excerpts contain examples of (1) modulation to the dominant and/or the dominant of the dominant chord and (2) modulation to the relative major and/or the VII–III progression. Choose the analysis you believe to be most appropriate and give reasons for your choice.

Bach, *371 Chorales*

Major: No. 4, fifth phrase
          No. 107, fifth and sixth phrases
          No. 156, fourth phrase
          No. 217, fourth phrase

Minor: No. 112, third phrase
          No. 242, measures 1–3
          No. 321, last two measures
          No. 324, third phrase
          No. 356, sixth phrase

Beethoven, Sonatas for Piano

Major: No. 4 (Op. 7), second movement, measures 1–8
          No. 11 (Op. 22), fourth movement, measures 129–135
          No. 14 (Op, 27, No. 2), second movement, measures 1–8
          No. 16 (Op. 31, No. 1), first movement, measures 3–11

Minor: No. 15 (Op. 28), third movement, Trio, measures 1–8

Chopin, Mazurkas

Major: No. 2 (Op. 6, No. 2), measures 9–16, 17–20.
          No. 23 (Op. 33, No. 2), measures 49–57

Minor: No. 1 (Op. 6, No. 1), measures 1–4
          No. 7 (Op. 7, No. 3), measures 26–32
          No. 43 (Op. 67, No. 2), measures 1–4

Mendelssohn, *Songs Without Words*

Major: No. 28 (Op. 62, No. 4), measures 32–36

Modulation in the Melodic Line

In a melody, a modulation becomes apparent when the implied harmony forms a cadence or a cadential progression in a new key. In Figure 20.12, measures 5 and 6, the melodic line C♯ D♯ E implies the chords IV–vii°–I, a cadential progression in the key of E major. This key is confirmed in the final cadence of the phrase.

Fig. 20.12.

German Folk Song (MSS 421)

It is not always possible to depend upon the appearance of an accidental in the melodic line.

Fig. 20.13.

German Folk Song (MSS 269)

Only the implied harmony here reveals the existence of the modulation. The new accidental (D♯ in this case) will appear in one of the lower voices when the harmony is written out in full. (The presence of an accidental does not necessarily imply a modulation. Review *Music for Sight Singing*, Chapters 8b and 13b.)

Assignment 20.5. Analysis of modulation in melodic lines. Using Figures 20.12 and 20.13 as models, analyze melodies from *Music for Sight Singing* as assigned: Chapter 10a, melodies begining in a major key; melodies 288, 289, 290, 417, 418, 419, 422, 429, 431.

APPLICATION

Written Materials

Writing the Dominant of the Dominant Chord

The dominant of the dominant contains a chromatically altered tone, an accidental not found in the key signature. Writing altered chords is covered by Part-Writing Rule 10.

Part Writing Rule 10. Use of altered chords does not change normal part-writing procedures. Do not double any altered note. If unusual doubling occurs, follow Rule 6A.

In the dominant of the dominant chord, all members function as though its chord of resolution were actually the tonic of a key. The third of the chord therefore acts as a leading tone and must be treated with care identical to that accorded the actual leading tone of the key. In a minor key, the fifth of II (VofV) is the raised sixth scale step of the actual key, but in relation to its chord of resolution it actually functions as a second scale step, and therefore may descend. In C minor, for example, the A♮ of D F♯ A♮ acts as a second scale step to G major and therefore often descends, contrary to its usual function in C minor as an ascending tone. See Figure 20.8, measures 1–3. The inner voice of the left-hand accompaniment figure progresses C♯–A♯– G♯, A♯ being the raised sixth scale step in C♯ minor.

The third of the dominant of the dominant may descend in one particular situation: when it is followed in the same voice by a note of the same letter name with a different chromatic alteration. This will occur when II or II⁷ (VofV or V⁷ofV) progresses to V⁷. This may occur in any voice: in Figure 20.14, A♮ to A♭ in the bass voice, in Figure 20.8, F✗ to F♯ in an inner voice. For an example in arpeggiated style of writing, see Figure 20.7: the B♮ of measure 2 descends to the B♭ of measure 3.

Fig. 20.14.

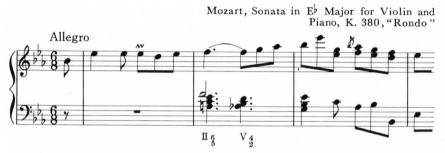

Mozart, Sonata in E♭ Major for Violin and
Piano, K. 380, "Rondo"

The II⁷ (V⁷ofV) may be found complete or incomplete, having characteristics identical to those of the V⁷ chord as described in Chapter 19.

Assignment 20.6.   Write examples of the dominant of the dominant chord. Place harmonic analysis below each example.

Assignment 20.7. Part-writing modulations to the dominant and to the relative major. Fill in inner voices and make harmonic analysis. Add non-harmonic tones where appropriate. Where no figured bass is given, add figured bass before filling in inner voices.

Assignment 20.8. Melody harmonization. Add alto, tenor, and bass voices to these melodic lines. Include harmonic analysis.

Assignment 20.9. Melody harmonization in keyboard style. Following directions given in Assignment 19.10, harmonize the following melodies, as assigned, using the dominant of the dominant or modulation to the dominant: *Music for Sight Singing,* 3, 19, 43, 66, 109, 270, 271, 274.

Ear Training and Music Reading

Harmonic Dictation

Exercise 20.1. Sing in each major and minor key the harmonic progression I–II–V–I and I–II⁷–V–I (I–VofV–V–I; I–V⁷ofV–V–I). Sing with letter names, always including correct accidentals.

Exercise 20.2. Harmonic dictation will now include examples of the dominant of the dominant triad and seventh chord.

Exercise 20.3. Singing modulatory progressions. Sing only roots of chords, using either chord numbers (Figure 20.15 *a*) or letter names (Figure 20.15 *b*). Example: sing the modulatory progression from E♭ major to B♭ major, using the pivot vi = ii.

Fig. 20.15.

a)	I	IV	V	I	vi = ii	V	I
b)	E♭	A♭	B♭	E♭	C	F	B♭

Sing modulatory progression to the key of the dominant from all major keys, using the formula in Figure 20.15 and the two following:

I–IV–V–I   I = IV–V–I

I–IV–V–I   iii = vi–ii (or IV)–V–I

Sing modulatory progression to the key of the relative major from any minor key, using these formulas:

i–iv–V–i   i = vi–ii (or IV)–V–I

i–iv–V–i   III = I–IV–V–I

i–iv–V–i   iv = ii–V–I

i–iv–V–i   VI = IV–V–I

Exercise 20.4. Harmonic dictation. In taking harmonic dictation that includes modulation, it is usually not possible to hear the modulation until the pivot chord is passed. This is because the pivot chord functions in the old key; it sounds as a chord in the old key, and when the new key becomes apparent the pivot is no longer sounding. Follow these suggestions for listening to modulation, particularly when taking down chord numbers only (without staff notation).

a) Sing aloud or to yourself (as instructed) the tonic of the new key. Sing the tonic of the old key.

b) Compare the tonic of the new key with the tonic of the old key. The interval between the two tonic notes will indicate the location of the new key.

c) In subsequent hearings listen for a chord immediately preceding the first cadential progression in the new key—a chord that seems to function in both keys. This will be the pivot chord.

Self-Help in Harmonic Dictation

Modulation to the Dominant

Angel Voices	4–8	M–2
St. Thomas	1–2	M–5
Old 113th	7–8	M–12
Duke Street	1–8	M–14
Vom Himmel Hoch	1–2	M–281
St. Theodulph	9–12	M–424

St. Asaph	5–8	M–498
Melcombe	1–4	M–499
Winchester Old	1–4	E–13
Ebeling	all	E–32
Quem Pastores	all	E–35
Horsley	1–4	E–65
St. Prisca	1–4	E–79
Bedfore	all	E–116
Frankfort	1–6	E–329
St. James	all	E–361
Swabia	all	E–375

Modulation to the Relative Major

Southwell	1–4	M–284
Bangor	1–2	M–427
Llangloffan	1–6	M–482
Bangor	5–8	E–68
St. Cross	1–4	E–74
O Traurigkeit	all	E–83

Melodic Dictation

Exercise 20.5. Writing a melody with modulation from dictation. The principles involved in harmonic and melodic analysis and in the sight singing of modulation apply here. Listen for the cadential progression in the new key and establish mentally the new tonic pitch. The interval relationship between the old and new tonic will indicate the name of the new key. Check this information against the name of the new key as found in writing the pitches by interval relationships. In the second phrase of Figure 20.12 the new tonic is *heard* as a fifth above the old tonic; therefore the new tonic is E. If the melodic intervals are written correctly, the note E will be written in the melody at the point where the new tonic is heard in the melody.

After the melody is written, make harmonic analysis, as in Figures 20.12 and 20.13.

Sight Singing

In singing a melody in which a modulation is involved, it is important to recognize the new key as soon as possible, since it is difficult to sing in one key while the music is written in another. Always look far enough ahead in the music while singing; when the new key becomes apparent, visualize the new tonic triad on the staff and establish its pitch in the mind. See page 87 of *Music for Sight Singing* for additional helps in singing modulations.

Keyboard Harmony

Exercise 20.6.   Play at the keyboard a modulation to the dominant from each major key. Use any one of the three formulas listed in Exercise 20.3. Example: modulate from E major to B major, using the pivot vi = ii. Begin in any soprano position.

Fig. 20.16.

I IV V I   vi =

ii V I

Exercise 20.7.   Play at the keyboard progressions including the dominant of the dominant chord. (For the symbol "II," "VofV" may be substituted.) Start in any soprano position.

I–II–V–I

I–II^7–V–I

I- II$_6$$_5$–V–I

I–II$_6$$_5$–I$_6$$_4$–V–I

I–V^7–vi–II$_6$$_5$–V–I

I–II$_4$$_3$–V–I

I–V^7–vi–II$_4$$_3$–I$_6$$_4$–V–I

I–IV–II$_6$$_5$–I$_6$$_4$–V–I

I–II$_4$$_2$–V$_6$–I

I–vi$_6$–II$_4$$_2$–V$_6$–I

i–II–V–i

i–II^7–V–i

i–II$_6$$_5$–V–i

i–II$_6$$_5$–i$_6$$_4$–V–i

i–VI–II$_4$$_3$–i$_6$$_4$–V–i

i–iv–II$_6$$_5$–i$_6$$_4$–V–i

i–VI$_6$–II$_4$$_2$–V$_6$–i

Exercise 20.8.   Play at the keyboard a modulation to the relative major from each minor key. Use any one of the four formulas listed in Exercise 20.3. Example: modulate from F♯ minor to A major, using the pivot, VI = IV. Begin in any soprano position.

Fig. 20.17.

i	iv	V	i	VI =		
				IV	V	I

Exercise 20.9.   Melody harmonization. Harmonize at the keyboard melodies from Assignments 20.8 and 20.9. For additional practice, many melodies containing modulation to the dominant or to the relative major can be found in folksong collections and in elementary school songbooks.

Appendix 1

The Essentials of Part-Writing

THE SINGLE CHORD

Approximate Range of the Four Voices

Soprano: d^1—g^2 Alto: a—c^2

Tenor: f—f^1 Bass: F—c^1

Triad Position

In *open position*, the distance between the soprano and tenor is an octave or more. In *close position*, the distance between the soprano and tenor is less than an octave. The distance between adjacent voices normally does not exceed an octave, although more than an octave may appear between bass and tenor.

Normal Doubling

Diatonic major and minor triads

    a) root in bass: double the root

    b) first inversion: double the soprano note

    c) second inversion: double the bass note

    d) exception, minor triads, root or third in bass: the third of a minor triad is often doubled, particularly when this third is the tonic, subdominant or dominant note of the key.

Diminished triad (usually found in first inversion only): double the third; when the fifth is in the soprano, the fifth is usually doubled.

Augmented triad: double the bass note.

Seventh chord: normally, all four voices are present. In the major-minor seventh chord, the root is often doubled and the fifth omitted.

Altered triad: normally, same doubling as non-altered triads; avoid doubling the altered note.

CHORD CONNECTION

Triad Roots

When the bass tones of two successive triads are the *roots* of the triads

Triad roots are repeated.

Rule 1. Both triads may be written in the same position, or each may be in different position. Triad positions should be changed

    a) when necessary to keep voices in correct pitch range.

    b) when necessary to keep correct voice distribution (two roots, one third and one fifth).

    c) to avoid large leaps in an inner part.

Triad roots are a fifth apart.

Rule 2A. Retain the common tone; move the other voices stepwise.

Rule 2B. Move the three upper voices in similar motion to the nearest tones of the next triad.

Rule 2C. Move the third of the first triad up or down the interval of a fourth to the third of the second triad, hold the common tone and move the other voice by step.

Rule 2D. (Exception) At the cadence, the root of the final tonic triad may be tripled, omitting the fifth.

Triad roots are a second apart.

Rule 3. The three upper voices move contrary to the bass.

Triad roots are a third apart.

Rule 4A. Hold the two common tones; the other voice moves stepwise.

Rule 4B. When the soprano moves by leap, the second triad may be in either close or open position.

Rule 5. When it is impossible or undesirable to follow normal rules for triads with roots in bass, double the third in the *second* of the two triads. But if this third is the leading tone or any altered tone, double the third in the *first* of the two triads.

Triads in Inversion

Progression to or from a triad in *inversion*, a triad with a *doubled third*, or a triad with any *unusual doubling*

Rule 6A. Write the two voices moving to or from the doubled note first, using oblique or contrary motion if possible.

Rule 6B. When first inversions of triads are found in succession, each triad must have a different doubling to avoid parallel octaves, or the same doubling may appear in different pairs of voices. Avoid doubling the leading tone or any altered tone. Approach and leave each doubled tone using Rule 6A.

Position Changes

Rule 7.   Triad position may be changed
   a) at a repeated triad.
   b) using Rule 2C.
   c) at a triad in inversion or a triad with unusual doubling, following Rule 6A.

Non-Harmonic Tones

Rule 8.   A non-harmonic tone temporarily replaces a harmonic tone. Write the triad with normal doubling if possible and substitute the non-harmonic tone for one of the chord tones. Approach and leave the non-harmonic tone according to the definition of the non-harmonic tone being used.

Seventh Chords

Rule 9.   The seventh of a seventh chord, its note of approach and its note of resolution comprise a three-note figure similar to certain non-harmonic tone figures: passing tone, suspension, appoggiatura, and upper neighbor. The seventh usually resolves down by step.

Altered Chords

Rule 10.   Use of altered chords does not change part-writing procedure. Do not double altered note. Follow Rule 6A if unusual doubling occurs.

General Rule

Rule 11.   In situations not covered by Rules 1–10, observe the following:
   a) Move each voice the shortest distance possible.
   b) Move the soprano and bass in contrary or oblique motion if possible.
   c) Avoid doubling the leading tone, any altered note, any non-harmonic tone, or the seventh of a seventh chord.
   d) Avoid parallel fifths, parallel octaves and the melodic interval of the augmented second.

Appendix 2

Instrumentation:
Ranges, Clefs, Transposition

Range

The range given for each instrument is approximately that ordinarily used by the average player. Neither the lowest nor the highest note playable by the instrument is necessarily included. These ranges will be found satisfactory for purposes of this text.

Clef

Each instrument regularly uses the clef or clefs found in the musical illustrations under "Range." Exceptions or modifying statements are found under the heading "Clef."

Transposition

Unless otherwise indicated under this heading, pitches given under "Range" sound concert pitch when played. (Concert pitch: $A^1 = 440$ vibrations per second; the note A^1 on the piano keyboard is concert A). All transposing instruments sound their name when written C is played; for example, a clarinet in B♭ sounds B♭ when it plays a written C.

STRING INSTRUMENTS

Violin

Range

Viola

Clef. Alto clef is used almost exclusively. Treble clef is used occasionally for sustained high passages.

Violoncello ('Cello)

Clef. Bass clef is ordinarily used. Tenor clef is used for extended passages above small A. Treble clef is used for extreme upper range (not shown).

Double Bass (Bass Viol, Contrabass)

Transposition. Notes sound an octave lower than written.

WOODWIND INSTRUMENTS

Flute

Oboe

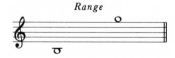

Clarinet: B♭ and A

Range

Transposition.

    a) Clarinet in B♭. Notes sound a major second lower than written. Use signature for the key a major second *above* concert pitch.

    b) Clarinet in A. Notes sound a minor third lower than written. Use signature for the key a minor third above concert pitch.

Bassoon

Range

Clef. Bass clef is ordinarily used. Tenor clef is used for upper range.

English Horn (Cor Anglais)

Range

Transposition. Notes sound a perfect fifth lower than written. Use signature for the key a perfect fifth *above* concert pitch.

Horn (French Horn)

Range

Clef. Treble clef is commonly used.

Transposition. Notes sound a perfect fifth lower than written. Key signatures are not ordinarily used. Write in all accidentals. In many published horn parts, notes written in the bass clef sound a perfect fourth higher than written. Consult with player of instrument before writing horn part in bass clef.

    Horn parts are occasionally written in D, E♭, and E.

Saxophones: E♭ Alto, B♭ Tenor, and E♭ Baritone

Transposition.

a) E♭ Alto Saxophone. Notes sound a major sixth lower than written. Use signature for the key a major sixth *above* concert pitch.

b) B♭ Tenor Saxophone. Notes sound a major ninth (an octave plus a major second) lower than written. Use signature for the key a major second *above* concert pitch.

c) E♭ Baritone Saxophone. Notes sound an octave plus a major sixth lower than written. Use signature for the key a major sixth *above* concert pitch.

BRASS INSTRUMENTS

Trumpet or Cornet, B♭ and C

Transposition.

a) Trumpet or Cornet in B♭. Notes sound a major second lower than written. Use signature for the key a major second *above* concert pitch.

b) Trumpet or Cornet in C. Non-transposing—sounds as written.

Trombone

Clef. Both tenor and bass clefs are commonly used.

Tuba

Appendix 3

Harmony, Scales, and Keys
in Western Music

Harmony in its broadest definition is the relationship of two or more tones sounding simultaneously or in close proximity. As a specific area of study, harmony can be defined as the study of chords, their formation, their succession, and their relationships to each other. Simple examples of harmony can be seen in typical church hymns and in such pieces as "America."

Fig. A3.1.

Henry Carey (?), *America*

GBD   EGB   ACE   DF♯A

Using the definition of a chord as found in Chapter 1, paragraph 18, we arrange in thirds the letter names of each note of the chord. The chord is then identified by the name of the lowest note in this series of thirds and by the size of the thirds as explained in Chapter 1, paragraph 19. Thus, the first chord in "America" is a G major triad (G B D), the second an E minor triad (E G B), and the third an A minor triad (A C E), A being the lowest note when the triad is spelled in thirds.

A musical composition usually contains several other elements besides harmony: *melody*, the succession of pitches, which forms the tune; *rhythm*, the duration of each of the pitches and the patterns formed by these durations; *form*, the patterns of musical construction; *intensity*, the loudness or softness of the sounds; and *timbre*, the quality of the sound (for example, the difference in sound that occurs when the melody of "America" is played first on the violin, then on the trumpet).

Why, then, is this study of music entitled simply harmony? This book is a study of musical composition during a period of time when a system of harmony was a unique and vital element, a period of approximately three hundred years, c. 1600–1900. This era encompasses the Baroque, Classic, and Romantic period of music history and includes most of the best-known names in present-day concert repertoire, ranging from the forerunners of J.S. Bach (1685–1750) through Haydn, Mozart, Beethoven, Chopin, and many others, to the end of the nineteenth century with Brahms and Wagner. The music of this era utilizes all the elements listed above, but it is a system of harmony that principally differentiates this music from that of earlier and later times.

Harmony, however, is not exclusive to this period, but can be present in any period of music history when the music contains two or more notes sounding simultaneously. Up to the ninth century, known music of Western civilization was *monodic* (single line melody). The only music surviving from this time is a large body of religious chants, such as the Gregorian chant below.

Fig. A3.2.[1]

Gregorian Chant

Li - be - ra - me, Do - - - - mi - ne

Harmony first appeared in Western music when someone discovered that two persons could sing the same melody, but one at the interval of a fifth above the other, a device known as parallel organum.

Fig. A3.3.

Organum, c. 850

sit   glo - ri - a   Do - mi - ni,   in   sae - cu -

You will note that the only harmony (the notes sounding simultaneously) at any point in the piece is the interval of a fifth. Clearly, the harmony is of less interest as a compositional device than the melody. Though the importance of melody was challenged by this first rudimentary harmonic usage,

---

[1]Figures A3.2-A3.6 are reprinted by permission of Harvard University Press, Cambridge, Mass., from Davison and Apel, *Historical Anthology of Music*, Vol. 1 (1949), where may be seen the complete compositions from which these excerpts are taken.

melodic considerations remained of primary importance in music composition up to c. 1600, during which time the factor of harmony assumed a growing importance.

The art of combining two or more melodies simultaneously is known as *counterpoint*, the most elementary type being organum as shown in Figure A3.3. Following the lead of this discovery, music composition developed through the use of counterpoint, first by allowing two melodies to move in independent directions,

Fig. A3.4.

Organum, 11th century

then with independence of rhythm,

Fig. A3.5.

c. 1200

and followed by the addition of more and more melodic lines.

Fig. A3.6.

c. 1250

By the end of the sixteenth century, contrapuntal music was commonly written in two to seven voices, with examples of greater numbers of voices being found rather frequently.[2] It should be pointed out in looking at these

---

[2]Thomas Tallis (c. 1520–1585, English) wrote an unusual motet, *Spem in alium*, consisting of forty individual, non-duplicating voices.

examples that through the sixteenth century, most music was written for voices and was written without bar lines; each voice part was placed on a separate page, as with band and orchestra parts today, and not in score form as shown here.

Fig. A3.7.

Palestrina (1525-1594), *In Dominicus Quadragesima*

We have said that contrapuntal writing is made up of individual melodies. But could each voice line be composed without any regard to the others? If so, only by chance would the melodies sound well together; more likely they would clash with each other. In writing melodies that are to sound well together, it is necessary to plan in advance how they will come together. The simultaneous sounding of notes at any point in the piece constitutes the harmonic element of contrapuntal writing.

Harmony in pre-seventeenth-century music was determined by calculating the distance of any note in any voice part above the lowest sounding note, usually the bass note. It was necessary that these distances be consonant intervals, which, in the sixteenth century were: major and minor thirds, major and minor sixths, the perfect fifth, and the perfect octave. Any other intervals were dissonant and could not be used above the lowest sounding note except in certain well-defined situations.

To observe this principle, see Figure A3.7. In measure 4, we would today look at the notes above the D in the bass, arrange them in thirds, and call the sonority a D minor triad. There was no such concept in the sixteenth and earlier centuries. This sonority was simply an octave, a fifth, and a third above the lowest sounding note D. The fourth half note of this measure to them showed an octave, sixth, and third above C, but to us this is an A minor triad with the third in the bass voice.

The idea of a chord as a separate entity rather than as a coming together of several melodic lines was slowly emerging throughout the latter half of the sixteenth century, but received its principal impetus near the end of the century as the result of a practical performing necessity. Most music up to 1600 was written without designation of performance media (except that for keyboard), though the music usually included words for vocal perfomance. But it was common practice for melody instruments to play along with the singers, and in the case of church music, for the organist to accompany the group using the singers' parts. The difficulty of playing from a large number of separate voice parts led an anonymous Italian organist to prepare bass parts with figuration above or below the notes to indicate intervals above the bass part. This musical shorthand is known as *figured bass* or *thorough bass* and first appeared in printed form in 1594.[3] In application, the organist read the bass note, computed the notes to sound above it, and played a vertical sonority that we call a chord. By repeating this process on successive bass notes, he was actually playing a succession of chords.

About 1596, Lodovico Viadana (1564–1627) capitalized on this idea by writing original music for voice and figured bass, for the express purpose of providing music that could be performed with organ by one, two, or three solo singers. This procedure, revolutionary in its time, became immediately popular and led to imitation by many other composers.

The song in Figure A3.8 is an example from a collection printed in 1600 and entitled *Le Nuove Musiche* ("The New Music").[4] Only the vocal solo line and the bass line with figures were written by the composer. The rest of the

---

[3]Early examples of figured bass show only limited use of figuration, to help the organist in questionable places. Figured bass was never an exact science; each composer placed or omitted figures to suit his own purposes. For further information, see Chapter 8; also, in music dictionaries, articles entitled "Figured bass" or "Thorough bass," and a complete survey in F.T. Arnold, *The Art of Accompaniment from a Thorough-Bass* (London: Oxford University Press, 1931).

[4]This style of writing actually led to the "invention" of opera. In the late sixteenth century, a group in Florence, Italy, known as the Camerata and headed by Vincenzo Galilei (father of Galileo Galelei, the astronomer) was searching for ways to produce drama through music. It was impossible to declaim a dramatic text in counterpoint since the several voices would be singing different words at the same time. The Camerata recognized the usefulness of figured bass, and one of its members, Jacopo Peri (1561–1633), wrote the first opera (*Dafne*) in 1597. This score, now lost, was followed by an *Euridice* by Peri and another *Euridice* by Caccini in 1600, these written in a style similar to that of Figure A3.8.

notes in Figure A3.8 represent one possible interpretation, called "realization" of the figured bass. In the practice of the time, the keyboard player would improvise an accompaniment, using the figured bass line as a guide, with the probability that no two performances would be identical. The writing and spontaneous realization of figured bass accompaniments for solo vocal or instrumental performances continued until about 1750, culminating in the works of Bach and Handel. In modern editions, a realization is often included as part of the score, as in Figure A3.8.

Fig. A3.8.

Giulio Caccini (1550?-1618), *Sfogava con le stelle*

From this beginning, harmony as a systematic device of music composition developed rapidly during the seventeenth century, but it was not until 1722, that a reasonable theory of harmony was conceived. After a century of conjecture by many theoreticians about this new style, Jean Phillipe Rameau (1683–1764), a leading composer of his time and one of the most famous theoreticians of all time, presented his theories of harmonic music in his *Traité de l'harmonie reduite à ses principes naturels* (*Treatise on Harmony Reduced to its Natural Principles*).

Two of his discoveries are of particular interest to our discussion. First is the Theory of Inversion. In spite of the widespread use of chords since 1600, these chords were still thought of as being constructed using intervals above the lowest sounding note. Rameau thought differently; he felt that all chords using the same letter names, no matter in what arrangement, were one and the same chord; e.g., C E G, E G C, and G C E are all forms of the single triad, C E G. To prove this, he observed that in the interval of the octave, both notes sound identically; therefore, the octave actually represents a single pitch of the same name (Figure A3.9). It should follow that any interval of a chord that is changed only by an octave transposition of one or more of its notes has not really been changed at all.

Fig. A3.9.

Thus E G C is C E G, the same triad but in a different form, the first inversion, and G C E is C E G, but in second inversion (Figure A3.10).

Fig. A3.10.

But why is C the fundamental note of this triad rather than E or G? The answer to Rameau was based on an acoustical phenomenon well known as far back as early Greek times, and said to have been discovered by Pythagoras (sixth century B.C.). We take a string that when played sounds C. If we press a finger at the half-way point on the string and play on one half of the string, the note produced is another C an octave higher. If we place the finger to divide the string in thirds, and play on one third of the string, we get a pitch G an octave and a fifth above the original note. Figure A3.11 shows the pitches derived from the first six divisions of the string.

Fig. A3.11.

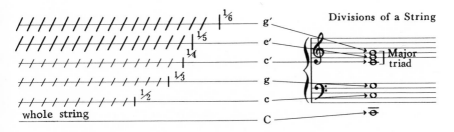

Rameau observed that each note created by dividing the string was directly related thereby to the entire string, the source from which the upper tones are derived. In our illustration, the triad c^1 e^1 g^1 is derived from the division of an original string sounding C. c^1 is in an octave relationship to the original C; it therefore represents the fundamental or generating tone and becomes the root or fundamental of the triad, no matter in what order the triad notes are arranged.

Another acoustical phenomenon, the *overtone series*, displays similar characteristics. When any given pitch is produced, other pitches called overtones, partials or hamonics,[5] and usually inaudible to the human ear, sound simultaneously with the given pitch. These are higher than the original pitch, and in the same intervallic relationships as found in the successive divisions of the string,[6] When C is sounded, the pitches c, g, c^1, e^1, and g^1, plus an indefinite number of higher pitches, are also present (Figure A3.12).

Fig. A3.12.

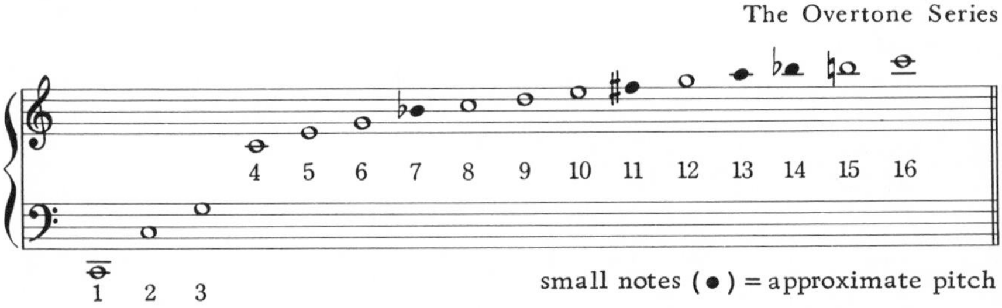

The Overtone Series

small notes (•) = approximate pitch

Here again we see a triad, C E G, each tone of which is related to a progenitor, C. This acoustical information was sufficient to convince Rameau of the nature of the triad and its invertibility.[7]

Intervals are invertible in the same manner. C up to G, a perfect fifth, inverts to G up to C, a perfect fourth. The only difference in the two intervals is the octave location of C. Note also that in the overtone series, a perfect fifth shows the ratio 2:3 and the perfect fourth 3:4. The ratio of the two C's, 2:4, when reduced becomes 1:2, the ratio of the octave. All other intervals can be inverted in a similar manner; for example, the major third, 4:5 inverts to a minor sixth, 5:8, C up to E and E up to C.

---

[5]In Figure A3.12, "1" is the fundamental, while "2" is the first overtone, etc. When using the terms "partial" or "harmonic," "1" is the first partial or harmonic, "2" is the second partial or harmonic, etc.

[6]These overtones determine the quality of a sound, for example, the difference between an oboe sounding A and a trumpet sounding the same note. The difference in quality is caused by the difference in the intensities of the various overtones.

[7]It must be said that the existence of the minor triad cannot be proven in this manner, nor was Rameau successful in finding a reasonable explanation. Once established, however, any type of triad can be inverted according to Rameau's theory.

Having found that all chords have roots and that the root remains constant when the notes are rearranged, Rameau next sought to discover the underlying principle governing the progression of one chord to another. Rameau said that these progressions are based upon movement of the roots of chords, whether or not these roots are in the bass. In looking at the intervals from the division of the string and from the overtone series, he noted that the first interval to appear above the fundamental and its repetition, the octave, is the fifth. Therefore, root movement should be best when the roots are a fifth apart. This can be shown by taking a piece of music and extracting the roots, placing these on a third staff, as in Figure A3.13. It should be kept in mind that there are three possible root movements, by fifth, by third, and by second. According to the theory of inversion, the effect of the fourth is the same as the fifth (C up to F is the same as C down to F), the sixth is the same as the third (C up to A is the same as C down to A), and the seventh is the same as the second (C up to B is the same as C down to B).

Fig. A3.13.

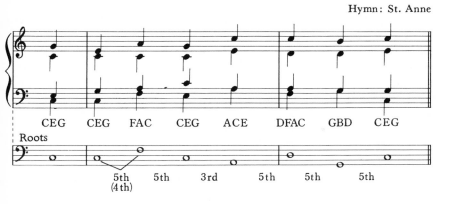

Hymn: St. Anne

In this part of his theory, Rameau was correct; subsequent analysis has shown that in the music of almost every composer during the years 1600–1900, the majority of root movements were by the interval of the fifth. Rameau's reasoning that root movement by thirds should be next best and root movement by seconds least best has been reversed by the practice of composers.

But on the whole, Rameau was eminently successful in discovering satisfactory principles of chord construction and chord progression. Chords have roots that may or may not be in the lowest sounding voice, and chord succession is a function of the movement of these roots, movement by the fifth being the best. These principles allow us to identify a chord by numbering the chord according to the location of its root in the scale,[8] and to study the relationship of chords through the movements of their roots.

Music written after the time of Rameau and up to c. 1900 can, for the most part, be studied and analyzed by the principles first outlined by Rameau. It is because of this fact, and in spite of the large number of composers and diverse styles in this three-century span, that we can study the music of this period under the single subject heading of harmony.

SCALES AND KEYS

It is helpful in the study of harmony to understand the derivation of the system of major and minor scales and keys, the framework within which the harmonic system operated in the seventeenth through nineteenth centuries. Scales were not always major and minor; rather, they were derived from older scales commonly used before the seventeenth century. Key and key signature are concepts that came into being only after major and minor scales were established.

Scale systems can be observed in music of most cultures and can be traced back to the earliest times in music history. In Western music, scale formations were known and described by the ancient Greeks as early as 300 B.C. By A.D. 900, the use of four basic scales was firmly established. These scales are similar to major and minor in that they are made up of whole steps and half steps, but differ in that each scale has a different arrangement of whole steps and half steps. These scales, commonly known as *church modes* or *Medieval modes*, begin on the notes D, E, F, and G, each progressing up stepwise without the use of accidentals to a pitch an octave higher than the starting note.[9] These four scales can be played on the piano using only the white keys. They are shown in Fig. A3. 14 with their names and locations of half steps (all other intervals are whole steps). You will observe that the half steps always occur between E–F and B–C, but the scale-step location of the half step varies in each mode. These modes could be transposed up a perfect fourth (or down a perfect fifth); by placing a flat on B, each mode retains its original half step and whole step characteristics.

---

[8]For example, in C major, to identify a chord with the letter names A, C and F, we arrange the letter names in thirds to find F as the root, and locate F as the fourth scale step in the C major scale; the chord is IV in C major.

[9]Each scale was found in two forms, the *authentic* and the *plagal* (*hypo*) forms, for a total of eight scales. The difference between the two forms was merely the melodic range in which the scale was used: *authentic* from the root of the scale to its octave and *plagal* from the fifth of the scale to its octave.

Fig. A3.14.   The Medieval Modes

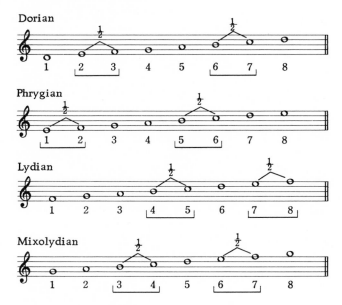

Fig. A3.15.   The Transposed Modes

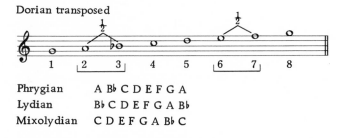

Phrygian	A B♭ C D E F G A
Lydian	B♭ C D E F G A B♭
Mixolydian	C D E F G A B♭ C

These scale forms were rarely used in their "pure" forms shown above. Very early in medieval times, performers altered certain notes to produce what they felt to be a better sound. Composers sometimes indicated these changes in the music, but more often omitted them, assuming the performer would make the changes on his own. These alterations, which consisted of adding a sharp or a flat to certain tones of the scale, were known as *musica ficta* or "false music." Among the common alterations were: (1) lowering B to B♭ (transposed, E to E♭) in any mode when the melody contained the pattern A B A (D E D) and (2) raising the seventh scale step that precedes the eighth scale step at the end of a musical phrase (Dorian and Mixolydian only), converting the whole step progression into a half step progression.

Fig. A3.16.

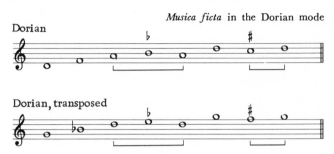

Musica ficta in the Dorian mode

Since these accidentals were often omitted by composers, present-day editions of pre-seventeenth-century music are often found with accidentals written *above* the notes, indicating the *probable* location of altered scale tones. The following piece, in transposed Dorian, shows at (1) the progression D–E♭–D with E♭ written in by the composer and at (2) F♯ at the end of the piece added by an editor in conformity with known sixteenth-century practice.

Fig. A3.17.

Joannes Stahl   (1545), *Ich will zu Land*
ausreiten (abridged)

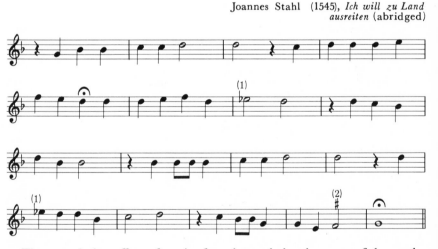

The cumulative effect of *musica ficta* changed the character of the modes (except the Phrygian, in which the whole step 7–8 remained) to that of our present major and minor:

Adding a leading tone
   Dorian = Minor, melodic form
     D E F G A B C♯ D

Mixolydian = Major
    G A B C D E F♯ G
Adding B♭
    Dorian = Minor, natural form
        D E F G A B♭ C D
    Lydian = Major
        F G A B♭ C D E F
Adding a leading tone and B♭
    Dorian = Minor, harmonic form
        D E F G A B♭ C♯ D

As an example, the almost constant use of E♭ (transposed B♭) and F♯ (leading tone) in Figure A3.17 changes this Dorian (transposed) melody to minor, except for measures 4–6. The next time you hear "Greensleeves," a Dorian tune, listen carefully to the sixth scale step in the first phrase. It is commonly performed today with either B or B♭.

Fig. A3.18.

In 1547 it was recognized by Heinrich Glareanus in his treatise, *Dodecachordon*,[10] that two additional modes and their plagal forms existed, the Ionian mode on C (like the present C major scale, C D E F G A B C) and the Aeolian mode on A (like the present pure minor scale on A, A B C D E F G A). Between this time and 1750, the date of the death of J.S. Bach, music became more and more characteristically Ionian or Aeolian and the use of the other modes gradually disappeared.

Beginning early in the seventeenth century, composers began to write transposed major and minor scales at locations other than a fourth above the original forms. This produced more accidentals in the scales; for example, transposing the Ionian mode from C up to E necessitates sharps on the notes F, C, G, and D. These new accidentals were sometimes placed in the music, sometimes at the beginning of the piece, or some at the beginning and the rest during the piece, as in Figure A3.17, where we see B♭ in the signature and E♭ written in the music. Such a signature could not be called a *key signature* in the sense that this term is used today. Not until approximately 1750 did the use of accidentals at the beginning of a piece become standardized so that by looking at the signature one would know on what pitch the Ionian (major) or Aeolian (minor) scale begins. In eighteenth-nineteenth

---

[10]Greek for "twelve strings," but referring to twelve modes.

century terms, *mode* indicates the kind of scale being used, in terms of the locations of its half steps and whole steps, these being limited to two, major and minor. *Key* indicates the letter name location of the first note of the mode. Major mode and minor modes are usually referred to today simply as major and minor scales, while the term mode is reserved for the ancient church modes.

SUMMARY AND A LOOK FORWARD

This survey of the two principal characteristics of music in the seventeenth-nineteenth centuries can be summarized as follows:

1. Chords
   a) A chord is a vertical sonority built in thirds.
   b) The lowest note of the series of thirds is the root of the chord.
   c) A chord is invertible, and its root always retains its identity, regardless of its placement in the vertical sonority.
   d) Chord progression is determined by movement of chord roots, that of the fifth being the most common.
   2. Scales and keys
   a) Scale formations are reduced to two: major (Ionian) and minor (Aeolian).
   b) The original C (Ionian-major) and A (Aeolian-minor) scales can be transposed to any pitch; the accidentals necessary to maintain the scale formation are placed at the beginning of the piece and called a key signature

Summarizing broadly the periods of music composition by the basic compositional characteristics of each, we find

1. up to c. 800	monody	modal scales
2. c. 800-c. 1600	counterpoint	modal scales, *musica ficta*
3. c. 1600-c. 1900	harmony	major and minor scales and keys

What of the present day, the period following 1900? At approximately the end of the nineteenth century, it became obvious to serious composers that the resources of the major-minor harmonic vocabulary had become virtually exhausted, that is, it was increasingly difficult to write original music that did not sound similar to music written before 1900. Even as composers around 1600 experimented with new ideas such as figured bass, chord formations, and chord progressions, composers around 1900 began to experiment with new sounds and new musical devices.

This is not to say that music has ceased to be written in the familiar harmonic style. Actually much twentieth-century composition such as popular music, Broadway show music, church anthems, and music for vocal and instrumental pedagogy continue to utilize the resources of the nineteenth-century harmonic vocabulary and the major-minor key system. But composers of today who are trying to write music that does not sound like that of the previous century are finding it necessary to create new resources or to utilize older neglected resources for this purpose. The study of these resources and the results derived from them is usually known as *modern harmony* or *contemporary harmony*, and properly follows the study of traditional (seventeenth- through nineteenth-century) harmony as presented in this text. *Advanced Harmony: Theory and Practice*, will include a brief outline and survey of the transition from traditional to contemporary harmony and of the principal practices of contemporary harmony.

Index